"Paul Spinrad takes us on a magical journey through the looking-glass of video performance. Engaging interviews introduce us to modern Mesmers practicing the ancient ritual of bending minds with light. The revolution may not be televised, but it's certainly being projected."
 —David Pescovitz, co-editor of BoingBoing.net, contributing writer to *Wired*

"History, technical specs, overviews of VJ gear, interviews—wow, *The VJ Book* will become the bible for video artists for years to come. Paul Spinrad even dives head-first into the copyright concerns that VJs have to cope with as both aggregators and producers. It's a great handbook for VJs, experimental filmmakers, or anyone else who's interested in interactive media control. And after reading all the interviews, one thing is clear: there is no one way to approach the art of VJing."
 —Grant Davis (VJ Culture)

"Recommended reading for anyone who's interested in the ongoing evolution of human expression, as we continue our dialogue with technology. Gives a sense of the real human personalities that drive a technologically-mediated art form."
 —David Last, musician, VJ, and co-curator of "Synaesthesiologists" for
 the 2004 New York Video Festival

"VJing is often viewed as a 'lower' art form, but it subverts both mainstream media and the art world, and blurs 'high/low' cultural distinctions. It's the beginning of a new audiovisual language; a prologue to how we'll communicate when thought-projection is the norm."
 —Thomas Williams (VJ Biomorphica)

THE VJ BOOK

© 2005 Paul Spinrad
A Feral House Book
ISBN: 1-932595-09-0

Feral House
PO Box 39910
Los Angeles, CA 90039

10 9 8 7 6 5 4 3 2 1

www.feralhouse.com
info@feralhouse.com

DVD by Melissa Ulto
Technical Advisor: Jon Schwark
Technical illustrations by Tom Giesler (www.tomgiesler.com)
Design by Hedi El Kholti

THE VJ BOOK

INSPIRATIONS AND PRACTICAL ADVICE FOR LIVE VISUALS PERFORMANCE

■ ■ ■ ■ PAUL SPINRAD

ACKNOWLEDGEMENTS ■ ■ ■ ■

I was completely unqualified to write this book when I started. Perhaps I still am. But I faked it by bugging numerous people who know much more about VJ than I do—a list that includes but is not limited to VJ Aix Magnetic Eagle, Benton-C Bainbridge, Craig Baldwin, Philip Alden Benn, Mark Coniglio, Sue Costabile, Bill Cottman, Holly Daggers, Grant Davis, Ben Discoe, Scott Draves, Ivan Dryer, Eugene Epstein, Emmett Feldman, Meredith Finkelstein, Dave Fleischer, Kathleen Forde, Stefan G., Steve Goldsmith, Toby Harris, Yusei Horiuchi, John Humphries, Walter Karmazyn, Jaybill McCarthy, Peter Mettler, Norman Perryman, Chris Pirazzi, Rob Read, Michael O'Rourke, Jon Schwark, Jay Smith, Olivier Sorrentino, George Stadnik, Jade Steele, Samuel Stoller, Pall Thayer, Reinaldo Torres, Melissa Ulto, Lori Surfer Varga, Paul Vlachos, and Henry Warwick.

Many friends of mine also helped, first of all by being friends, but also by pointing me in interesting directions: Laura Baron, Cynsa Bonorris, Adrian Cotter, Ernesto DiSabatino, Leslie Felperin, Mark "Remarq" Johnson, Ezra Kenigsberg, Muffy Srinivasan Rood, Edward Spiegel, and Audra Wolfmann. My original inspiration for this project came from my friend Jordan Romney, who ran fantastic visuals for our 2003 Love Project fundraiser party. Thanks, Jordan, for expanding my consciousness in a healthy and legal way.

Neil Salkind of Studio B helped me enormously from the start with support, advice, and encouragement. Thanks also go to Ben Sawyer for consideration and helpful discussion, and Katie Conley, who really went to bat for me with her editorial board.

I'm also indebted to Wendy Seltzer of the EFF and Eric Bjorgum for generously having taken time to vet the Legal Issues chapter.

Andrea Juno and V. Vale (although they may not like being mentioned in the same sentence) have my thanks for showing me what a culture book can look like. This book clearly carries much of their DNA. I'm also indebted to everyone I worked with at *Wired* magazine, especially Bob Parks, for improving my writing and showing me the ropes of technology journalism.

At the core of any cultural movement, there always seems to be at least one place where generous, creative, dedicated, and visionary people take it upon themselves to build up a community. This requires a ton of hard work, but it's one of the most beautiful things that people do. For VJs in San Francisco, that place is Dimension7, and all of us owe them our deepest gratitude.

Finally, I'd like to thank Wendy Becktold and my family for their unflagging encouragement and interest (and for the time they spent reading and commenting on early drafts).

Dedicated to the Love Project / LPU
for all the inspiration

TABLE OF CONTENTS

FOREWORD

By Jon Schwark (Videojon), LightRhythm Visuals

THE APPEAL OF BECOMING A VJ is obvious: we are junkies for power and flash. We imagine ourselves as Zeus or Thor at the eye of the hurricane, casting our lightning bolts above the fray. We look out with satisfaction across the swirling clouds.

We are born with an innate will to create visible action at a distance. It's the rush of shooting bottles off a fence with a rifle. It's calling someone you're about to meet on their cellphone when you can already see them across the café. As children, who didn't want to be the construction crane operator or the railroad engineer the first time they realized such dream jobs existed? You push a little button here and you see something big happen over there. It's a primal thrill.

Maybe it comes from a behavioral tendency—rooted way back in our evolution—to appear larger than life, as a way to attract mates or frighten predators. Many animals carry out these bluffs instinctually, and it seems to succeed in saving their skins and passing on their genes. On the other hand, it's the basic drive of *Homo sapiens* alone to construct, to add complexity, to think big.

So back to VJing, this relatively new art form. It is a tendril of modern culture evolving in the fertile soil of technology, energized by our primal desire to affect visible action at a distance. That's the theory, but where has this mixture of desire and technology taken us in actual practice?

In spite of our aspirations of Zeus-like omnipotence, VJs often feel more like the Sorcerer's Apprentice from *Fantasia*. Our magical objects take on a life of their own, with only occasional unskilled input from the protagonist mouse who summons their performance.

These humorously juxtaposed metaphors, Zeus and the Sorcerer's Apprentice, hint at where we're going: Mickey needs better command of the medium—tools that offer finer and finer grained control. Zeus wants to create whole new environments, alternate structures for the audience's relationship to moving pictures, contexts that go beyond the one-way, streaming rectangles of canned cinema and television.

If we look deep inside ourselves, we can sense the perfect medium. Imagine a galaxy of glowing stars. Your presence envelops the space, from a point of choreography at the center. Your consciousness becomes a vortex of glittering eels swimming with one mind, each of them a pixel choosing what to reflect. You see the visible in every direction, and control it fluidly at all levels—from the conceptual and editorial, through the composition of the image, right down to the pixel level. Most difficult of all, the Holy Grail, really: your performance is dynamic, and can change on a whim.

The process of getting there has been a hard one for live visual artists, and its perfect form it will always remain elusive. Musicians, actors, and orators have been generating environment-enveloping performances for ages directly with their minds and bodies. Producing sound is natural, a byproduct of our breath. With visuals, it's been a centuries-old struggle against the laws of physical reality, waged with rigging, props, pyrotechnics, light, and shadow. And only relatively recently did we nail down cinema, photographic representation with a time component.

The hard-fought spoils? Cinema and television, with the cameras, projection systems and economic models they're linked to. Early, silent film, with its portable cameras, and early television, with its 100% live format, both promised a dynamic future. But artists who worked in these new media were captivated, understandably, by radical new powers of representation—at the expense of spontaneity. At the same time, the businesses that owned these media systems sought the profitability of duplication and mass-production. As a result, through most of cinema and television history, only scattered effort has gone into capturing the improvisational aspect of performance, the uniqueness of the present moment, and of each individual audience.

The history Paul delves into in these pages, then, begins with a process of evolutionary false starts and one-offs. The fingers of *Cultura* have been searching for a natural modality—the base stalk that will survive to be the proto-species from which the next generations will spring. In VJing, we have seen an accelerated snap into such a new modality. Over the last decade, the form has quickly evolved into a standardized medium that takes the best aspects of film and television, and opens them back up to spontaneity and live human interaction.

Just as in evolution, it was change in the environment that drove the new form into existence. Niches opened up in the culture, begging to be filled, while artistic resources became available as byproducts of other processes. Grazers, predators and scavengers roiled in a new, unexplored landscape of mixers, projectors, laptops, and software. Technology is our meteor. So, yes, it is obvious why someone would want to become a VJ at this point in the cultural timeline; there were rats before, scurrying between their holes at night, but the smart rats are stepping forward into the age of mammals.

INTRODUCTION ■ ■ ■ ■

WHAT IS VJING? It means improvising with visuals, specifically those rendered via projected light. The expression originally referred to the Video Jockey (as a counterpart to a Disc Jockey), but it's more accurately Visuals Jockey—a general descriptor that encompasses older, non-video avocations such as "running the light show." Martha Quinn and Kurt Loder notwithstanding, the term VJ, as used here, has nothing to do with appearing on television to introduce advertisements.

Faster laptop computers and digital projectors now offer VJs fundamentally new powers of visual improvisation. In fact, those two are all you need: a laptop and a projector, along with some free software. Some have compared these developments to the invention of musical instruments, or at least of a new class of instrument. But let's not go too far; the ability to generate visuals on-the-fly is nothing new. Puppeteers, theaters, circuses, and operas have been doing it all along (within the constraints of the physical world, despite all the clever rigging). In the 1890s, the color organ created moving visuals without the physical constraints (but all of the subsequent tinkering with masks, lenses, and filament shapes still couldn't make the definition sharp enough to create recognizable pictures). Film was always clear and infinitely controllable (too bad it's a dead, stored archive rather than a live experience). Video and computer graphics did finally make it possible to manipulate imagery arbitrarily, liberating a basic form of expression from long-endured limitations (yet the equipment was, until recently, prohibitively expensive). Okay, maybe this *is* like the invention of musical instruments—live musical instruments, somehow coming after the invention of recordable ones.

So what's the big deal about its being live? As we're flooded by well-produced, mass-marketed, canned media product, this is easy for us to forget. The big deal is, every moment is unique, just like in life. And with apologies to Plato, the truest reality is the one we're living in, the world outside our door, rather than any flickering shadows on the wall. VJing connects with the moment and connects with others. It's a gift for the people you're with, never to be duplicated. Yes, you're using video technology, As Seen on TV, but it isn't meant to earn you future glory, to be delivered through a one-way channel to people you'll never meet. It isn't for a detached audience, sitting somewhere else.

Today, VJs perform most often in dance clubs to accompany a DJ. This lineage is a blessing and a curse. Clubs offer a fun atmosphere and a receptive crowd, but, as an audience, they aren't paying much attention to the visuals on the screen. People are there to dance, so the DJ has the power, and the VJ plays second fiddle. There is no visual substitute for the physically energizing, visceral power of a beat, and audio scratching has a magical ability to evoke the inflections of speech without using words. Video scratching, meanwhile, is more likely to evoke the instant replay on *Monday Night Football.*

But there's another side of DJing, its cultural collage—selecting, mixing, and juxtaposing music and other sounds to draw parallels and distinctions among the sampled components. And for this creative intent, VJing blows DJing away completely. The VJ's palette is far broader, encompassing any imagery at all, recognizable or obscure, abstract or representational, iconic or ambiguous. The elements can also be combined more freely, anything mixed with anything, without worrying about key, or beats per minute, or whether they sound good together. The dissonances a VJ creates are cognitive, not musical.

Furthermore, VJing has far more subversive potential than DJing. This characteristic is essentially built-in, thanks to intellectual property laws. A DJ in a club that pays its ASCAP dues is legally covered, but for VJs, the best performances happen in private or at non-commercial events, because they have fewer legal limits on source imagery. VJs who sample need to operate beneath the culture industry's radar. Any VJ who performs at a superclub knows that in the meantime, someone else is putting on a more diverse and challenging show for friends in their living room.

So VJs are spreading their wings and traveling in new directions, out of the club and into places where audiences sit and pay attention. Some perform solo, while others work with dance troupes and musical ensembles. Others add live video to karaoke and improv comedy. And most of them would probably be up for all of the above.

Major creative shifts are happening as well. VJs are beginning to experiment with narrative, which the field has been mostly lacking. There's nothing about live video that precludes storytelling—it just hasn't been done much yet. We have plenty of Man Rays, but who will be our D.W. Griffith or our Orson Welles? Who will be our Chuck Barris? This vast new territory needs pioneers.

With all of its media and electronics, VJ could pass for the next phase of advanced, technology-fed alienation. But underneath, it's more like cooking. You collect the best, freshest ingredients you can find, mix them together the way you and your guests will like them, and then you serve it up and enjoy the special time together.

After the photograph and the phonograph, after television and radio, sight and sound lost some of their authenticity. We can now no longer be sure if we saw something in person or on TV. But we don't have smell-a-vision, and a delicious meal is always a direct, unmediated experience. And when we remember it, we know that our senses had engaged with the world in a living moment, that we weren't just tasting someone else's characterization.

That's what VJ does with all the fantastic new video technology we have. It takes it back from Big Media, serves it up just for us, and makes it delicious.

San Francisco, 2005

16

HISTORY ▪ ▪ ▪ ▪

LIGHT PERFORMANCE has always occupied a funny place between science and art, influence and irrelevance, high culture and low culture, dependence and independence. It has always been driven by technology, which perpetually attracts dreamers looking for the next revolution and tinkerers who prize demonstration-value above more intuitive aesthetics. At the same time, it answers many longtime artistic yearnings and its potential really is only just now beginning to be realized. Like any self-conscious avant-garde, it has functioned as both a breeding ground for creative innovators and a comfortable cocoon for the talentless seeking an excuse for their unpopularity. For some performers, it has been an all-consuming passion; for others, merely a gimmick they tried in order to distinguish themselves. Some of the field's greatest names, such as Thomas Wilfred, became embittered outsiders, and yet the field's influence on visual culture has been enormous, far exceeding its recognition. Finally, its long and uneasy relationship with music has inspired several breakings-up and gettings-back-together over the decades.

COLOR CONCERTS, 1893–1950s

Contemporary VJing evolved most directly from the psychedelic projections of the 1960s, but artists, inventors, and crackpots have been putting on light shows since the late 1800s and earlier. During the field's long, half-forgotten early development, it centered around the "color organ," a device which embodied the light-as-music metaphor that continues to influence the field today. The first color organ was designed in 1743 by Louis Bertrand Castel, a mathematician and priest who may have been inspired by the power of stained glass and pipe organs. Castel's harpsichord-based *clavessin oculaire* associated the seven notes of the major scale to seven different colors, which were displayed by colored papers moving in front of candles. Others subsequently developed this idea with devices that projected beams of sunlight or light from oil lamps through colored liquids or glass, and then reflected them onto the wall. Most of these inventions were add-ons to the pipe organ, which because of its complexity attracted a lot of engineering talent.

The field remained a sidelight until A. Wallace Rimington patented the first standalone color organ in England in 1893 and promoted it later with his book *Colour-Music: The Art of Mobile Colour*, published in 1912. This invention started a mini-revolution, which viewed projected color as the new music—and enabled the non-musically inclined to perform recitals. Optimistic adherents flocked to this cutting-edge mix of technology and culture, including physicist Albert Michelson. Meanwhile, plenty of high-flying theory came out to support the field, including systemizations that mapped notes, scales, and other aspects of music to analogous structures defined within the field of color and light. These systems never caught on, but some within the music world recognized great promise in the new territory. Russian composer Alexander Scriabin, for example, wrote a symphony that he scored for both orchestra and light organ, giving it the portentous name *The Poem of Fire: Prometheus* (1908). But Scriabin's atonal score never gained the broad appeal of George Frideric Händel's *Music for the Royal Fireworks* (1749), an earlier example of music written to accompany live abstract visuals.

Color performances boomed during the 1920s, met by a flurry of new color organ, kaleidoscope, and projector patents. The most popular recitals were given by famous inventor-performers who toured the country with portable devices showing off the spectacular new effects they had developed. Leading light organists in the U.S. included Mary Hallock-Greenewalt and Thomas Wilfred. In 1926, Wilfred accompanied the Philadelphia Orchestra with his patented Clavilux, under the direction of the young Leopold Stokowski. Meanwhile, in England, the most successful inventor-performer was Adrian Bernard Klein, who wrote several subsequent editions of Rimington's text, renaming it *Coloured Light*—before renaming himself Adrian Cornwell-Clyne.

Other people who were drawn to the light saw it in a supporting role as a mood-enhancer, rather than in the lead. This view turned out to be the better near-term cultural prediction. In his 1932 article "Light as an Art" for *The Builder*, English engineer Fred Bentham envisioned a revolution in stage lighting enabled by an organ-like color console. Bentham soon got the go-ahead to pursue his vision, and by 1939 it was realized in the King Street Strand Electric Theater. The Strand's console was a success, and it became the model for numerous subsequent Strand Light Consoles, which were installed in top auditoriums throughout Europe and in South America.

Walt Disney invited Leopold Stokowski and the Philadelphia Orchestra to take another foray into visuals, collaborating on *Fantasia* (1940). This was a movie, not live performance, but its visual-music sensibility grew out of the color concert tradition, while adding the control and detailed resolution that were only possible at that time with animated film. Disney's spellbinding imagery, which includes Mickey Mouse as a mischievous sorcerer's apprentice, has remained an animation high-water mark. In one geek-friendly touch, the film's "Meet the Soundtrack" intermission segment features an "interview" with an oscilloscope-like line that transforms into an expressive character of its own. Some years later, video artist Steina Vasulka introduced a live version of similar music-as-electronic-input imagery to the New York art world with her pioneering performance *Violin Power* (1970–8).

The inventor-performer tradition was carried on in the U.S. by Cecil Stokes, who in 1942 patented the "Auroratone" process based on the rainbow effects that result from shining polarized light through crystals grown on a glass slide. When the crystal slide is made to vibrate, the visuals synchronize with sound. During World War II, Stokes successfully promoted his invention as a breakthrough relaxation method and as therapy for mental patients in Army hospitals. He later took the Auroratone on tour, performing live light-show concerts with Bing Crosby and others (Crosby and his brother Larry were investors in Stokes's Auroratone Corporation).

DIY COLOR ORGANS, 1960–1970s

In 1960, *Science and Mechanics* magazine published "Play Moving Color Tunes with Your Records," a how-to article on building a color organ, a device which switched colored lights on and off automatically in response to music without a human player. The article was written by Maurice Wetzel, who owned a couple of related patents, and it anticipated a spate of color organ articles in hobbyist magazines such as *Electronics World* and *Popular Electronics*. Building your own color organ became a popular home electronics project until such forces as the rise of the Japanese electronics industry (which manufactured finished products that were actually cheaper than building your own Heathkit) and the home computer made such tinkering a thing of the past. During the 1970s, commercial color organs briefly became a favorite fixture in state-of-the-art bachelor pads, but they shared their demise with such fellow technologies as the waterbed, quadraphonic sound, and the 8-track tape.

WET SHOWS, 1952–

The light show took a fateful turn in 1952 when the creative potential of a common piece of classroom equipment, the overhead projector, was discovered by the newly-simmering counterculture. At an art-education conference that year, Seymour Locks, an art professor in San Francisco, gave improvised visual accompaniment to a jazz combo by using an overhead to project wet paints that he swirled around in a glass dish. This was the beginning of a dynamic, abstract-expressionist technique that came to be known later as "wet shows" or "liquids."

During the 1950s, light artist Elias Romero ran liquids at small concerts, gallery openings, and other underground happenings in Los Angeles and, later, San Francisco. Artsy beatnik types soon picked up the technique, which caused a revolution in light-show culture similar to the influence that Jackson Pollock's wet-paint splattering had on the easel painting of the same era. But unlike Pollock's paintings, light-show performances could neither be sold to collectors nor reproduced in *Life* magazine—which meant that the artists who created them had less economic value. One result of this was that the medium remained underground, where it still exists today.

In broad terms, the Beats of the 1950s taught liquids to the Hippies of the 1960s, who immediately discovered the technique's natural affinity with drugs and rock 'n' roll. The dripping, swirling colors recalled visions of melting that reportedly come from LSD, bringing revelers further out of their oft-vacated heads as they gyrated their bodies to the throbbing, amplified beat. Light artists augmented liquids with slide and film projectors, color wheels, mirror balls, strobes, ultraviolet, and fluorescent colors—all of which combined to create the psychedelic light-show look that still defines the era. These visuals were performed at Ken Kesey's Bay Area "Acid Test" parties in the mid-'60s and at other events, notably Stewart Brand's Trips Festival at San Francisco's Maritime Hall (billed as a "non-drug re-creation of a psychedelic experience") and Andy Warhol's Exploding Plastic Inevitable happenings in New York, both in 1966.

At SF's Avalon Ballroom, light artist Bill Ham made the wet show a regular feature, using multiple overhead projectors to prevent the muddying that inevitably comes from mixing colors in the same dish. The Avalon, along with the rival Fillmore West and the Fillmore East in New York City, brought the psychedelic light show to new levels of sophistication. Each venue had its own visual style, and trained eyes could recognize who was running the show that night just by looking at the liquids. Meanwhile, Virgil Fox ran "Heavy Organ" concerts, where Bach was played against a psychedelic background.

Hollywood soon brought psychedelic visuals to film. Roger Corman's *The Trip* (1967), written by Jack Nicholson, was another "non-drug re-creation" of an LSD experience. Its visual effects were designed by Bob Beck, who literally wrote the book on psychedelic light shows (see Resources). For *The Trip*, Black used an array of techniques including liquids, subliminal flashes of Jungian and Crowleyan imagery, and special methods of timing strobe lights to synchronize them with film. The "Star Gate" sequence from Stanley Kubrick's *2001: A Space Odyssey* (1968), more commonly referred to as the "trip sequence," relied on many of the same psychedelic effects.

"Wet show" traditions have been carried on ever since by hippie culture. The Grateful Dead and other bands rooted in the '60s continued to run psychedelic light shows, which have become a visual shorthand for the era as a whole. Liquids reached a new audience during the big raves of the early '90s. Event producers such as SF's Toon Town employed the latest video and laser effects, but they had the cultural intelligence (and the heart) to hire aging light-show hippies to run liquids alongside their computer video projections. And today, post-'60s musicians such as Beck use liquid projections onstage, visually reinforcing their ties to hippie musical tradition.

CLUB VIDEO, 1970s–

A few light artists used live and recorded video during the late 1960s. In 1969, Nam June Paik began experimenting artistically with the Sony Portapak, a mobile video unit developed for television reporters covering the Vietnam War. But for the most part, the technology was too expensive to catch on widely. As Herbert H. Wise's late-'60s handbook *Professional Rock and Roll* (1967) describes, "…the most up-to-date [light show] technique involves the setting up of a closed-circuit television system, preferably with a TV projector [. . .] This is about as expensive as anything could get and is only possible at a university or other facility which owns such equipment."

The tipping point came in the late 1970s with affordable VCRs, which opened up vistas of video source material for capturing, trading, and simple two-deck editing. During this "Last Days of Disco" era, forward-looking New York dance clubs such as the Peppermint Lounge installed video monitors and began playing underground video mixes as part of their décor. Meanwhile, a new wave of professional video mixing hardware was coming to market, which put a lot of used video equipment, newly obsoleted but still workable, into amateur hands—especially in broadcasting cities. From this primordial soup of technology, urban density, and unexplored creative territory emerged a thriving community dedicated to club video. Video artists in New York wound up defining the look of the influential '80s club scene, just as their hippie predecessors had authored the visual style of the '60s.

New York's Peppermint Lounge club became a sort of "VJ University," training the video staff in the young art form. To symbolize their breaking new ground, the Pep's video control team added the club's logo to the famous image of Neil Armstrong planting the American flag on the moon. The resulting collage became an all-purpose identifier on the club's screens.

MTV launched in 1981 and became an immediate success, which had enormous effects on the VJ scene. The young cable network redefined the term "VJ" as a broadcast VJ rather than a club VJ, borrowing the distinction from "radio DJ" (host) versus "club DJ" (turntablist). To the rest of the world, "VJ" came to designate an onscreen personality rather than a relatively anonymous performer, collector, and technician. In recent years, the original sense of the term has grown.

More significantly, New York-based MTV drew a lot of talented video artists away from the local VJ scene—the Peppermint Lounge in particular—with the inevitable bad blood and accusations of "sell-out." In return, however, MTV vastly expanded interest in video production (if not live video performance) as a creative medium, and attracted talent into the field from all over the world. In addition, the New York club-video "look" that informed MTV became a new standard of cool, embraced by advertisers. This led to many high-paying Madison Avenue gigs for struggling New York video artists.

In the post-MTV universe, any bar anywhere, no matter how "uncool," could show far-out videos on the tube. This posed a problem for the dance clubs of '80s New York, which survived by staying ahead of the curve. Steve Rubell and Ian Schrager's Palladium, which opened in 1984, took the path of going even further with video. Above the Palladium's dance floor hung two huge, movable banks with twenty-five CRT monitors each, taking coordinated inputs from a stack of thirty-three VHS decks, among other things. (The Eidophor video projectors of this era were prohibitively large and expensive.) Other clubs joined a backlash, including Irving Plaza, which prominently exclaimed "NO VIDEO" in its advertisements.

Another technical mini-revolution happened in 1984, when Australia's Fairlight Corporation came out with the Fairlight CVI (Computer Video Instrument), a dedicated video-processing unit that cost around $6,500. The Fairlight could run its effects on video in real-time, which made it a favorite of high-end club VJs and television studios as well as video production houses and ad agencies that didn't operate live. Fairlight operators could superimpose graphics, produce solarizations and other color effects, show "trails," and do lots of other things that you see an awful lot of in videos of the mid-1980s. As with Adobe After Effects (and even Photoshop), the introduction of the Fairlight opened a brief window of opportunity during which designers could satisfy clients by simply pressing the right button on a new tool, before over-use rendered the results recognizable and uninteresting.

Video effects became more accessible with Commodore's Amiga, a home computer which boasted sophisticated video capabilities thanks to a legendarily innovative operating system. Amigas challenged Mac and PC platforms during the late '80s and early '90s, and Newtek's Amiga Video Toaster, introduced in 1991, brought dazzling video effects to the consumer desktop for the first time. Although Amigas haven't been manufactured since 1993, they retain an international cult following.

Meanwhile, in the '80s art world, Nam June Paik's work evolved away from pure video and towards the construction of sculpture that incorporated video screens. By building museum-friendly insider art around video screens, he challenged the arts establishment to begin considering video as a serious art form. He won his case, thereby carving a niche for himself as a pioneering artist and bridging the way for other video artists. Some club VJs of the era didn't think the video in Paik's work was anything more than totem screens designed to say "this is video" within a sculptural context, but they appreciated the cultural vision and social dedication Paik applied toward getting the elders' blessings for the new medium.

SCRATCH VIDEO, RAVES, AND VJ, 1980s–

From the VCR onwards, the newly-accessible technology brought more people into video. They tended to split into two different currents. The angry, solitary artistes edited video at home, producing dense, complex "scratch videos"—collage compositions which often carried political or social critiques. These were traded around on tapes and shown in basements and clubs. Meanwhile, the mellower, more social video geeks pursued live VJing, using simpler tools to play with video or generate abstract patterns on the fly, without sound, in order to accompany music from the DJ. These people jumped naturally into the rave scene after it emerged in the late 1980s.

Scratch video grew up underground alongside audio remixing during the 1980s—especially in London, where cheap VCRs provided an answer to high unemployment rates among young malcontents. But the form is rooted in the collages of appropriated footage created by experimental filmmakers such as Walter Merch, Stan Brakhage, Bruce Conner, and Craig Baldwin—and even mainstream directors like Frank Capra, whose 1943 propaganda film *Prelude to War* (the last of the Army-commissioned *Why We Fight* series) is constructed entirely from stock and newsreel footage. (In one quick sequence of two-second clips, Capra reviews the entire history of the U.S., from conquering the land to electrifying the cities, backed by an inspiring Gershwin score.)

Audio remixing was more common than its visual counterpart during this era, because producing it required less equipment, and it was easier to distribute. But the two shared an ethos. This was the golden age of pirate radio, before the newly-accessible Internet offered an easier distribution channel. But pirate television stations popped up as well, such as London's Thameside TV, which broadcast briefly in 1985.

Around 1990, producers of scratch video and sample-based music began catching heat from the legal arm of the culture industry for using others' intellectual property. The punchline came with U2's 1992 "Zoo TV" tour, when the band hired video artists Emergency Broadcast Network (EBN) to perform improvised assemblages of live commercial video satellite feeds, just one year after U2's own record label had sued the band Negativland for stealing intellectual property.

Raves happened later, beginning in the late 1980s. The canonical recounting explains that London DJs vacationing in Ibiza discovered the synergistic experience of ingesting the drug Ecstasy and dancing to up-tempo "house" music. They brought word of this home, and within a couple of years, the hedonic combination's popularity had exploded, fueling the huge "rave" parties of the early 1990s, held in warehouses, hangars, and open fields around London, San Francisco, and other cities. The raves were disturbing (read: fun) enough to inspire specific legislation against them in Britain's Criminal Justice Act of 1994 (full title: The Criminal Justice and Public Order Act—see Part V, "Powers in relation to raves").

Old VJs look back fondly on 1992, the peak of the rave era, as a time when top VJs were billed prominently alongside the DJs. But VJing was harder back then. DJs had standardized the basic equipment setup on two Technics 1200 turntables and a mixer. This convention enabled any DJ to jump on deck anywhere and begin spinning immediately. VJs, in contrast, had no standard setup (and still don't). They had to arrive first to put everything together and leave last after packing everything away—while the DJ got all the glory.

Many gave up, but others wrote software to make it all easier. The British DJ/VJ duo Coldcut collaborated with Camart to build a video-triggering application called VJamm, which they began performing with in 1997 and distributed to the public in 1999. Meanwhile, Sebastian wrote a MIDI-triggered video app that was released in 1997 by music tech company Steinberg as X‹›Pose. A stripped-down version of this software was distributed with the Jean-Michel Jarre CD *Odyssey through O2* (1998), and Sebastian soon released the application himself as ArKaos VJ.

Over the next few years, ArKaos and VJamm were joined by scores of other VJ applications running on all major platforms. By happy coincidence, these new-millennium years also witnessed an explosion of bandwidth, video capture tools, video archives, and digital video technology, plus dramatic declines in the cost of laptops and digital projectors.

During 2003–2004, Edirol, Korg, and Pioneer began manufacturing VJ hardware, further nourishing the field. The units sold at professional prices, but consumer hobbyists started buying them anyway. In the meantime, the consumer electronics industry hasn't clued in to VJ yet. They haven't noticed (as beginning VJs routinely joke and sympathize about) that the avocation has an uncanny ability to part people from their money. But when they do catch on and steer their ship around, VJ culture will change, and perhaps people will start having the same "I was a punk before you were a punk" arguments that have characterized so many co-options in the past.

The rest, as they say, is history.

Catchy Names from the Golden Era of Light Instruments

In the 18th century, Louis Bertrand Castel was alone with his *clavessin oculaire*. But the 20th century saw dozens of visionaries inventing new light instruments, and then giving them futuristic, scientistic names.

Musical Chromoscope—James Loring, 1901

Mutichrome—C.F. Smith, UK patent in 1924

Sarabet— Mary Hallock-Greenewalt, 1920s

Clavilux—Thomas Wilfred, first patent in 1930

Colortron—Tom Douglas Jones, 1930s (also **Sculptachrome, Chromaton** (formerly **Symphochrome**), and **Celeston**)

Auroratone—Cecil Stokes, first patent in 1942

Polartoscope—Carranza, patent in 1947

Lumigraph—Oskar Fischinger, 1951

Musiscope—Nicholas Schöffer, 1959

Dreamachine—Brion Gysin, 1959 (not an instrument per se, but nice to include)

Musicolor—Maurice S. Wetzel, 1960

Thyratron Colorsound Translator—Royal V. O'Reilly, patent in 1962

Colorgan—Donald Lancaster, 1960s (also **Musette, Psychedelia I**, and **Hi Fi a Go Go**)

Scopitone—French music film jukebox company, early 1960s

Fanflashtick—Gerd Stern and Michael Callahan, 1960s

Lumonics—Mel and Dorothy Tanner, 1969

INSPIRATIONS

INTERVIEWS ■ ■ ■ ■

VJING, LIKE OTHER EMERGING CREATIVE FIELDS, has no established canon or pantheon. There's no consensus about what the territory covers and how it's mapped, and people haven't even agreed on what to call it. (This book prefers "VJ" as a general term for both practitioner and practice, but some restrict "VJ" to the dance club and prefer Video Art Performance, Performance Cinema for the more general practice, and Visualist for the practitioner.) This newness is part of what makes the field exciting. People in and around live video performance have come to it from diverse backgrounds, and they offer a breadth of perspectives beyond that of what you'll find in more mature fields, which typically indoctrinate their novitiates with textbooks and introductory courses.

Some of these perspectives follow, but this set of interviews is by no means exhaustive, and I'm sorry that time, space, and circumstance did not permit me to include dozens more, including:

242.pilots (performance ensemble)
Jerry Abrams, Visualist for Jefferson Airplane, Blue Cheer, etc.
Matt Black, Coldcut, VJamm Developer, VJs.net Founder
Russell Blakeborough, Camart, VJamm Developer
Animal Charm (performance ensemble)
Fred Collopy, Professor of Information Systems, RhythmicLight Webmaster
Matthew Biederman, (VJ) DelRay
Broker/Dealer (performance ensemble)
Joshua "Kit" Clayton, Cycling '74, Jitter Developer
Larry Cuba, iotaCenter—Director
Holly Daggers, FORWARD Motion Theater, Eyewash
Grant Davis, VJ Culture, Dimension7
Jessie Deep, ArKaos VJ Developer
Johnny DeKam, Vidvox, VDMX and Grid Developer
Scott Draves, VJ Spot, *Spotworks* DVD author, Electric Sheep Developer
David, Mr. E., Audiovisualizers.com webmaster
Eric Dunlap, FORWARD Motion Theater, Eyewash
Dave Fleischer, Puppet3D—Co-Founder, VP, and Creative Director
Dave Foss, (VJ) Davy Force!
Lowell Fowler, High End Systems—Chairman
Ryan Geiss, Geisswerks—Founder, MilkDrop, Geiss II, and Smoke Developer
Josh Goldberg, VJ, Dervish Developer
Breck Haggerty, Concert Lighting Designer, NEV 7 Developer
Toby Harris, VJ *spark, AViT conferences—Founder

Greg Hermenovic, VJ El Kabong, Derivative, Inc.—President
Ralph Hocking, Experimental Television Center—Director
Sherry Miller Hocking, Experimental Television Center—Assistant Director
Nathan Janos, EJ Enterprises—VP Development
Charles Kriel, VJ Kriel
The Light Surgeons (performance ensemble)
Marita Liulia, Media Artist
John Laraio, (VJ) Mobius 8
Magnetic Poets (performance ensemble)
Radley Marx, Electronica-Optica, VJTV
Mark McCall, VJ Eniac
Robert Mokry, *Total Production US*—Columnist ("The Visualist")
Jonathan More, Coldcut, VJamm Developer
Alexander V. Nichols, Stage Lighting Designer
Michael O'Rourke, Dimension7
Steve Parr, Oddball Film—Director
Sunit Parekh, VJ
Chris Pirazzi, MEZ Developer
Rick Prelinger, Prelinger Archives—Founder
Radiant Atmospheres (lighting collective)
Rev-99 (performance ensemble)
Rob Read, Edirol USA—National Sales Manager
Sébastien Rosset, VJ eXhale, VJCentral.com founder and webmaster
Dave Richardson, Hyperdelic Video, 111 Minna Gallery
Shirley Shor, Media Artist
Station Rose (performance ensemble)
Samuel Stoller, VJ Science
Bob Stratton, VJ Umm These Waffles Sure Do Taste Delicious, Remote Lounge
Bec Stupak, Honeygun Labs
Mickey Tachibana, Drum Machine Museum
Emile Tobenfeld, (VJ) Dr. T.
Steina Vasulka, The Kitchen—Co-founder, Video Artist
Video Kasbah (performance ensemble)
Vello Virkhaus, VJ V2
David Zicarelli, Cycling '74—President, Max/MSP Developer

Many of these people live in New York, in either NYC or upstate in the Albany/Troy/Schenectady area. When I think about how many of them I never talked to, I can only cry. And please don't even mention Japan, where there's been a huge VJ scene for years—with lots of great people that few in the U.S. have ever heard of.

The list above is just the folks I happen to know about, mainly from local San Francisco circles and English-language VJ websites. I know there are hundreds more doing amazing things throughout the world. If you happen to meet any of the people I've listed at a party (or the many others who should be, but aren't), then hopefully you'll enjoy an interesting interview of your own.

OLIVIER SORRENTINO ■ ■ ■ ■

Olivier Sorrentino, AKA VJ Anyone, performs live video and curates new media at the Institute of Contemporary Arts (ICA) in London.

PS: What kinds of material do you look for as a VJ and a curator?

OS: I'll begin with the curating—that's much simpler. When I started, I put together a few screenings, just to say "this is VJing." But I quickly realized that this was too broad, so I added themes, which gave more detail about what people could expect to see that night. We had one about female VJs, another one about found footage—the whole sampling culture. There's one coming up about computer graphics and another one about VJ festivals. That one won't be creative works so much as documentary pieces about AVIT, Cimatic, Machinista, Contact Europe—all these VJ festivals in different parts of the world produce some kind of archive, so they're a rich source for a screening.

So my first conclusion was that you might call it all "VJing" from the outside, but as soon as you go within the boundaries, you see a lot of branching—different genres and subgenres, categories, styles. Some people work within specific areas, but many more work multiple genres at once. There's not that many contracts to live off of, so VJs will produce stuff in their own bedrooms, and then work anywhere they can. Like on a Friday they'll do a Drum 'n' Bass night, on Saturday, they do a House night, and during the week maybe a corporate gig somewhere and an editing job someplace else. The keywords are versatility, variety. I think the word "Jockey" is very important in VJ—it's a visual jockey. A jockey rides different horses, improvises, works by the seat of their pants. The term fits the occupation very well.

PS: People have historically produced video to be broadcast and duplicated, so it's worked out in advance. What's the effect of live audience and improvisational ability on the form?

OS: This makes all the difference. At a cinema, the audience comes in around the same time, they all sit and look in the same direction, the film starts, and everyone has the same experience. At a club, people come at different times with different friends, and maybe they want to drink or dance or see the DJ. Each individual experience is more customized, and the video component is ambient, in Brian Eno's definition of ambient: it's a low-attention type of art that caters to an audience that isn't there specifically for your product but for a whole environment. You're part of this global experience.

When you went to raves in the early 1990s, the DJ wasn't the main focus—everyone was just looking around at the crowd. Then the music industry began presenting the DJ like a band on the stage. But there wasn't much to look at. How exciting is it to watch a DJ shuffle through his records? So there was this visual gap to fill, and that's when VJ came about. The music industry created this artificial role because they wanted the DJ to be this central personality, this big money-maker.

Now you're seeing this again with VJ—promoting these personalities in order to move more merchandise. That's why VJ DVDs are coming in. These do have potential, though. You can put movies on DVD, but the VJ is the creative person who can take full advantage of the medium with its branching and navigation.

PS: It's a star system—making money by maximizing the distance between celebrities and everyone else.

OS: Well, if you live within a system that you can't change, you just have to adapt. You can be political about it, but at the end of the day, it is a capitalist society.

PS: You were saying that in the early days of raves, it was more about the group and people coming together, rather than the superstar DJ. One thing that I like is how a lot of VJs use live camera on the crowd. That's a way of keeping the original focus—here we are in this place together, and this is about all of us.

OS: I totally agree. I've started to use stills of the crowd regularly in my performances. I'll run my visuals on automatic or have a friend help me out. Then I'll go down onto the floor, take some pictures, then come back five minutes later and mix with them. Live video doesn't work the same way, because when you're looking at the camera, you can't see yourself on the screen. Moving images are always fleeting. Pictures make a stronger statement—they're more official, a captured moment from two minutes ago.

Going back to curating and VJing, I honestly don't see much difference between the two. A VJ, like a DJ, is fundamentally a curator. A DJ goes out and buys records and curates a mix. They produce an original experience that's constructed of other musicians' work. A large portion of VJs produce their own clips, of course. But if you want a close-up shot of exotic insects and you live in a cold country that doesn't have these, you're going to have to sample one of those nature shows on the telly. So there's a large aspect of collecting. You could say that the filmmaker or the band is like a hunter, while the DJ and VJ are more like gatherers—it's a hunter/gatherer dichotomy.

And even if they do produce their own source material, VJs and DJs focus on what other people like. If you're into this culture, you'll notice that a DJ doesn't come to a gig with a fixed set. He'll have a range of possibilities, and he'll lift his eyes, look at the crowd, and ask, are they dancing? Are they enjoying it? If they are, he'll give them more of the same, and if they're not, then he'll go somewhere else, explore different avenues, make it faster or slower or warmer. Same thing with the visual side, although people still pay more attention to the music. You trigger different samples and watch to see if people are looking at your visuals or not.

On the other hand, if people stop dancing and just stand there with their jaws dropped, staring at your visuals and drooling, then you're also not doing your job. If the crowd is watching the screen as cinema, then they're not enjoying the rest of the experience, interacting with other people, stuff like that. So it has to be subtle. And you have to keep in mind that vision is frontal and directional, whereas music is immersive. When you travel through a room, the music sounds more or less the same, but your vision will change and can be distracted. It's important to keep all these factors in mind.

A lot of people decide they want to be VJs, so they buy the technology and think that's it. Too many promoters can't tell the difference, so they'll hire one of these people for cheap, because they need to pay extra for the brown M&M's for some big DJ. So the guy comes up, strobes the same image for two hours, and you get people with epileptic seizures. I'm exaggerating here, but these sorts of dynamics do play out. So we need to educate not just the audience, but also the promoters, the people who make the events happen. The meat of the event is obviously the music, the DJ, or the band—and I don't think we'll ever be questioning that. But there's also the wine and the vegetables which add to the whole experience. And I think we've come to a tipping state where people are beginning to expect visuals, and are disappointed when they aren't provided.

PS: There's an older tradition, going back to color organs and color concerts, of people performing projections for seated audiences, sometimes without any music. Where do you see that fitting in?

OS: That was around long before VJs even had a name. Nam June Paik, John Cage, even Expanded Cinema—all those performances were in galleries, for audiences watching. You can see some of VJ's roots in these areas, and I personally think that's part of the culture, but not everyone agrees. The core of VJ is club culture, which is a mix. Some VJs are artists, but there's also a lot of designers and a lot of geeks. I think it's natural to tie VJ into art, but you might offend some people if you say that VJ's primary origin is in the visual arts.

PS: There's also the tech point of view.

OS: And game culture has contributed a lot as well. There are multiple origins, not only back and forth, but also up and down. There's high culture, which art relates to, but there's also the street aspects of VJing. When I started VJing, I heard anecdotes about VJs coming to the club with their Playstation and just playing a driving game on the screen. That was it, and it was fantastic—people loved it.

PS: Capcom's driving game *Auto Modellista* has a VJ mode, so you can apply filters to games you've saved, to present them as eye candy. I didn't know that people had already been doing this!

OS: The gamers and the game producers have been listening to this audience a lot, maybe even more than the art world. I've got a Master's in Fine Arts, so I understand that lingo, and I know for a fact that a lot of those people want to keep their distance from VJ culture, to maintain their status. Art is object-based. You sell one object to one individual, and you can live off of that for the next three months. It's the same principle with paintings. I know new media artists who produce limited-edition DVDs that they sell in a gallery. They'll make ten DVDs, then delete the source files so that the work only remains on the DVD. But, obviously, you and I could just rip off the DVD and produce other copies. How can you pretend that a DVD is a limited edition?

VJ, in contrast, is about the method, rather than an object or limited-edition objects that you sell to high society or people with lots of money who want to legitimize their business with culture. I'm not saying that art has only this role, but VJing performs a different social function. How art works, the system within the art world of serving and consuming art, is completely different from the world of visuals.

PS: If someone came into the ICA as a VJ and did nothing more than play a driving game, I might think, wow—that's kinda like what Duchamp did. It's recontextualizing something, which is interesting.

OS: I know what you mean—like a Readymade. But we've come a long way since Duchamp. In an art context, I think something like that might possibly work, but only if it were very well framed.

PS: You would need to include enough signposts to show that it's being done consciously?

OS: Completely. It is fair for art to use a VJ tool, but you can't really answer yes or no to that question. There are all these shades of grey, and the VJ world is a young enough form of expression that its place in the culture might change dramatically in five or ten years' time.

But in practical terms, VJing is about flexibility. You can perform at galleries, clubs, theaters, or corporate events, and it's friendly to all these things. You can say it's art, design, technology, or some type of popular, street-level culture. It's also tied up with the Internet, because you can download starter applications and source materials for free.

PS: You said it has the sensibility and attitude of being a curator, watching and listening, taking what you like, noticing how people respond, just being a watcher and a chooser.

OS: That's it. In an information-rich, global society, we need ambassadors to go further out and decide what to take into our society. With visual culture, you can be quite creative and inspired in your sampling. There's obviously a whole legal aspect around this which hasn't been sorted out. What's saving us at the moment is that it's not a huge industry. If you sue a VJ, the money you might get will amount to less than the legal fees.

PS: But if it grows in the future, that might not be true anymore.

OS: We'll have to see. The reason a DJ can legally play someone else's records is because the venue pays a fee to a licensing office that grants limited performance rights. There's no direct analog for video yet, but the UK does have a license, the Video Production License (VPL), which allows bars and pubs to play MTV. We're anticipating that this license will be extended to cover all types of visual material produced in a public venue.

But even if you are producing all of your own clips, how original are they really? Is it you, or is it because you have this funny filter in Photoshop or After Effects? Who made the camera? Getting back to Duchamp, at the end of his career he said that everything is an assisted readymade. A tube of paint is a tool to produce a readymade. And you can get inspired by different designs. Like, if you put blue strips at the top and bottom of the screen, then you're copying IBM commercials. It's a blurry line.

So for me, you can put the question of originality aside and talk about more important questions, like what a VJ actually does. It's someone that's curious and savvy of the visual culture, puts it all into a blender, and gives you an experience that's less alienating than television, and it's not necessarily narrative. I think "art" is not the right word for it now, but it may apply in the future. It isn't strictly "design" either, because that implies an object made for a specific use. But it's close to the idea of design—you can take familiar visual strategies, like a navigation menu on a website, to deliver your own messages. Visuals and graphical interfaces are a language, and rules apply to them. And the VJ is there to recognize those rules by breaking them.

KATHLEEN FORDE ▪ ▪ ▪ ▪

Kathleen Forde is an independent curator based in New York who has developed new-media exhibitions and performance series for institutions and festivals including SFMOMA, the Philadelphia Museum of Art, the Kunstverein Dusseldorf and Cologne, Eyebeam Atelier and the Transmediale Festival in Berlin. Her current exhibition titled "What Sound Does A Color Make?", produced in conjunction with Independent Curators International, is scheduled to tour internationally in 2005–6.

PS: What is *What Sound Does A Color Make?* about?

KF: In a nutshell, the exhibition looks at contemporary audio-visual artists who manipulate sound and image in relationship to one another, within the context of work from as far back as the 1970s, when the first video synthesizing devices allowed electronic artists to manipulate sound with image and vice-versa. The exhibit itself shows work from the last thirty years, but the catalog and related texts contextualize this recent work within the over three-hundred-year history of creative interest in fusing the senses of hearing and vision.

In the very early years, and even to a certain extent in the 1970s, the fusion of sound and vision or a dialog between the two was more metaphorical. For instance, in the early 20th century, Kandinsky produced paintings that he called "compositions," which suggested that you could see the rhythm, hear the music in a silent painting. In the 1800s, "instruments" like the color organ displayed lights that corresponded to notes in a composition. But before the '70s, more often than not, it was one element, either visual or sonic, representing the other—visual interpretations of music, or sonic interpretations of color. Since the late '60s and early '70s, technology and software that developed out of the first video imaging devices has made it is possible to fuse the senses and make these translations more dynamic. All of this is also wrapped up in perceptual psychology and the idea of Synaesthesia that has been around for ages. The idea isn't new—only the strategies.

PS: I'm still unclear—what happened in the 1970s that makes it a good place to start the exhibition?

KF: In the late '60s and early '70s artists started using equipment which directly plugged sound into video and video into sound, allowing them to electronically manipulate them together. For example, one of the early, seminal pieces is

Violin Power, by Steina Vasulka. She's an early video artist who trained as a violinist. For that piece, she plugged her violin into a video imaging device, an oscilloscope, and when she played it, you saw all of these squiggly lines up and down the screen. So you're actually *seeing* her violin music. Steina terms this procedural work "a demo tape on how to play video on the violin."

Nam June Paik was another video artist with a background in music composition who is regarded as a pioneer of this movement. When once asked to comment on the difference between sound and light, he replied, "Sound goes up to 20,000 hertz. Video goes up to 60,000,000 hertz. That is the only difference." He and all of his cohorts, like the Vasulkas and even Gary Hill, began experimenting with ways of seeing sound on video.

After the tools were created, this medium really started to explode—and it continues to do so today. The domino effect of this work takes us to the early '90s club culture, VJ/DJ collaboration, which also focuses on the live manipulation of image as it relates to sound. And now, a crossover has evolved between the two worlds. A lot of artists who are working in video installations and in image and sound sculpture are also creating tools and software for VJing. For some artists, it's like the dance club functions as a studio, where they can test out the technologies which will later make their way into museum/gallery-type installations and performances. There is a nice back-and-forth dialog between the two. VJs are getting more validity within the club world, being seen more as artists, and general audiences are learning that VJs and their tools are an important creative force because some of them are either coming from or finding their way into established art spaces.

PS: That is healthy—when people associate VJ exclusively with the dance club, it limits the whole thing in their minds. So the art world's influence brings it all out to where it should be.

KF: It's also about the evolution of the genre. We might expect or hope to have fully developed genres just a few years after a new technology develops, but that's simply not the natural progression. What we're seeing is that it's more like ten years down the road that things really start to come into their own. A huge boom in DJ/VJ software emerged in the early '90s, and only now is it developing into a genre in and of itself, a more established art practice, where there's a nice two-way interplay between visuals and sound, and where more and more, the images are not merely a backdrop for the music.

Additionally, one sees a lot of electronic musicians nowadays working really closely with one VJ, so it becomes more like a team. That's another way the field is developing and gaining a bit more weight. Fewer musicians just hire somebody who shows up with a random set of video clips.

PS: They're like a member of the band.

KF: Absolutely. Like, do you know Broker Dealer? They're a duo of electronic musicians on Asphodel Records. For the three-plus years they've been together, they've always worked with Del Ray, a VJ and artist who lives in San Francisco and exhibits in galleries, etc. He practices with them and has a real sense of what the music is about, what atmosphere they want to create—so he's always working on ways to visualize the sense of their music, both visually and conceptually.

PS: I always think of the classic four-piece band in rock. Different roles match different archetypes of personality and function within the whole. It seems that with instrumental music or electronic music, if you're not going to have a vocalist singing any lyrics, there's still a role for someone to convey symbolic meaning or non-musical content—and that's what the VJ or visuals person can do.

KF: I agree. Years ago, people complained that it was boring to watch someone behind a laptop on a stage. So in some cases it became a commercial necessity to have a VJ to draw in the audience. But that's developed into a more unified dynamic. It's not separate entities anymore, where the visuals are always taking a back seat.

PS: How did you come up with the idea to do *What Sound Does A Color Make?*

KF: At SFMOMA, I worked a lot with Benjamin Weil to increase the presentation of live arts, bringing in sound art, expanded cinema, and sometimes a VJ/DJ performance appropriate for the context. We were pretty careful about that—to make it suitable for a seated theater in a museum, and not just bring in club culture for the sake of being hip. We got very positive reactions from partners, curators, artists, and the press. At that point it became pretty evident that by simply bringing this kind of artwork into an institution with that level of esteem, all of a sudden an audience sees it as more valid. And deservedly so.

So I tried to keep my ear to the ground regarding the image/sound work that wasn't just whistles and bells or wallpaper. I started noticing that some of the best contemporary work in this genre was rooted to the idea of confounding the senses, which is a concept I've had an interest in from an art-historical perspective for quite some time. So it seemed to make sense to attempt to visually and sonically illustrate the story of this work, and show how it fits into an art historical context that spans three hundred years. I wanted to explain that this art form did not come into being only because we have new technology to play with; on the contrary, it's an interest that has inspired artists for centuries. I wanted to present a story that roots this contemporary work in its ancestry and suggests that it isn't new news.

I hope the exhibition conveys a broader understanding of the conceptual nature of this work. I was pretty careful to try to select work that goes beyond the spectacle of the latest software and brings to the fore ideas of physicality, spirituality, and an awareness of one's own senses—things that people were talking about in the 1800s. I tried to present and discuss this artwork without fetishizing how it was made. In fact, in the catalog and other texts that go along with the pieces, I veer away from describing what technology was used to make the work and instead speak about them in terms of their aesthetic sense and what they're trying to say.

I also wanted to select works that would engage a general audience. A lot of people are put off by media work, and feel that they just don't get it. I purposefully selected work that you can "get" from many different levels—psychological or physical for example. One doesn't have to be a tech geek to be able to get something out of this work.

PS: People of all ages.

KF: Exactly. People of all ages. But also, people of various levels of artistic interests and background. I hope people who might be interested in a Rothko, this sense of a vast color that you can dive into and feel a metabolic relationship with, or people who might love Kandinsky, can relate to this work.

PS: Some VJs are going to be interested in documenting themselves and having their work preserved and some aren't. And I think there's a basic difference between those two approaches. Would museums only be interested in performances intended to retain relevance in the future, rather than something that's created just for the moment to be experienced by the people there?

KF: Not necessarily. There are different ways of documenting a performance, and some ways are respectful to the artwork and some ways aren't. I think the key is to be flexible and creative in terms of a wider understanding of what documentation of the work could be that is appropriate for that piece.

For example, Scanner and Carsten Nicolai opened a show with a four-hour performance with projections that filled the atrium of SFMOMA. We recorded all four hours on DAT, and then the artists sent it back and forth between themselves, and edited it down into a twenty-minute piece that they thought represented the span of their performance. We put that onto a CD, and that CD is now available in music stores and at the museum as a piece in and of itself.

A lot of artists also create performance work that can live on in a different iteration as an installation. For example, another artist who lives in San Francisco, Scott Arford, has different versions of his piece that is going to be in *What Sound Does A Color Make?* called "Static Room." He has a standalone installation version, he can perform the piece from within the installation, or he can just perform it by himself, in a theater.

Meanwhile, there've been lots of symposiums, conferences, and workshops on the issue of media preservation that are addressing these issues of how to preserve or archive live work. It looks like we are reaching a point where it is more on people's minds, artists and curators, so I hope this means we will not be losing "moments" as much anymore.

I think that when something is ephemeral, there's a need to create a discourse around it—to have that performance then becomes the launching point for a symposium, a lecture, or a text. For me, that's a profound moment in museums, when these moments that you schedule inspire more moments, more dialogue. And then the discourse becomes the record of that moment.

Capturing ephemeral work is also not just about performance either. So much of what is going on in contemporary art is by its very nature ephemeral—the questions of how to document live arts can also be applied to networked projects or creative, software-based research. One thing I possibly foresee, although we need to be farther along to assess this, is that when we look back at this period of time, we might view the creators of the software and equipment as meta-artists in a way. The artists/programmers who created Jitter are a good example. I think Jitter is an interesting moment because of many things, but one is the way they allow other artists to create with what they have created—once you buy the software, you become part of this network or community. All of the artists who are using Jitter are also, in a way, the developers of it. The artists are debugging it, and there's this online community where people comment on how they would like it to be updated, what works, what doesn't, etc.

PS: So it's run like an open-source software project?

KF: Absolutely, and it's really listening to what the artistic community wants to be able to do. So to me, something like Jitter is a profound artistic moment, in terms of both what the software is enabling the artistic community to do, and also the way that it's going about it—the way it's a community, like an open-source movement. That's just one case. And often the people who are creating the software are also using it. So, perhaps the people creating the software, the programmers, will be seen as the meta-artists of our time, not unlike the artists who created video imaging equipment in the '70s.

PS: In the art history sense, it sounds like what you're describing is like "schools" of art—a bunch of people who work within a set of shared techniques or doctrines. So maybe Jitter and other pieces of software are the centerpieces of their own schools.

KF: If you look at the development of the software that live visual artists use from a timeline perspective, you can see a real influence of what came before and what after, a clear evolution. Research and design and programming and software are their own art form. In my opinion, it's not necessary for an art-work to be an object or a product anymore, although you can make one with it. Creative process is, in and of itself, often a "work" as well. This is an extension of what's been happening since the 1960s in performance: Performance as Object. Fluxus, for example, or in the '70s, with artists creating video imaging equipment, synchronizers etc. We're getting to a point where the research and the process of creating tools that enable more artwork to be made is, to me, almost an extension of Performance as Object—sometimes that's as much of an artistic moment as many of the objects, performances, and scores, that come out of it. Process- and research-based creative practices are now finding validity within the art institution's walls as never before. Artists have always creatively reflected the sociopolitical culture in which we live. And today it is no different.

40

STEFAN G ■ ■ ■ ■

VJ Pioneer Stefan G. has been a professional VJ and videographer for over twenty-five years.

PS: You've been a professional VJ for a long time. How can you survive in the business?

SG: It takes both love and commitment. I've seen many generations of kids go blurry-eyed when they first look at the screen; you can see that they're thinking of all the things they want to do. So they'll try VJing for a little while, but it's often a brief infatuation, and you can expect a drop-off point after about a year. But if they're committed to it, just like in romance, they'll start putting the necessary work in, creating original content and developing a performance style. If you connect with a medium, that doesn't necessarily mean you can create excellence—for example, I enjoy great keyboard playing and have tried it a little bit, but I'd make a fool of myself if I tried to perform. So, some people learn that they have something to contribute, and some people learn that they don't. It's at the two-year mark that you really see who's still standing.

To be a top VJ, a "consummate VJ," you need a very broad set of skills— and it's a moving target, of course. It isn't all just video; you also need to understand cinema, lighting, and many other disciplines. As with jazz, knowing the rules then gives you the ability to break them selectively and meaningfully.

Cinema comes first and foremost. During the twentieth century, film was the consummate art form because it combined many elements. Multimedia does this today. To do either of them well, you need to understand art history, composition, design, photography, lighting, even graphics—for instance, every VJ should be familiar with Saul Bass, the great title maker of our time. He's a big influence on me.

You also need to understand music and how to construct it to serve a narrative. And you need rhythm. I took drumming lessons from an African folk drummer, and they've influenced my work ever since. Film has three rhythmic elements: motion in front of the camera, motion of the camera, and the cut. The cut is like the kick drum, defining the overall pace. The other two are like the snare and hi-hat or the snare and toms—secondary paradiddle elements between the marking of the beat.

The consummate VJ should have a sense of both the language of film, and how features are actually made. These days, you can get some of that information from the extras on DVDs. I was fascinated with the process when I was first learning it, and it would be fascinating to learn in film school, but there's no substitute for actually working in a production office and being on a set—even if you can only get a job as a production assistant. I discovered that personally, after having worked with small crews for years on guerrilla music videos. There are a lot of protocols and efficiencies you can pick up that make the whole process far easier.

So that's the filmmaking side. On top of that, a consummate VJ needs to know the basic engineering issues of video. This may seem obvious, but some VJs today lack this knowledge. For example, for one event in England last year, I sent some NTSC video along with simple instructions on how to convert it to distribute through their PAL system. But nobody there had the background needed to put the patch together—and there were many VJs there. I was fortunate to go through the early days, when you had to Gen-lock all your sources to sync them up, because it gave me a deep understanding of how the medium works.

You need to understand the hardware issues and have a basic understanding of roadie skills and rigging skills, down to the proper way to wrap cable. I'm not saying that every VJ needs all of these skills. Some are more focused on content creation. But in terms of being the consummate VJ, these are all a part of it.

Naturally, you also need to understand the dynamics of performance and how to apply your own personal style, what you prepare ahead of time and what you leave open. Every good performance features structure and your improvisation, the skeleton, and the optional extras which give it life, give it room to breathe.

Finally, VJs must be able to read a light meter. That's the only way to evaluate the light levels you're working at and communicate them to others in precise, quantitative terms, in order to control the environment. You need to understand the light density and light refraction of the space you're working in—everything from giant halogens lighting up buildings in the background to little inkies lighting up the teacup that a character is drinking from in the foreground—and coordinate it all with the lighting designer. A common bad experience for VJs is to spend a week creating some animation that a corporate client has paid many thousands to produce, only to have the effect ruined by a sixty-dollar par can hung in the wrong place and washing out the screen. Another common problem is backlights reflecting off of the drummer's cymbals and throwing big, ugly splashes onto the screen.

Coordination is essential, however it's done. LDs have a certain primacy over VJs in the event production world because that business is more established, but in my experience, a lot of event lighting professionals lack sophistication. They're good at illuminating performers onstage and making lights flash, but they need to have the understanding required to make a large arena feel like an intimate space, or create a special sense of theater, or a movie set, or something other-worldly.

I honestly believe that because of the breadth of their skills, in many instances the VJ is a prime candidate for overall production management. They understand sound, light, video, and how they all interact. The most aesthetically-effective productions that I've been involved with have had a production manager who has a vision and knows every department—whether it's me or someone else who has those basic filmmaking, VJ, lighting, and roadie skills. You need a person to know and coordinate everything in terms of lighting and color, so it looks coherent. And someone needs to champion the video, because that's the element that can potentially add the most to the production.

Moving head systems such as Kaleidovision, the Koil system, and the Catalyst from High End Systems are a great step forward in terms of coordinating lighting and video, although in my opinion they have not yet realized their potential. The industry has its established customer base of lighting designers, and although many have basic cinematography skills, they aren't as oriented toward image, pattern, composition, and timing as VJs are. So they tend to get these systems with only the basic content package—a lot of which is really good, but it's still very limited. I think VJs are the ones who would make best and most interesting use of this technology, but it's considered lighting equipment, not video, and ultimately it's the LD who prices out the lighting rig, not the VJ.

Another part of the VJ skill set is live camera work, which is another whole department. The concert tour industry calls it i-mag (short for image magnification) or visual amplification, and it involves giving the audience close-up views of the strings as the guitar is played, or letting them see the bead of sweat running past the singer's eye, or another audience member's reactions—reinforcing the emotional connection between performer and audience.

I-mag originally developed as a facet of VJing, and we really played with it back then. For example, at many New York clubs, such as Interferon and Danceteria, after soundcheck in the afternoon I would shoot members of the band standing and applauding in different places around the room. Then, during the show that night, after a song finished, we'd sometimes cut away to a live shot of the audience, and sometimes we'd cut away to these clones of the band, laughing and cheering.

Today, i-mag is associated mainly with the big screens in large arenas, but companies that specialize in it often don't hire VJs or even people who work with music—like, they'll get someone who directs infomercials. It's turned into a drier, less creative, more conservative form, and for most of the major arena bands, their video is a couple of steps behind the front edge of club VJing.

Ultimately, people with big budgets tend to be more risk-averse. A band that's playing to 50,000 kids may be shouting about tearing down the system, but at the end of the day, they're a business enterprise upon whom people's paychecks depend. And that demands a serious element of conservatism, which runs into the production decisions. For a long time, audio engineers didn't use computers because they were considered riskier than tape machines. Now hard drives have found their way into high-end i-mag rigs, and the result is a great new tool, but a lot of professionals won't use them because they're afraid of a system crash, like they might get on a computer.

One example: at the first Green Spirit Dance in November 2002, we had about a $5,000 budget for video. That was a rave that took place at the Concourse Exhibition Center on the same night that the Rolling Stones played at Pacific Bell Park, just a few blocks away. Hundreds of people walked over after the Rolling Stones show was finished, and the universal comment was, wow, these visuals are so much better! The video on the Rolling Stones tour was just typical i-mag, while we were really trying to push the technology and conceptual framework. It also helped that we could do whatever we wanted to and didn't have the unavoidable music industry bureaucracy in the way.

Last year I went to see one of my favorite acts, and they had a beautiful, high-resolution video wall, but the basic formula that the video followed—steady i-mag, a little bit of B-roll thrown in, and some video feedback off of the screen—was exactly what we were doing over twenty years ago. In the i-mag world, it's still considered current. This was a forty-dollar per head show, but you could never get away with that kind of minimalism at a ten-dollar dance party.

But with audiences becoming more sophisticated, the gap is closing, and many VJ techniques are being reintroduced into common i-mag practice. Now that half of Madonna's audience have been to raves and seen the video there, the video on her tours has of necessity become more elaborate. Still, the touring industry has its old habits, and people who want to push the video find it a hard sell unless the band itself suggests it. That's how it usually plays out—you get some new band on their first major tour, and they want something like what they saw at the rave. Like, they want an enormous 3-D octopus to look like it's eating the drummer at the end of the encore, or whatever. That's when things get interesting, and when they need to hire a real VJ.

Meanwhile, I have seen some of the best acts in the world on major tours where the video people just relied on generic video packages, such as Motion Backs. These are backgrounds with wobbly lines and such that come off of a twenty-five-dollar, royalty-free DVD. If you know video, it's embarrassingly cheesy. It's like going to see a great singer, and they're backing her up with royalty-free music from some industrial CD. I would never do that, although some can obviously get away with it.

It comes down to fear. Where you have money, you tend to have more conservatism and fear and less of an exploratory attitude. And where you do have the early adopters and a more exploratory attitude, you often don't have the resources.

Like the touring industry, Hollywood can learn a lot from VJs in terms of efficiency of producing graphics. We're approaching a post-rendering age, and I believe that many of today's CG skills are going to be considered pretty antiquated. Rendering will be replaced by real-time mocap, motion-capture, for many applications, and to do mocap you have to make decisions quickly and think on your feet, which are very much the purview of the performance VJ.

PS: Not to mention the sheer physical puppetry, the ability to gracefully move your muscles as input to sensors during takes.

SG: Yeah, the skill set that VJs have been developing independently will replace a lot of the skill set that animators now use in Hollywood. In the film industry, people probably wouldn't believe that you can produce twenty minutes of finished animation, keyed, from scratch, in just three weeks. But within VJing, it's a necessity—it's how you stay in business. The pressure of live performance forces you to make choices about what's possible, and gives you a lot of practice creating things in one pass, rather than tweaking frame-by-frame.

In some ways, it will be like a return to the days of motion control, of doing multiple passes using an IMC system, slowly running a camera past a physical model like they did for the opening shot of *Star Wars*. Even though it's "old school," I actually love motion control. It has a meditative quality. Many years ago, I did a ten-second piece that actually took about six days to shoot, apart from the model-building. I got one of my favorite artists in the world to make this really beautiful model. It was a city on half a planetoid, with a figurehead that winked at the end of the shot. So you swooped in really slowly, and in the background is a checkerboard of space and clouds. The clouds were actually time-lapse films of real clouds. So, that was one exposure level. Then we had our starfield, the basic little lights—that was another exposure level. We had our beauty pass, which was the main lighting on the main object, and everything else would be black. We used Scotch reflective tape with a light above the camera to get the lights on the buildings in the city. Each one of those passes was a separate take at separate exposure levels, but they were all combined physically onto one piece of film. It took a crew of five people six days to create a scene that today I could do on my own in an afternoon with SOFTIMAGE—although it wouldn't have the same character or look.

In 1981, I antagonized some people in the motion-capture community with an article I wrote for *Reality Hackers* magazine. I argued that with advances in computers and bandwidth, much of the work that was then done with physical models, the "kit bashing," would soon be done by computer graphics. A lot of people didn't want to hear this at that time.

I also wrote in the article that certain stories could only be told onscreen once we had computer modeling and 3D animation, such as Harlan Ellison's "The Silver Corridor," or *Doctor Strange* from Marvel Comics. With the tools that were available in 1981, you could not tell *Doctor Strange* properly, get those magnificent interdimensional landscapes. They tried, but it didn't work. I may be a technophile in many ways, but I believe in appropriate technology. Some stories are impossible to tell without three-dimensional computer graphics, but others are best told around candlelight or firelight with just the human voice. There's a huge range in between with a huge range of creative decisions you can make, depending on the resources available. If you wanted to remake

Jurassic Park but you only had two hundred bucks to spend, you could do it with glove puppets. There are always options.

Another thing the article predicted was that after a first wave of CG-based neo-realism, we would see stylistic variation explode in film. We've seen this recently with films such as *O Brother, Where Art Thou?* There isn't a single monster or spaceship in that film, yet pretty much every frame was digitally processed. I wrote that with computer graphics, stylistic exploration in the mode of the great painters would finally be possible in motion media, i.e., film. So I was very enthusiastic about computer graphics back then, and some of the people who originally turned their backs on me for celebrating these changes are now well-established doing CG for features. So you've got to laugh.

But that's the nature of many companies. Many in the upper echelons of Hollywood are separated from people who have real ideas by a middle management layer that takes ideas that filter up and presents them as if they were their own. That's happened to VJs thousands of times. But they're ultimately cheating themselves. A company can successfully steal ideas from a person, but they're ignoring the mother lode that would be available if they actually hired them. I think this is one of the things that's holding culture back. You can be the greatest visual storyteller in the world, but professionally, you're no competition for somebody who above all else "wants to direct." People often just work with the people they're familiar with, and so it becomes a matter of self-promotion.

PS: I've seen some of that myself, and I think it will always be an issue. But, as successful as those people might be, I think that coming up with your own ideas is a more fun way to go through life.

SG: It gets back to the idea that there's no limit to what you can accomplish as long as you don't mind who gets the credit. It's legal to steal ideas in this society, but it is not legal to steal money. This means that where art and finance mix, there isn't a level playing field, and the person who controls the money can steal the ideas. It's basically rule by force—not physical force, but economic brutishness, with Adam Smith's invisible hand of the marketplace acting as a fist. As a result, a lot of nice people in the ivory towers of industry are somewhat sad figures because they're isolated from the things that they love, from the very things that would inspire them. VJs have a huge advantage in this area, as they are by necessity always in the "cultural mix" and are interacting with audiences, getting direct feedback.

Within creative communities we see a different model, allocating resources by merit rather than force. So it's not the kid with the rich parents who has the Steinway; it's the kid who can play piano best.

PS: Open-source software operates that way.

SG: Exactly—and that's relevant to VJing because historically, every time the medium takes creative leaps forward, the scene has enjoyed a collaborative atmosphere. Whereas when the VJ scene has been tighter and more competitive, the creativity stalls or even loses ground. I say this with the long view of having been through several of these cycles, a couple of booms and a couple of busts, and I've seen it corrupted commercially a couple of different ways, initially with MTV's willful misinterpretation of what music video was about.

So I've been on a rollercoaster, as every freelancer is—sometimes having lots of money in the bank, sometimes wondering where next month's rent is gonna come from. Some people may consider that a lack of success, but my personal definition of success is accomplishing what you've set out to do with your priorities still intact. To quote *Citizen Kane*, making a lot of money is easy to do if that's all that you want to accomplish in life.

PS: I'm impressed by how throughout your career, you've had an unerring eye for where the interesting new stuff will come from, sensing what's going to heat up next across different disciplines.

SG: There's a great scene in *Highlander* where Connor says "1783 was a very good year." And then he goes into all the events that happened in 1783. There was no foggy "Well, around that time…" He knew that was when the Montgolfier Brothers flew their first balloon and what else happened that same year. That's when you realize, my God—this guy really did live through those times, and really has been alive for hundreds of years! That historical context strikes me as something that I can give you for this book—during the early days of VJing, what else was brewing, what the rest of the media landscape looked like. But although I have great respect for the past, and will learn every lesson that the past has to teach, my eye is firmly on tomorrow, and on the trillion-year adventure that the human race is just starting out on.

Actually, I have one old photo for you that someone took a long time ago, of me and Milton Berle, both in tuxedos, at a sort of private event. At the time it was like, "Here's the guy who pioneered television and the guy who pioneered performance video together—two generations of the same thing."

Going back to my childhood, growing up literally in the shadow of London's main television broadcast tower, two major influences on me were my cousin Josephine and my uncle Bogdon. Josephine worked as a production assistant on a lot of well-known British television shows. Through her, I became familiar with the lingo and the production environment, particularly the demands of live television. My uncle Bogden showed me that if you looked at the grooves on an LP, you could tell where one song ended and where the next began, and also where certain parts were, where the music changed—all of which I found fascinating.

Some years later, after my initial schooling, I wanted to work in television. But there were only two TV stations in England at that point and no place to work. I got a job in Screen Gems' audio studios on Wells Street, cutting acetate.

While I was there, I was fortunate enough to see them upgrade from the '50s style of recording to 24-track, so in my early months I learned the old miking techniques. I also learned how music related to film, and how the creative production process worked on an industrial scale.

At the same time, during the early '70s, I started getting stints as a DJ. This was pre-cassette, so being able to cut acetates was a real boon, and I became very familiar with the cutting process. If somebody wanted a particular song, I could just run off an acetate and give it to them. But after a while, working in the studio got boring. I love it now, but in my younger days it made me feel too isolated from the universe, and it was driving me nuts. So I ended up road-ie-ing around for a while, loading equipment, touring, learning those skills. It was probably a terrible career move, but the whole hands-dirty work ethic had a great influence on me.

I was also collecting little music films and shooting in Super 8. Meanwhile, I was inspired by John "Hoppy" Hopkins' TVX at the London Arts Lab, which showed that video could be more than television. Once in a while I'd get a black-and-white 1/2-inch Portapak and experiment with that.

Some years later, by a fluke, I ended up being a house DJ at Dingwall's in Camden Town, which was an influential club; radio DJs would go there, and you'd sometimes see Pete Townshend and Richard Branson come in. I was able to break or champion a lot of good music—Bauhaus, Killing Joke, Dennis Brown, Fela Kuti. I also played hip-hop acetates and dub plates that I got from friends in New York, but it was a little too early for that to be accepted. Meanwhile, I brought in and projected my Super 8 animations and reels from the film co-op down the street.

After the Betamax hit the market, I started using video. I no longer had to carry pounds and pounds of film cans, and I could switch from one VCR to another instantaneously, reactively, rhythmically. Visual artists had sought a performance medium for centuries, and now that video was available, the form could really be invented. This was in 1978, two years after the Sex Pistols broke through, and the atmosphere was very countercultural. The most heroic thing most young people thought any English person had ever done was play "God Save The Queen" in front of the queen herself. New wave hadn't been invented yet; "Blue Monday" wasn't out. If you wanted to see a music film back then, you'd have to catch it in the theater during the three days that it would run, or else go to a screening at the ICA that people like John Marshall used to put on—he's a great guy and a great filmmaker who made some concert films with Jimi Hendrix.

Dingwall's was the first club in the area to put in a permanent video installation, a few monitors and a stack of VCRs, so it became a laboratory for developing the medium. Then more clubs started putting in video, and that's the business I went into. For the first few years, until the warehouse party thing, VJing was strictly club video, driven by club owners wanting bragging rights about having the fattest system in town and then hiring the best person they could to run it.

I decided to relocate to New York, which had a club scene that's now legendary. I worked at places like Danceteria and the Peppermint Lounge, which operated as a sort of VJ university at the time. I even worked at Studio 54, which was a memorable place, although it wasn't important to the development of the VJ medium. I had far more fun at Negril, on 2nd Avenue near 11th Street, working with unknown acts like Afrika Bambaataa, Grand Wizzard Theodor, or Jazzy J. The club was owned by Bob Marley, but when he went off the road, his tour manager Ken Williams took over running it.

VJ and hip-hop emerged widely at the same time, although they had different gestation periods. That's important to know if you want to understand the history of the medium. Hip-hop had actually started decades before, and if you watch *Absolute Beginners*, there's a scene toward the end, from the 1950s, where a couple of Jamaican guys are jamming with microphones and congas over a DJ playing a Miles Davis record. That's the origin, turntables and a microphone, and you'd see it in Jamaican neighborhoods in London. For hip-hop DJs back then, it was all down to working the breaks. It wasn't like you could put on the instrumental side from some major record company, and that's how you got your rhythm.

When I first got to New York, hip-hop had not come downtown yet, and actually, most of the people below 125th Street who listened to hip-hop were English. Punk bands over from London would ask me where the turntable action was, and it was embarrassing to admit that there wasn't anything downtown. We'd have to go out to some park where people would plug into the light socket—no permits, nothing—and that's how we gave them the kind of Saturday night out that they expected in London. But by 1981, hip-hop records were coming out, and there were clubs full of VJs all over New York City. Some places, like Mudd Club, CBGB, and Max's Kansas City, wouldn't touch hip-hop. But DJs like Don Letts at the Roxy recognized that punk and hip-hop were a perfect fit, both the cry of the oppressed, so in between a punk band's sets he'd play heavy dub from Yabby You or Lee Perry. What punk rock was to dinosaur rock, hip-hop was to the overproduced R&B of the time—both were reactions against things getting too pompous.

So it was great to work with Grand Wizzard Theodor just last week. I used a lot of classic graffiti and street art imagery for that. Grand Wizzard Theodor and I emerged at pretty much the same time in New York—he was in the front of the hip-hop wave, and I was at the front end of the video and VJ wave. I hadn't talked with him for almost twenty years, but there we were in the same place again, and we had an interesting conversation. We've clearly shared a lot of experiences on our respective journeys—both of us are still plugging away at what we do because of a love of the art, while others who were less committed made fortunes off of techniques that we developed. I mean, Grand Wizzard Theodor is the person who invented scratching! So both of us are doing fine, but neither of us as rich as we possibly deserve to be, at least in my opinion. But that's just the curse of the early adopter.

MTV, which started broadcasting in 1981, is a great example of that. Before MTV launched, Bob Pittman, who created it, used to spend a lot of time in various clubs studying VJ culture. Then, after MTV, everyone outside the club scene thought that VJs were screen personalities who played the latest fifty-thousand-dollar video from A Flock Of Seagulls. The MTV people explained to the VJs in New York that there were now two kinds of VJs, club VJs and broadcast VJs—just like there were club DJs, who mix and perform live, and broadcast DJs, who play songs on the radio and act as hosts.

But MTV was new and exciting, and there's a whole era in there, slightly post-MTV, where there was a huge demand for people to play music videos. But there wasn't a video for every song, so when there was a track that the scene liked but that the record companies weren't trying to push, that's where the live VJ art came in, and you would play the song and improvise some ambient visuals, as we called it then.

Players were cheap enough at that time, but producing video effects was prohibitively expensive. The standard digital video effects unit was the Quantel 5000, and it cost up to $750 an hour to sit in a room with one of these and do simple video effects. A few valuable people, like Dean Winkler at Teletronics, were in the fortunate position of being able to work with DVEs day in and day out. They shared those skills and resources with me and other early VJs, and had a major role in raising the standards of the form. There were people who built video synthesizers, worked at studios, worked with flight simulators and let you in after work so you could tape some fly-throughs, all of whom contributed to the creative community.

But when you rented equipment or borrowed people's time after hours, you had to decide in advance what effect you needed. You'd say, "I need a certain stop-frame and colorization on this, in shades of orange, somewhere between fifteen and twenty frames per second." Then, after $1,500 and two hours in the studio, you'd get a loose approximation of what you were imagining. When the Fairlight CVI came out in 1984 it changed all this.

The Fairlight was a real-time digital video effects unit. Something that required two weeks of optical printing work with film could be done on the Fairlight with a couple of keystrokes, or at least a couple of passes. More importantly, it cost six to eight thousand dollars, depending on the options package, which was far less than the Quantel—and it was even somewhat portable. This meant that motivated individuals could actually own one, practice on it, and take it to performances. It gave you time to refine your shots, get the exact shade of orange that you envisioned, and figure out that seventeen frames per second was that magic point, not sixteen or eighteen. You could experiment with the Fairlight between soundcheck and showtime, adjust the palettes, adjust the timing, refine your technique, and get more practice time in than you would in months of working on professional music videos in studios. You could become an instrumentalist, a performer. Two years later, Video Toaster on the Amiga made video effects even more accessible, raising the art even further. It all comes down to access to tools and familiarity, the old Buckminster Fuller thing.

PS: You use the word "art"—what role did video art play in all of this?

SG: Video art, like in galleries and museums, has for the most part stayed in its own separate world, which is unfortunate, I think. When VJing started in the late 1970s, Nam June Paik had been producing video art for years, but his work had more to do with the sculpture around the screen than the content of the video itself. It was conceptual art, really, although it was positioned as video art. There were some great video artists working then, like Stephen Beck, but Bill Viola and others seemed more focused on the gallery mentality, even though it was a time of technologically-inspired visual upheaval. And a lot of early VJ style was actually a reaction to the sterility, patronage-whoring, and gimmicky nature of the first generation of video arts.

During the late '70s and early '80s, David Ross was a very important figure in the video arts. He started the Whitney Biennial, and back then, he was a truly great curator. He visited everywhere, from the Fun Gallery, which was owned by Patti Astor, to graffiti shows downtown. In the Lower East Side, on Avenue B, in all these dives with receptions with boxed wine, he would be there hunting out the art. He was like a good A&R man at a record company; he would find talented unknowns and build up their marquee value. He headed the Whitney until 1998, and then he came over to San Francisco to head the SFMOMA, but unfortunately he didn't repeat here what he'd done earlier in New York. In fact, from what I gather, he rarely moved more than about ten yards away from a bottle of champagne or a plate of caviar the entire time he was here—which discouraged a lot of people who had looked forward to his broadening the local artistic horizons.

And, frankly, the kind of video art that you see at SFMOMA and other museums is often way below minimum professional VJ standards. A museum might keep something that looks like a test shoot looping for hours, whereas in a club you'd only get away with showing it once for a few seconds. I've been severely disappointed at the mainstream art world's take on multimedia. One installation I saw at SFMOMA was an enclosed space with two projectors dedicated to showing the front and rear view of a beach, and that's all. This has nothing to do with the heights of creativity you can see in warehouses, nightclubs, and small studios. There's a wide gulf between these two worlds in terms of both inspiration and execution, at least as far as I've seen—and I'll admit that I haven't been to every video exhibition or screening out there, so I may have missed some excellent stuff. But there's great video going in this area. This really is one of the mother lodes of interdisciplinary media talent, the nexus of Silicon Valley and the Haight-Ashbury, the computer and the light show. Yet pretty much everyone in the VJ scene who is well-regarded by their peers is locked out of SFMOMA. It's like they don't even investigate what's out there.

In 1998 they put together a huge exhibit of Keith Haring's public art. Now, it so happens that I have some of Haring's very early baby paintings, and I used to shoot all of his chalk stuff on the subway. I probably have the largest collection of early Keith Haring video in California. So despite my being an outsider, I had several unique works and documents that seemed worthy of consideration for the show or at least to project during the launch party. I let the museum know what I had available, but they never got back to me, and they got their friends to do visuals for the reception. This isn't just a personal thing; I've talked to many others who've had similar experiences.

So I think it comes down to profile and positioning. But I don't believe that the arts community is being served by two camcorders on a beach while so many other artists are producing very detailed, well thought-out work.

PS: In terms of curating local art, it seems to me that the SFMOMA spends far more money to do a far worse job than does the Burning Man organization. The best video at Burning Man is light-years ahead of work I've seen at SFMOMA, and the same is true for sculpture.

SG: For the past few years, I've done a show that same weekend, MegaBuzz, where there's maybe 15,000 people and a budget to match. The promoter pays a buck a head, and he wants great video, not just good video. So which do I choose? Any VJ who has the stature to have a club residency, to be on tour, to be working on animation for a serious project, can't afford to take two weeks off during the peak summer touring season, or to miss SIGGRAPH, to go to Burning Man.

So Burning Man gets a lot of people who are just building their reputation. I'm not putting them down because the second-string VJs today, with a little experience, are our superstars of tomorrow. But you see the people who are focusing on self-promotion, on building up their name recognition—essentially people who aren't already booked that weekend. People there may be the early adopters, but they're generally not the ones that record companies or agencies are booking professionally.

I think the world is a better place that Burning Man exists, and I would welcome the experience of performing there, but even if I've had major tours and have paid my rent for a couple of months, I just can't afford to turn down paid gigs in order to groove around in the desert.

PS: Most of the live video imagery you see at Burning Man seems to derive from rave culture, rather than club video—more abstract, less collage.

SG: That was the next phase of it, starting in the late '80s. With the warehouse parties, the business model changed. You had to own your own equipment and bring it to the event, and this broke the social contract that VJs and promoters had in the club world. Previously, it had been that they picked you because of your merit, and then you'd get to play with a quarter-million-dollar video installation for the night. Instead, people competed on what hardware they had and what they were willing to work for. It was like, "Oh, my buddy's got a projector and some old cartoon reels—he'll come and do visuals for beer money."

But in the early '90s with producers like Toon Town, raves and their audiences became far more sophisticated. This was another boom time, with big budgets for video, film, and choreography. Working with dancers is great. At Hellball at the Giftcenter which is one of the circuit parties I do, we had a couple of dancers rappelling down the walls. I shot them in silhouette and did video feedback with a fairly long delay to make it look like they were multiplying, so after a while, I was showing this big crowd of rappel dancers moving around. It just comes down to careful lighting, like so much else in VJing.

In general, any imagery you're mixing with should be designed against a black background, and if you do anything else, it must be for a specific reason. Like at the Kennel Club we did a lot of bluescreen effects, so we had a "house blue," which was the color you saw looking through the camera at a bluescreen with the follow-spot on it. I used that exact hexadecimal color point as the background for any animations I created to use there. That way, I could do a chroma key that fit everything. Meanwhile we avoided using that color or anything close to it for the go-go dancers' costumes. That's important because otherwise you can't insert any backgrounds behind them.

Some of my video isn't even designed for the screen. It's for aerial beam effects, extrusion effects, in rooms with a lot of haze, fog, or smoke and where I'm not doing rear projection. The beam is more visible in the air than where it finally lands, so I design it to look good from the side. Like, it might just be some colored dots moving slowly against a black background. Bounce it off of a DMX mirror you're controlling, and you can make the beam pattern dance around on the floor like a person.

Anyway, budgets for VJs dropped again in the mid- to late-'90s, and the main thing that suffered was production coordination. People no longer scheduled production meetings before events; everyone just showed up in the afternoon, rigged up their equipment, and played their content. So the whole thing became less coordinated, although the people themselves were as professional as ever.

In reaction to this, I've come up with some strategies that bring back a level of communication and coordination without requiring a budget for pre-production. MegaBuzz with Trancefusion at the SF Civic Center a few years ago is a good example of what can go wrong and how to fix it. We had excellent people working there—the laser guy was great, the lighting guy was great, all the DJs were great, I thought I was holding my own. We were all doing our absolute best in isolation, but the lack of coordination made the overall effect a little bit sploogy.

We did have one cue for the night, for when the band Trancefusion came on. I'd designed some animations for them which showed a magician working over a cauldron. So we decided to begin showing the animation only in shades of green, black, and white, while the lighting guy switched to all green shades. Meantime, the laser was already green. As soon as we did that, the whole place was bathed in a green glow, and a hush came over the audience. Then we gradually brought in more shades, starting with blues. I would introduce a new color to the video, the lighting guy would immediately follow, and each time, you could hear the audience gasp. The effect was magical, and it was simply a matter of deciding what not to do, how to compress our palette. It was like the way *The Matrix* has no reds—there's another example of a compressed palette. We didn't bring the reds back until about two-thirds of the way through Trancefusion's set, when I switched the video over to use a full palette.

VJs as a culture have proven that just taking the money away won't shut a field down or prevent its evolution, although it might guide its direction. It comes down to the art of the possible, and you develop your creative ability from the tools and budgets that you have available. If you have to compromise, do a tape-based show, or prepare more of the material ahead of time. Instead of choreographing a dozen dancers, pre-shoot one and work with that. Yes, you lose the excitement, the sense that everything could go south at any given moment, but you can still produce a damn fine result that's aesthetically valid and creatively unique. VJs will persevere no matter what, as long as they can eat and pay the rent, because there is that drive, that need for the medium to exist.

After budgets shrank, VJing retreated to the laptop, became more solitary, and VJs developed fantastic new software tools. That's where it's been for a while. What I see happening when production budgets expand again is that these new tools will be applied to large-scale theater that breaks down the fourth wall. A lot of this stuff will converge—filmmaking, lighting, and new video technologies will recombine with early '90s video skills like compositing, blue- and greenscreens, and motion capture, and we'll see live dancers in front of the greenscreen, giving the sense of working without a net, all being done in real time. That's very important, because I've seen shows where people worked their butts off to produce everything real-time, and yet because they're stuck in the back, the audience thinks they're just playing an old *Mind's Eye* DVD. They're sweating away, creating all of these layers, and the people don't even know.

I'm working on an interesting performance project now, creating animation for Jade Steele's *Tales of the Rondo*. It's sort of a rock opera, like *Tommy*, but it's designed to be presentable in a number of ways, using the EJ system on a turntable.

PS: What's the background on that?

SG: The project began with Jade's music, which I really like. The lyrics tell a sci-fi story, about an enslaved race called the Weeds who serve as caretakers for an ancient, powerful object called the Rondo, during a time of interplanetary war. The music combines basic rock 'n' roll with elements of drum 'n' bass, hip-hop, and techno, and it's the first rock music that has actually inspired me since the days of Nirvana. Rock becomes most interesting, I think, when it hybridizes, assimilates other elements, and that hasn't happened in a long time.

Jade got a great comic book artist, Marc Nordstrom, to draw illustrations for the story, and I've been working with these to create an animated version on DVD, which will include backing audio and MIDI cues for lighting and sound effects. Using this disk and the EJ system, a turntablist will be able to control the animations and tell *Tales of the Rondo* visually. We know we want to perform this way with Jade Steel's band, but it could also run with just a DJ, actors, a reader, or any combinations of the above. So, it's an animated film that can be performed live off of turntables, accompanied by any kind of audio you want. One thing about VJing is that it's revived the old skill of purely visual storytelling, which you had with silent film.

I have several irons in the fire right now. There's the Jade Steele project, I've got a couple of gigs this weekend, including a spring-themed fashion show at Ruby Skye that I need to create graphics for. Next week I'm down at Stanford University, where I do a lot of video work. I love working at Stanford—it's like a little slice of heaven to me. I discover a lot technologically, and can work with and measure myself against some of the best minds of our time. Meanwhile, I have some trade shows coming up. I have to design the screen layouts and the content for them. Doing the screens is a design job in itself, but if you ever saw Pink Floyd perform with a circular screen in the '70s, you know it can really add to the production value. And that was fairly primitive by contemporary standards.

I'm so busy and deep into the work that I don't have time for self-promotion. As you're discovering, VJing is one of those fields where you have to do some digging, because the most accessible people aren't necessarily the ones doing the most interesting things. I'm certainly not out there handing out business cards at receptions or placing ads in magazines. In fact, the only two times during the past week when I was not either at home or working here in the studio were when I was doing the Mixmaster Mike and Grand Wizzard Theodor shows. And for every person like me that you talk to, I guarantee that there are at least five more people whom you don't even know about who are doing equally interesting projects.

CRAIG BALDWIN ■ ■ ■ ■

Craig Baldwin makes and curates independent film in San Francisco. His docu-
mentary Sonic Outlaws *(1995) uses appropriated film material to explore issues*
of sampling and intellectual property in the music world.

CB: So, you're on the VJ tip? That's cool; I'm into visual appeal. I actually
worked my way through school doing lights and projections for clubs. You
know, a lot of other film people in the Bay Area came out of doing light shows
as well—Bruce Conner, Jerry Abrams, Karl Cohen. It's one way to make a living
and still stay in the art world. I don't dismiss it, but ultimately I'm not into
escapism. I mean, eye candy is OK, but I'm a filmmaker—I want to deal with
ethical issues. With abstract visuals, it's hard to ask questions. I want a visual
language where you can speculate or interrogate.

PS: Maybe it's just terminology, but I mean "VJ" in the broadest sense—not
just showing dazzling visuals, but also using film clips to improvise with.

CB: Well, I've done a lot of that. I used to publish a catalog, "Sub Cinema,"
with 16mm montage reels and loops that I rented to clubs. Better yet, I would
also sell services, come and set up projectors and show mix films all night. I
rode a moped around town with a couple of 16mm projectors between my legs
and a backpack stuffed with film reels. Club Townsend was the best gig—that
was three nights a week. I also worked at 1015 Folsom (Das Klub) for many
years, and the DNA Lounge, the Paradise Lounge, and the Oasis back then.
Also a place called Oz, which was in North Beach, above the Mabuhay Gardens.
   16mm projectors are cheap now—I must have five. You can get one for thirty dollars at a garage sale, and the last two or three I've gotten for free.
Schools often have them taking up closet space and they're happy to get rid
of them. It's just like with old footage—you can rescue it and make art out of
it. I don't think anything in my studio was bought new, and I'm proud of that.
   I've gotten film from all sorts of places: collectors, hobbyists, and projec-
tionists, pawnshops, flea markets, dumpsters—especially dumpsters outside of
television stations. A lot of government films are public domain and sometimes
easy to get your hands on, even military material. One time I was up at the
Presidio library and found a couple of reels about counter-insurgency operations
in Latin America. They actually let me sign them out under a false name, the name
of a dead friend. I just kept them, and cut them up into some of my own films!
   For a long time, it was cheaper to bring 16mm projectors into a place rather
than video projectors, and you could find more material in 16mm. Film has a

more sensual look and it conveys a sense of history, but with video you can apply filters, layering, windowing, and graphic overlays—effects that are very interesting for their own sake. For some venues, video can be more convenient, and in the early '80s, I transferred a lot of my films over to VHS and then Stephen Parr folded them into his Club Generic Video catalog. Today you see more digital projectors in clubs.

Some people realize that 16mm celluloid is probably in the last few decades of its active lifetime, so a lot more artists are picking it up for its value as media archaeology. It's like the enlightened appreciation that people have for vinyl records, wire recorders, and tube amps. Also, film is an archival medium. I've got stacks of VHS, and I don't know if you'll be able to show it in twenty years. The film you can show in 120 years.

I'm dedicated to educating people on what was going on in the history of visual culture. It's not nostalgic or camp—it's critical consciousness, how we got here, media literacy. Americans are obsessed with media. You can tune into different radio stations for '20s music, or '30s, '40s, '50s, etc. All these eras are becoming omnipresent, and we navigate around among them. It's all open to deconstruction. I'm going to a conference in Germany this summer to teach a class where we'll be cutting up old East German propaganda films, and I expect that it'll be a great history lesson for all of us. Or sometimes people call me because they're having an event, like a '40s night, where everyone dresses '40s and I'll show films from that era. There are a lot of these, like Bardot-a-Go-Go does with '60s French pop culture. It's typical of the VJ scene, where they'll open up a virtual space in history.

Film collage is nothing new—Hans Richter made film collages during the Dada era, just as John Heartfield was cutting and pasting his photomontages. A later example is in Frank Capra's *Why We Fight*. This was a series of propaganda films that the government hired him to produce during World War II. He creates a sort of dialectical montage that compresses all of the history of the U.S. into just a few minutes. Capra created this by mixing newsreel footage, narrative scenes from Hollywood movies, re-enactments that Capra shot himself, and animations which have since become famous—like the one showing arrows and concentric circles stretching across the Pacific from Japan, which has a big octopus on it. Mixing fact and fiction like this was radical at the time. He uses fast cuts and backs it up with a pop musical score by Gershwin; it's beautifully effective, and it anticipates all of the VJ stuff. You see immigration and all the different ethnic groups, then you see workers building Hoover Dam. When it's finished, the water surges through, and you see the power lines across the desert, and then the lights in the city all go on. Without words, it sweeps you up and communicates an epic narrative. You can look at this film and say, wow, this is something America produced, and we can be proud of it.

And then there's Bruce Conner. I call him the bad conscience of Capra. He shows how you can use the exact same imagery—tanks, Hoover Dam, whatever— and make it either critical or sympathetic. It's like jiu-jitsu, using the weight of the enemy against himself. He also creates jarring new interpretations for materials that come from a completely different context. For example, Conner's *Report*, a montage film about the assassination of JFK. In a couple of places, he shows some high-speed lab footage of a bullet passing through a light bulb, going a little further each time you see it. What does that mean? In context, it's obvious that it represents the bullet going through Kennedy's head. And this isn't just being artsy. Bruce Conner is an extremely popular filmmaker; he's not elitist, not precious at all.

PS: In your film *Sonic Outlaws*, one of the members of Negativland describes appropriation art as "electronic folk culture." I liked that—it reminded me of using extra fabric in making quilts, or appropriating the image of Elvis in needle-points or a million other things, like Greil Marcus talks about in *Dead Elvis*.

CB: Yes, it's folk culture—just like scratching and hip-hop, which came out of kids growing up in cities surrounded by cheap record bins. The quilting thing reminds me of Thad Povey from the Scratch Film Junkies. He has a studio near-by. People from the neighborhood come in, and he gives them old film and has them scratch it up and color it with fingernail polish, which looks great when you show it. This is "Cinema Concrete"—that's the term for where you're actually modifying the material of the film itself. Nam June Paik did a kind of video version of this when he took a big magnet to a picture tube. Anyway, Thad calls these get-togethers "quilting bees."

But the main thing *Sonic Outlaws* brings up is intellectual property, which I think is issue number one in the creative arts today. It's the biggest impediment to building audio-visual compilations. In the ideal electronic folk culture, everything would be available for sharing and collaboration. That's why Creative Commons is such a fantastic communitarian resource.

If you're just performing at a club, though, I wouldn't worry about it. I think you can get away with using proprietary materials for most live performances, and even in large venues I don't think the copyright police would notice. Broadcast is where you run into trouble; that's often off-limits.

IVAN DRYER ■ ■ ■ ■

Ivan Dryer created Laserium in the early 1970s at the Griffith Observatory in Los Angeles. It became the city's longest running show and was performed continuously until the observatory closed for renovations in 2002. Dryer's company, Laser Images, has brought Laserium to cities around the world and is currently developing Laserium Cyberdome, an intensely immersive, interactive entertainment complex. The company also produces laser imagery for stage productions, trade shows, amusement parks, the special effects industry, and other sectors.

PS: How did you get into lasers?

ID: I started out in documentary film, actually. Back in the late '60s and early '70s, I was doing camera and editing work, and in 1970, I went to a conference at USC called "Experiments in Art and Technology." One of the presenters there was Dr. Elsa Garmire, a laser physicist at Caltech, and she showed how lasers could create Lumia, interference patterns that have a gossamer or cloud-like appearance. I immediately wanted to make a film about it, so I got myself and a friend invited out to her laboratory to shoot some of the visual effects.

At her lab, Dr. Garmire projected onto the walls with a helium-neon and a small argon laser. I was blown away—I could not turn the camera off. I just kept it running and running, going through hundreds of feet of film. But the moment I saw the developed footage, I knew that there's no way film could capture any of the immediacy of the experience, its scope, or the intensity of the color. It had to be seen live. I'd last worked at the Griffith Observatory a couple of years prior to this, and I realized that their planetarium would be the perfect place for live laser performances.

I approached them with the idea, and they agreed to see a demo. So we set up a little 15-milliwatt He-Ne laser and projected Lumia on the dome. We were originally going to do it for maybe ten minutes. We put on an album and watched for a while. Forty-five minutes later, we put on another and kept going, just watching Lumia and the stars. It was captivating. They thought so, too. But they said no, because it wasn't fitting for a scientific institution to host what was essentially an entertainment program produced by an outside company. So that's how it stood for a while with them.

Meantime, I invested in some small lasers and got other jobs. In 1972, we did the first lasers on a rock tour, with Alice Cooper. We also did an educational film, and the first laser effects for a feature film, *Medicine Ball Caravan*, which was edited by the young Martin Scorsese. For the grand opening of the

Bank of America building in Century City, we projected laser Lumia inside. Then for the building's ribbon-cutting ceremony, we were supposed to use our five-watt Argon laser to cut the ribbon instead of scissors. It was going to be a first. Unfortunately, when the designated ribbon showed up, it was made of this thick seatbelt-like material, and there was no way our laser could penetrate it. So we cut it with scissors beforehand, taped it back together, and put some black powder charges underneath the tape so that it would ignite and look dramatic, as if we cut it with the laser.

At the ceremony, Governor Jerry Brown and five other guys were holding the ribbon, three on each side. They kept wriggling back and forth, so the ribbon kept moving away from the proper spot, and we'd had to bounce the laser beam three times to get it outside there in the first place. Under these conditions, the beam just didn't have the intensity to burn that powder. I eventually just told them to pull the ribbon apart. Afterwards, at the luncheon, Jerry Brown treated us to the remark that a $1.98 pair of scissors would have been a lot more efficient than a ten-thousand-dollar laser—which tied in with his whole Small Is Beautiful campaign at the time.

But I was still making most of my living working with film, not lasers. Laserium finally happened at the Griffith Observatory in 1973, after Dr. William Kaufmann came in as the new director. At twenty-eight, he was the youngest director ever of a major planetarium—and it turned out that he was also pretty hip. I did a demo for him, and he thought it was worth giving it a shot. So he gave us four Monday nights as an experiment, beginning with November 19th, which was just nine days after I finished my last job as a film editor for the feature *Executive Action*.

On the morning of the day we opened, we finished building our projector at 5 a.m. Then at 7 a.m., I appeared on Ralph Story's *AM Los Angeles*, which was the big local television morning show back then. I was on for maybe ten minutes, showing Lumia effects with a little helium-neon laser, and based on that and my poor attempts at trying to describe Laserium, we had two half-full houses that night. At the end of the test run, on December 10th, we had to turn away 500 people from our second show. So we kept going, continuing under our original thirty-day operating permit for twenty-eight years.

PS: What did audiences make of the first show? Like, how did they categorize it? It's always interesting to see how people relate new cultural forms to the things they're already familiar with.

ID: They had no idea how to describe it. We recorded a lot of audience comments early on, which we used in advertising. A lot of people said that they couldn't explain what Laserium was, but they had to tell their friends about it. I've always thought that our opening in L.A. at that time was key to our success, because people here were ready for anything.

PS: From the beginning, the Laserium shows mixed musical genres. You had progressive rock, classical music, synthesizer music that we'd now call early electronica. It reminds me of how light performance has never settled down in terms of low vs. high culture.

ID: I see that as art vs. entertainment, and like any other medium, ours can be both. In March 1975, *Arts* magazine came out with an article on Laserium in which the writer articulated the art-worthiness of what we were doing. The tag line was, "Within Laserium... lie seeds of the high visual art of the future." Unfortunately, his forecast didn't bear out, at least not immediately, but I think he was on the right track.

PS: Was it difficult to get the rights to the music?

ID: We had a lot of interesting experiences—in some cases it was very easy, and in other cases it was a nightmare. Like, in 1977, three days before we were set to open in London, the management of Pink Floyd notified us that we couldn't perform until the band members, or at least Roger Waters, saw our show and gave their approval. We did a command performance the night before the opening. Fortunately, they gave their thumbs-up. The same thing happened with Aerosmith one week before our opening at the Hayden Planetarium in Boston. We had to do the show for Steve Tyler. I was here, sitting on pins and needles, because we'd already done all of our advertising.

Initially, some companies were very hard on us—especially Capitol Records for Pink Floyd. They wanted to sue us for this and that because we didn't get all the rights we were supposed to, other than performance rights from ASCAP and BMI. But then two strange things happened. First, their attorney discovered, much to her horror, that the album in question, *Dark Side of the Moon*, had never been registered with either ASCAP or BMI. They couldn't find it anywhere in the files. Then they noticed that after we opened in Toronto, local sales of that album increased dramatically. This was in 1982, for an album that originally came out in 1973. So after they saw that we were increasing their sales, they backed off entirely. Pink Floyd was actually a relatively unknown, experimental band when Laserium first started, so when we played "Echoes" and "Set the Controls for the Heart of the Sun," a lot of people were hearing them for the first time.

Meantime, we've done many listening parties for new album releases, starting in 1974 with *Tales of Mystery and Imagination* for the Alan Parsons Project. The industry typically has these launch parties in L.A. and New York, and we've done them in both places. We've done The Who, The Cure, a whole bunch of things. In 1993, we also did the 20th Anniversary *Dark Side of the Moon* party, held at the Wilshire Ebell Theater here in Hollywood. It was really a gas. Timothy Leary and three former astronauts came to that. We still have this huge banner from that performance hanging up in our studio.

PS: The whole issue of file-sharing and downloadable music hasn't completely shaken out, but there's obviously no way of duplicating the audience experience, the unpredictable experience of being physically present with a lot of other people reacting to a performance. Because of this, it strikes me that the music industry should focus on immersive, live experiences that can't be copied and sent around, and distribute recordings mainly as free or cheap advertisements designed to get people into shows.

With the first Laserium shows, I imagine that the laserists had to perform live because there was no way of automating it. But at some point later, you must have realized that the whole thing could be pre-recorded. I think it was an interesting decision, and the right one, not to go down that path. What was that like, and what was your rationale?

ID: Yes, we have always kept the live element, even as we've introduced more computer-controlled and computer-generated imagery, like laser-animation cartoons. The laserists could always change what was on the dome at any time, intercept or override it, or even play entirely live, as has happened when the computer failed. Some of the best audience responses have come from those conditions. When I performed, I would sometimes make a mistake or deviate from what I thought was the best choreography, and the audience would like it—so I'd do it again and incorporate that into the show.

There's always been a synergy between the audience and the performer. Each laserist has his or her own take on the interpretation of the music, and the audience responds more when they know that there's a real, live performer there, rather than just a button-pusher. They get off on that, and we encourage their response continually throughout the shows. We liked it when people would applaud, or hoot and holler, or whatever else—although the Observatory here always tried to suppress this.

PS: The Griffith Observatory staff tried to keep the audience quiet?

ID: They did everything they could to subdue the audience, so it wouldn't tear down the walls, demolish the seats, or whatever else they were afraid of. Laserium always had this tension with the host planetariums and their idea of audience decorum. It's primarily a rock 'n' roll audience, and they're used to the freedom of expression you find at rock shows. They come into a planetarium, and there's a hushed, temple-like quality to the space. It's this dome, with all sorts of high-tech equipment and a big planetarium projector in the middle. It's awe-inspiring. So everyone takes a seat, and then the planetarium guide staff comes in and does an introduction before the show, making it clear that they're in charge, and that you'd better heel to the rules and behave in an orderly fashion rather than allow your emotions to get the best of you.

I'll never forget, I was sitting next to Tim Leary the first time he saw Laserium. At one point in the show, he just reached up his arms, as if to gather it in. He just had this spontaneous reaction—and he was straight at the time.

PS: You've talked about the mental state that Laserium puts audiences in, an openness and awareness that's similar to experiences with meditation or biofeedback.

ID: In the 1970s, Bob Beck and I actually did some experiments with EEG measurements and galvanic skin response, gauging audience reactions to the music alone, the laser images alone, and the two together. We tried it with various images and musical selections. With the EEG we were monitoring theta and alpha waves, and GSR relates primarily to beta, of course.

The results were interesting, and altering each element caused clear differences in people's response. We got the highest activity when both music and images were playing, and some selections had a particularly strong effect. One that I was particularly fond of was "Awaken" by Yes, which was accompanied by these spinning dark and light spokes that radiated from the center of the dome, covering the entire thing.

PS: Kind of like a Dreamachine.

ID: But we could control the direction and speed of the spokes, their thickness, how many of them there were, how they were moving with respect to one another. The pattern changed continuously along with the music. And the lyrics at one point are: "Master of light, Master of images, Songs cast a light on you." It really was strong—the way the music, visuals, and lyrics all worked together to tickle people's brainwaves and put them in an altered state. I think we've exceeded that only a few times since.

PS: Bob Beck wrote one of the best references I've found about light shows. It's this self-published book from 1966 called *Light Show Manual*, and it's an amazing source.

ID: He was an old friend, although we fell out of touch. I think the last time I saw Bob was at the Electronic Arts conference in Pasadena in 1991. He had some very interesting ideas about electromagnetism and their effect on brainwaves, the Schuman Resonance frequency in particular. I experimented with it some myself back then.

PS: What's the Schuman Resonance?

ID: It's the frequency at which radio waves in the ionosphere encircle the earth, 7.83 times per second, or 7.83 hertz, which corresponds to high theta waves in the brain. Bob had very sensitive, low-noise measurement devices which he used to detect the Schuman Resonance, and he also measured the brainwaves of people who were in certain kinds of trances. One thing he found is that people with so-called paranormal abilities, healers and psychics and the like, had higher activity at this frequency than others—so they're tuned into a kind of global brainwave that exists as standing waves of electromagnetic energy all over the earth. He also went to locations that were traditionally considered places of power and found that the Schuman Resonance was typically stronger in those places, which implies that they could facilitate meditating and entraining at that frequency.

PS: Did you use this frequency in Laserium visuals?

ID: No, I avoided it for a couple of reasons. One is that it's within the frequency range at which strobe lights can cause seizures in epileptics, so it might be dangerous. Also, Bob once did an experiment at Knott's Berry Farm where he broadcast radio waves at 7.83 Hz from a small transducer that had a range of a few hundred yards. He said it introduced a lot of confusion into the area. It's not something you want to toy with in a public place with unsuspecting individuals. Bob told me that the CIA had been interested in his work. I've been out of psychotronics for quite some time now, but it's an interesting area, and I wouldn't be surprised if research is going on about trying to weaponize it. A couple of people who might know more about what's going on now are Michael Hutchison, who wrote *Megabrain*, and Michael Persinger, who's been relating atmospheric electromagnetic fields to insect behavior. But I'm looking for more direct interactive experiences, using technologies that we understand and have available to us now.

PS: I've been reading about laser video projectors, like the Lumalaser Colorburst. What advantages do they have over other projectors?

ID: One big advantage is that they're always in focus, no matter where you point them, since you're projecting tiny beams rather than focusing an image. Also, laser video has higher contrast than any other form, higher even than DLP, and you get better color saturation because of the purity of the laser colors. And, in theory at least, you can get a much wider frequency range. Typical video projection starts the low end at about 612 nanometers I think, so the reds are actually orange-red. Whereas with laser you can go to 650 or even 670, and get really deep reds. And it's the same on the other side—you get a deep blue-violet that's extremely arresting.

PS: So with laser video, is it the same principle as regular video, with a green gun and a red gun and a blue gun?

ID: Usually no, although it can be done that way. In most systems the color mixing takes place at a different level, by means of polychromatic acousto-optic modulators. Instead of producing a single emission line at one color, the laser diode generates a range of lines, eight of which lie within the visible spectrum. The PCAOM calculates the proportions for mixing those eight wavelengths together in order to create white light and any of a total of sixteen million other possible colors.

Also, there's a German laser video projector built by Schneider Laser Technologies and marketed by Zeiss that operates differently. It uses multiple laser diodes to produce the colors, which it combines by means of a complex filtration system. I've heard it creates a very beautiful white, ten watts of white light, but it's an expensive system—$250,000.

For Laserium Cyberdome, we're probably going to use one by Evans & Sutherland that's based on their Digistar III full-dome star and video projection system. Right now, that system uses five regular Barco projectors, but they're going to manufacture a laser version of it where two laser projectors create the entire field. Our dome will be pretty flat, with a short throw in the middle and a long throw at the edges. Without laser video, this would be a problem.

PS: When do you expect Cyberdome to open?

ID: Well, I expected it to be open by now, but we've had difficulty in the financing and in securing the location. It's a Catch-22; you've got to have one to have the other. We do have a great location in mind, but the financing people want it nailed down before they'll invest, and this costs a lot. Then it will probably take us six months to a year to deploy all this new technology, depending on what problems we have. For some of the devices, like the LightDancer, we have a working prototype in our studio, but it hasn't yet come out as a product. For Cyberdome's floor, we're ultimately going to need eighteen of those.

PS: What's the LightDancer?

ID: It's a system from a startup called BodyHarp Interactive that turns your body into a MIDI controller. You don't have to wear anything; it's all infrared-based. One broad beam, about eight feet in diameter, comes down from the ceiling, and as your movements interrupt it, sixteen infrared sensors below pick up what you're doing and translate it into MIDI. Those signals then control different parameters of the images and sound that's playing.

But it's hard to do something new, because nobody wants to be the first. We bootstrapped the original Laserium ourselves with a $10,000 laser and some home-built electronics. With Cyberdome, we're talking about five million dollars to get started, which is a whole other beast. It's tough to get people to grok the vision, first of all, and then go out on a limb to support it—even though they're willing to sink a hundred million dollars into some movie that can get blown away in two weeks if it doesn't fly. When we show visuals on a conference-room screen, it's hard for people to imagine what it would look like projected overhead at sixty feet across, filling their entire field of vision.

PS: L.A. sounds like a great location for Cyberdome, but I think Las Vegas might also work.

ID: Everybody says that, and I'm sure we're going to consider it as a second location, but Las Vegas has a more entertainment-oriented dynamic there, and I don't think that the show that we're planning to open with, *Timegate 2012*, would do as well over there. It's based on the work of Terrence and Dennis McKenna, who calculated that on December 21st, 2012, which also marks the end of the Mayan calendar, we will reach a threshold where the accelerating pace of technological development goes infinite, and the world as we know it comes to an end—commencing the Age of the Gods, according to the Maya. For that show, we want to create an overwhelming, transformative kind of experience that isn't like normal entertainment—something that has a spiritual dimension. I think the audience mindset in Los Angeles would be open to this, but in Vegas people just want to get down and party. They'd prefer Cyberdome after 11 p.m., when it turns into a dance club.

But in general, I think the pattern in our society will continue toward more and more cocooning, staying at home. People aren't going to get out and enjoy having a communal experience. Maybe Cyberdome can be one of the last bastions of that kind of interaction before we all go inside—as we must one day, when the ice creeps over.

PS: That's a cheery thought. Maybe, instead, it will be one of the first bastions of a renaissance of communitarianism!

ID: I don't hold out much hope for that, but I do want to prolong real-world experiences for as long as possible. Just wait until virtual reality kicks in on a large scale. Virtual experiences will ultimately overwhelm anything anybody can do. You'll be able to live in whatever world you want, much to the detriment of our society—or what's left of it. I don't have a very rosy view of the future.

PS: I'm surprised! One of the early events that I'm interested in is the Trips Festival in 1966, produced by Stewart Brand. He had the same kind of vision for that, as a big, communal, blow-you-away kind of group experience—but there was a hopeful, almost messianic, sense to it.

ID: There was, and I certainly had that too at the time. But intervening technological and political developments have changed my mind. I've been working on a book, *The Omega Convergence*, about how converging technologies threaten humanity as we know it. One of the fruits of technology, of course, is global warming, and I've believed for many years that we may soon enter another ice age, like in the movie *The Day After Tomorrow*. Immediately before the last ice age, global warming increased and reached a tipping point. Then temperatures oscillated wildly for a very short period, possibly only a matter of weeks, before the global climate settled into a colder base state.

The things leading up to that are happening right now. Glaciers are receding everywhere, and the western ice shelf of Antarctica is in danger of disappearing. Of course, our current administration is doing absolutely nothing to stop this, and if they get four more years, I don't see anything stopping it. So everybody left will go underground, but the dislocations that are suffered in the meantime will be the worst that humanity has ever experienced.

Combine that with people just wanting to hole up in their media cocoons to begin with, communicating via the Internet rather than in person. All these trends lead to the ultimate extinction of humanity, as I see it, and to takeover by the machines, whose hegemony we have set up for them (the Mayan Gods, perhaps?). They can keep us occupied with Virtual Reality, the perfect Soma, while communicating without us, via the Internet. And there are people like Rodney Brooks at M.I.T. who look actually forward to the time when we all become androids. The whole Transhumanism movement espouses the idea that humans will soon be replaced—and they're right!

PS: I know—I'm against it.

ID: I'm against it too, but I'm afraid we're fighting against the tide. That's why I think it's important that we do whatever we can to be true Humanists, to promote all forms of real human interaction for as long as possible. That way we can at least say that we didn't give up without a fight.

PS: Right on! That's one of the main themes of this book—making the case for real-life interaction. Otherwise, what you're describing reminds me of that great old science fiction story, I forget who wrote it, called "The Machine Stops."

ID: That's E.M. Forster. I quote that, actually, in *The Omega Convergence*. Forster envisioned exactly the kind of future that we have coming to us, and we're doing everything possible to accelerate it. All these sci-fi movies have been happening, like *The Terminator* and *The Matrix* series. Their particulars may be doubtful, but the general idea is absolutely true.

PS: Do you think these films make such futures seem more palatable or more inevitable? Obviously, these scenarios do resonate with people—they illustrate major issues of our era, and we're smart enough to realize this, which is why we all find these movies so interesting.

ID: I think they develop a hidden undercurrent of dread, while at the same time making people feel mute and powerless, because they sense the inevitability of it. That's why these movies don't elicit much serious public discussion or outrage. People don't want to confront these issues head-on because they're too momentous. Nobody wants to destroy their weekend soccer games. They want civilization to persist as it is, but even under the best scenarios, it can't.

PS: Yeah—everyone in China can't have their own car.

ID: Think about water. Even if global warming doesn't result in an ice age, doesn't result in famines and extinctions, water will still be a problem. In California, we talk about "water wars" euphemistically, but we'll have real water wars. Farmers will start arming themselves to protect their water supplies. And as long as they get it, then the cities won't.
    You don't want to listen to me. I'll ruin your whole day.

PS: Oh God, no—I agree with you on all this stuff! You're pessimistic, but I think you're fighting the good fight.

ID: All we can do is shine our candles in the darkness before it envelops us. Or, as I like to quote Dylan Thomas: "Do not go gentle into that good night... Rage, rage against the dying of the light."

NORMAN PERRYMAN ▪ ▪ ▪ ▪

Amsterdam-based visual artist Norman Perryman has fused music and painting for five decades. His paintings frequently express musical themes, and he has performed live, projector-based "kinetic painting" for the stage with ensembles such as the Netherlands Dance Theater, Circle Percussion, the Rotterdam Symphony, and the Netherlands Chamber Orchestra.

PS: You've said that light performance is something that tends to come back every twenty years or so.

NP: Well, way back in the 19th century, people were experimenting with light organs, people like Castel in France, and Rimington. And then there was a lot around 1910–1912. The great classic is Scriabin's *Prometheus*, which is still performed occasionally. It's very problematic music, and I'm not sure that what he prescribed is really a good illustration of what we're talking about, but his score actually included a line for light organ. Scriabin extended the multimedia concept even then; he also wanted to include colors in the whole performance hall, and even particular fragrances. Stravinsky, of course, was also very much a multimedia composer. This was an intense period of collaboration. Later we get Picasso working with Diaghilev on ballet designs.

Skipping ahead, we get to the Walt Disney era. Work on *Fantasia* started at the end of the 1930s, and the film was released in 1941. During that time, Disney brought many European refugees into California to work with him and sometimes used their ideas without crediting them. That was another classic period, and it blended with the experiments Thomas Wilfred and others in the States were doing with light organs and other light machines.

Interestingly, Jackson Pollock used to spend hours at the Guggenheim Museum looking at Wilfred's light machines before he began painting his drip paintings. Pollock was also inspired by music, and had he lived longer I think he might have become a sort of VJ figure. Movement was what interested him—that's what "action painting" was all about.

In the '60s, Rauschenberg, Cage, and Cunningham were the great trio, with Cage composing music that was based on chance, Rauschenberg doing really way-out designs, and Cunningham way-out dance. Their influence is still around. Then in the late '60s / early '70s there was a lot of experimental splashing around. I started in the early '70s, and others were doing the same. Much of it was sheer improvisation—often very messy and not very successful. But at that time you could do what the hell you liked and nobody cared— it was a very free period.

I had been painting dancers and musicians for some while and realized that I wanted to join the performance. I was a frustrated dancer or musician, if you like. But my technique was painting, so I realized that I needed to develop some way of doing it live. I discovered that an overhead projector was a very simple and economical way of throwing up large images. You could project them onto dancers or onto musicians as they sat and played, and you could paint around them and follow them in real time. That was back in '73— I was living in Geneva. Then I produced some videotapes, and the critics said, "Hey, this is like early, experimental film!"

My methods ultimately go back to the fact that I had no money and needed a very simple means of accomplishing what I envisioned. Rather than developing a technique which was based on video projections, synthesizers and other high-tech which was in its infancy at the time (but we now know as the beginning of the rave scene), I thought, let's keep this very simple, and use what we have in us: intuition, sensitivity, our body's sense of movement, our direct, spontaneous, emotional reaction to music. Let's package all of those instincts together and turn them into a performance.

In 1976 I had made my first major movie with Swiss television using these techniques. It was actually quite a mess, not a great success—but it was a wonderful fifty-minute celebration of the various ideas and techniques that I had been fooling around with. They work in live performance, but I haven't found a director yet who can give form to them on film.

PS: What is your technique now, in terms of the colors, the plates, and things like that? From your website I recall that you started out as a watercolorist. That's already a very fast, immediate kind of painting.

NP: Well, I learned to paint with oils, like everybody did in art college. As that became more fluid and transparent, I realized that watercolor was the way to go for me. This is forty years or so ago. Gradually I developed a name as a watercolorist, painting landscape and especially musical themes and portraits. And even in landscape watercolors I started to see symphonies—rolling hills, or the horizon of the flat Dutch landscape, for example, which is like a whispering rhythm, with tiny undulations.

Later, I thought let's use the watercolor technique, which is very risky, fluid, and difficult to control—let's use that on the projector. So I started using fluid colors on a glass plate, placed on top of an overhead projector. It's quite small, a square that's twenty-eight centimeters on a side. So I'm painting on a small scale, but I've developed skills as a painter which can be either illustrative and precise or else quite free, depending on what's necessary. In most of my performances, the images are enlarged to at least nine meters wide. Most people don't use the overhead projector that big, but you can. Even with a regular 400-watt light, you can get great image for a concert hall.

I usually put a screen behind the orchestra or ensemble or dancer and stand in the pit, if there is one—as with a ballet or opera—or else on the edge of the podium, if an orchestra is onstage. I turn the overhead projectors around so that instead of using them over my shoulder as most lecturers would, letting the audience watch the screen behind them as they speak, I face the same direction as the projectors. This means I have to paint upside-down and left-right reversed, which is hard work. I've tried constructions with mirrors to make the image go the right way up, but for now I still paint upside-down and it works pretty well.

PS: This is all on glass plates?

NP: Yes, small-sized glass plates with a little plastic dike around the edge so the color doesn't run off into your projector. And I've got five or six projectors lined up in a row. Each of them is connected to a dimmer, so I can cross-fade from one to the other or even have three at a time come up again. The cross-fading is an essential factor in the performance. You see a scene, whatever it might be—say, Mount Fuji if it's a Japanese piece, or the red sun—and suddenly you see some other image coming through it. It's just the dimmer mixing with projector number two, whatever it's showing, but it can be breathtaking. This is very much what VJs are doing today, using other means. They're mixing images.

PS: Definitely! So the dimmers are right next to the projectors?

NP: Yes. I control them with my other, non-painting hand. Or, more recently, my son, who's very musical and interested in images, has been performing the image-mixing for me. We recently collaborated on a show in Amsterdam for MTV, actually, with a DJ. It was a sort of fusion between classical and DJ type of music, using our images. My son worked as the VJ, doing the image-mixing, and I took a lot of my cues from him because he was more familiar with the sort of music that DJs typically play.

So there's usually at least one assistant at the side of me, either to change and sometimes clean the plates, or to mix the images. I've got a whole case of plates lined up like CDs that we can pluck out and put onto the projector. Some are pre-prepared with an image underneath, such as a basic shape, or a drawing of, say, a landscape or a city. Then you paint over that to make it more. That's all it is, really. As I've said, a child could do this—as long as he practiced for twenty years or so!

I've given lots of workshops and lectures on using this technique for young people. Sometimes I'll say, okay, today we'll run this workshop, and tomorrow you'll put on a performance. And they do! Because it grabs you, and it's relatively easy. You don't have to put on a high-tech, high-skill, detailed performance, but you can use these techniques very powerfully.

NORMAN PERRYMAN

PS: I find it interesting and not surprising that Jackson Pollock would watch Wilfred's machines. The light-show "liquids" of the psychedelic era are very Pollock-like, and I think the reason Pollock became more famous than light-show artists is because he left sellable commodities behind—the paintings themselves. Also, photos of him in his studio looked good for *Life* magazine, whereas light show people who were doing liquids in the Fillmore West in San Francisco were more anonymous and may not have had Pollock's photogenic star quality. But it seems that action painting is part of the same tradition.

NP: Well, Pollock spoke of getting into the painting bodily, walking around *in* it. And that is exactly the sensation you need when you're performing: to get inside the music, get inside the image, and move with it. I've done some painting on the floor, like Jackson Pollock, moving across a large area and having that filmed from above. I think there's something important about the fluidity of this that speaks to us—an organic fascination with water, which we've known since birth.

When people watch my fluid images moving on a huge screen, they just gasp because they feel something very deep. This is partly because they're magnified so large. You see a bubble of ink which is floating across the screen, and it's like a planet that's about to collide with another planet. It's hypnotic, the effect.

And it's all timed to go with the music. For me, that's an essential factor. There's got to be a real, inherent marriage between the two. This isn't just a light show. So, for example, I time the flow of liquid going across the screen. It may take a certain number of seconds, like five seconds, to go from one side to the other, and you time that to go with, say, ten notes of music. And if you slope the plate slightly, you can speed it up or slow it down. You can even make liquid float upwards, which nobody can figure out. People ask, "How do you do that? How do you make it float upwards?" Well, you just tilt the plates so it goes that direction!

There's something magical about it; it's like swimming in colored liquid. I think the color itself affects us emotionally. You've seen my photos with the Japanese drummers—they're drumming in a huge bath of color, and as it changes they disappear and reappear again, and then it looks like there's paint on them. People love this. It's incredibly theatrical.

PS: So when you're working on a piece or rehearsing with music, you have a score for the order of the colors?

NP: Definitely. I get the full score of the music. I can read music and I mark it up so I know for each section, even sometimes each bar, what I'm going to do. Then I listen to the CD, memorize the piece totally, and gradually work out a series of images. After this, I try them out to see how well they can move with the music. You can think of a nice image, but if you can't do it fast enough, you've got to change it—you've got to either adapt it or abandon it. That's the most challenging part.

So I develop a sort of storyboard to go with the whole piece, following the musical score. It shows sketches of each image for each projector and where the cross-fades happen, so that even the assistant can see what's going to come up next. Performing like this is pretty tense. You've got to have everything exactly lined up—all the colors, all the brushes. There are hundreds of brushes involved, and everything's got to be rehearsed in advance and memorized.

A little while ago I was doing a piece with the Rotterdam Philharmonic that was by Takemitsu, which is quite abstract.

PS: He's not rhythmic at all, right?

NP: Well, it's wild rhythm, it's very free rhythm. The musicians were really having to concentrate to play this stuff. I had memorized the whole thing, and they were curious, "How did you do this?" Well, it's the associations with the images that I've created that helps my brain see the whole thing connected. When you're actually working through the performance, there's no time to read music or even the storyboard. You've got to have it at your fingertips.

So I've moved from what used to be very free improvisation, in the '70s, to something which has detailed form and sequence to it—which ultimately is more satisfying.

PS: You were saying you see a new upwelling of interest in live visual performance, and I'm curious what are some examples you see. It sounds like you're doing some interesting new stuff, like with MTV.

NP: I've noticed that here in Holland and in Belgium, almost every concert manager seems to be looking for some visual accompaniment to whatever they're putting on. A lot of people are projecting films, like the great classics— Chaplin or whatever. Or they're using VJs to concoct various loops and they use beamers.

PS: What types of music are they showing Chaplin to and bringing in VJs for?

NP: Well, John Adams, for example. I recently saw a performance of his *Transmigration of Souls* here, his 9/11 piece. There was a lot of video projection in that—a few scenes of Ground Zero, but also abstract stuff that was rendered by computer. It was okay stuff, but not my cup of tea. I find that a lot of VJs are projecting cerebral ideas, presenting imagery and directing what we should think about. This takes you out of the music, I think. I'd rather enjoy the music and see a visual that flows along with it, rather than being steered towards thinking about a specific set of ideas, which can be heavy and tiring.

But I'm making plans to work with a composer who's probably going to be the best example of what we're talking about, and that's Tan Dun. He won an Oscar for the Best Score on *Crouching Tiger, Hidden Dragon* a couple of years back, and he's just done the film *Hero* with similar music backing martial arts. Wonderful drumming and string music—a combination of wild, abstract rhythm and romantic, haunting melodies. The music is slightly Chinese—he's Chinese—but it's a mixture of East and West. And he's a composer who believes that everything he writes should have a visual component.

I first met him in New York and then again last year in Amsterdam, where he was performing his opera *Tea*. He came to my studio, and we talked. I told him that my dream is to put together an opera with what I'm doing. That's the ultimate form—a major, evening-long performance that incorporates my techniques. And he told me that his dream is to make an opera about a painter!

PS: Oh, so this is *The Brush*, right?

NP: This is *The Brush*—that's right! So I told him that I have a film concept which already exists in script form. Maybe it should first be an opera, and then perhaps we can make a film of the opera. So we've been talking about that possibility. But I think what will probably happen is that we'll first work on some smaller performances together, like a visual concerto version of *Hero* or *Crouching Tiger*, and then we may move on to bigger things later.

But when he saw my studio, he said, "I just love this low-tech approach!" And the economics of it are so simple. He loves water percussion, too. He uses it a lot. Well, I'm using watercolor, so it really fits together. I hope that this becomes a significant collaboration during the next few years.

I'd also love to work with Michael Tilson Thomas in San Francisco. I did some workshops there, back in the '70s, but got sidetracked and didn't develop any big projects. But others were beginning to develop multimedia concerts then, like the Kronos Quartet. They often work with visual components. I would love to bring my techniques in their present form to the States. I think the sensational aspects of it would really appeal to American audiences.

MELISSA ULTO ■ ■ ■ ■

Melissa Ulto, AKA *VJ miixxy, is a New York-based VJ, DP, editor, filmmaker, writer, artist, and photographer.*

PS: How did you originally get into VJing?

MU: I was working at Columbia University as a senior digital video specialist. We produced a lot of documentaries, did live broadcasts of conferences and commencements, and created video material for publication online, for classes. Part of my job there was to keep up with new video technologies, especially for live video. In my researching, I came across MAX, which is the central program for many VJs, and I also started playing around with Jitter, a video toolbox for MAX. Then my friend Cynthia Lawson, whom I was working with, introduced me to Josh Goldberg—he created another MAX-based VJ app called Dervish. Josh came in for a job interview, and within ten minutes he gave me a copy of Dervish right off of his laptop. I started playing around with that and really enjoyed it.

Then someone else suggested that I try out Grid, by Vidvox, which has become my main performance software. I like it because it's purely a library player. You can manipulate some things and scratch with it, which is important to me because I love scratching. But it's basically a bank of clips that you can trigger to feed into a hardware mixer. The interface is great; it's got an animated representation of each piece, like a poster frame. I prefer a hardware mixer— I've got an Edirol V-4, which is a great unit. I do sometimes use VDMX and other mixing applications, but they generally aren't responsive enough for me, even on my G4, 17-inch, fully maxed-out laptop.

The club I perform at every week now, Spirit, has two V-4's. So when I work there, I'll string together eight sources: my laptop, two live cameras, and five DVD players—the three they have installed plus my two portable Koss players. Sometimes I run clips off of an Edirol production system they have, but it isn't that great; I prefer using Grid. So with all of these sources and these amazing mixers, I can do real-time responsive performing, reacting live.

People have been projecting visuals onto screens for generations, but it's become a live medium, like being a jazz musician. That's what's revolutionary. A musician learns the notes, and as a VJ, you create the images. Then when you perform, you work with the music, the room, the mood, the crowd, the theme of the night, and you bring it all together.

I've had friends who are video and film editors come and see me work, and they're amazed that it's all live. It's a completely foreign world to them, even a bit frightening. They're accustomed to spending an hour getting just the right cut, so they wondered, "what about your mistakes?" But the whole point is that there are no mistakes. The only mistake is if your mixer completely loses its signal. Other than that, it's free-form and fluid, which is more natural for me than doing film work. A friend once said that I'm in my natural state, my habitat, when I'm in the VJ booth mixing.

So that's how I originally got into it—through researching different video technologies. I had already been making Flash animations and experimental films, so VJing was a convergence for me, combining filmmaking, web technologies, new software, live performance, camera work, editing skills, and pure creativity.

Many VJs don't use original clips, and some don't use clips at all—they just generate images live as they're working, like from a MAX module they've put together. But I author new clips almost every day. I've got two hard drives filled with clips, probably over a thousand by now.

PS: How do you create them?

MU: It's all over the map: After Effects, Amorphium Pro, Maya, Artmatic, Final Cut Pro—sometimes even iPhoto. For example, I do a lot of fashion parties, and sometimes I'll have a client show up only an hour or two before I'm performing and hand me a disk that contains a long portfolio of model images. I'll bring the images into iPhoto to create a Quicktime movie, pop it into Grid, load it up on the screens, and mix it in with the other content. It works, and that's about as simple as it can get. I've even had situations where somebody says, "This logo needs to be on the screen in five minutes!" So I import the jpeg logo into Quicktime, export it as a movie, and boom, it's like a one-second loop that I can trigger and mix with like any other clip.

So I use everything in my arsenal. I'm not tied to one piece of software for anything, and I'm continually experimenting. Like, I recently learned about Studio Artist, and I really want to get a copy of it to play around with. It's absolutely like play for me. It's a box of different crayons, and I'm playing.

But mixing in live camera images makes the performances truly interactive. I'll point cameras at the performers onstage, or at the crowd. Everyone loves that—the performers, the crowd, and most importantly (professionally speaking) the club owner.

PS: And cameras make it all the more unmistakably live and distinct from a broadcast. It's for and about the people in the room, who are all sharing the experience.

MU: Yes, you create a live symphony of images that purely lives in the moment—unless you record it, which a lot of VJs don't. Once it's gone, it's gone. Some people are like, "You're not recording this?" And I tell them no, that's the whole point. I have recorded bits of my work in the past, but it's primarily a live performance. It belongs here, in this moment—not in a film festival, not in a screening series, not in an installation. Those are for different forms of expression. This is pure, live improvisation that exists in the moment, and that's where it should stay.

So I work at Spirit every Friday and Saturday night as the house VJ and video tech, and I get other gigs during the week, like the Psychedelic Furs show last Thursday and a magazine party this week. I also produce my own events, such as last night's Jezebel. That's a regular event for women multimedia and performance artists.

PS: You've noted that many women artists incorporate themselves into their work. Why is that?

MU: A woman artist's relationship to aesthetics is very personal. First of all, we create life, so we know that we're fundamentally creative beings. And our society sees the female form as the primary object of beauty—so we're not just the creator but also the form of art. That's why it's natural for many women artists to incorporate their own image, from Artemisia Gentileschi during the Renaissance to Cindy Sherman today. I started out this way, taking photographs of myself. It's a natural place to begin, because as a woman, you have a unique understanding of what it is to look at the female form. You're trained to look at yourself and say: this is beautiful, this is not beautiful. Every day, advertisements tell you to evaluate your skin—is it dry, is it oily? Are your eyelashes long enough? Is your body thin enough?

By using your own image, you take on your own objectification, create your own perspective as an artist and as a woman. It's a healing process—instead of looking at yourself through someone else's lens and seeing someone who has a dry "T-zone" and needs extra moisturizer, you start looking at yourself as a piece of sculpture. You bypass that neurotic ego sense that society creates. I think this is the ultimate goal of every artist, female or male. But for men, the process is usually more external.

PS: So you take the power of your own body, step forward with it, and say: This is me, this is where it's all starting, and I'm doing what I want here.

MU: You become your own muse; that's the key. It's not only about the body, but also the metaphysical idea of the body and the creative symbolism that's associated with the female image. Some women artists express views of femininity that they themselves embody. It's as strong, sensual, bold, and nurturing as they are, and the work really grabs your attention.

PS: Presenting the self in this way reminds me of some political actions, such as when Julia Butterfly Hill lived in that tree, Luna, to draw attention to environmental and forest management policies. She used herself physically, saying "here I am—now deal with it," or even, "this is my piece," not in a detached sense, but as a declaration.

MU: That's true—it's not only my piece because I've created it, but also because I'm in it and I am of it. You can say that all art is political because it poses questions and makes arguments, and society often finds it uncomfortable when a creative, sexual, self-determined woman poses difficult questions. The culture industry sometimes takes this threat and defuses it. Like, they'll select a woman for a reality show who has all the trappings of self-determination, the appearance and the right catch-phrases, and they'll manipulate the situation so her actions end up contradicting this. Like, she'll fall into the same old boy-saves-girl situation or some other ridiculous thing, revealing that she isn't really confident after all. It's more like Confidence Lite.

PS: They're taken back down, put in their place.

MU: Not even taken back down. They'll focus on somebody who never embodied much independence in the first place, but seems close enough that people who aren't paying attention won't know the difference. So, she'll be trying out the idea of free, creative expression—but if a guy comes along, she'll drop it all in a heartbeat. That's who they'll put on these shows. It's depressing.

Women artists and women in general fight against these crazy, silly stereotypes, which keep popping up in popular culture, art, and even in art criticism. For instance, I imagine *FHM* magazine coming out to a Jezebel event, meeting all these intelligent, amazing women artists, and then just mainly writing about how hot the crowd was.

I only expect this to change slowly, with no help from the media. It will come from our community of artists, our work ethic, and our ownership of the work and the criticism that surrounds it. Many art critics don't understand what we do, because it's completely outside their purview. So they'll focus on the surface, on what's obvious and sexy, because that's what makes the story and sells it to people. Women artists adjust to this. We have to accept that in order to get certain kinds of attention, we have to play our part in this game.

PS: I would guess that's a part of what you play with and very consciously use to manipulate the world.

MU: That goes back to owning your own objectification. You say, I am going to be objectified, I am going to be scrutinized, whether adored or hated. I'm putting myself out there, and I own whatever happens as a result. I'm strong enough to take this attention and turn it into something that works for me.

I have a self-portrait series called *unMade Movie* (*http://unmade.the-cataract.com*), where I play with the whole idea of objectification. I put on the roles of the blonde, the redhead, the brunette, the showgirl, the goddess, and I really had fun with them. And now I use these images in my video work. It's a catharsis for me, and meanwhile people have asked, "Wow—how did you do that?" Or even, "Who is that—I want to know more! Wow, that's you?" It's so concrete; people are relating to me directly in some way, whether it's sexually or even just about the wig I'm wearing. Abstract visuals can be entrancing, hypnotizing, but this adds in some actual reality.

PS: It also seems to me to be the perfect adjunct to the rest of VJing. When you improvise with your personal collection of clips, it's like a window into what you see and think, what associations you make, and what's going on in your head during the performance. It's a live window into your mind. Pairing this with images of your physical presence seems to be a natural combination, a complete personal expression.

MU: Yes, and not only are you viewing the VJ's work over time, but you're also usually viewing it in relation to another kind of artist, whether it's a musician or a dancer. So you're seeing what the person does in a sort of collaborative conversation. That's an artistic format that hasn't existed before.

It's not performance art, where I'm focusing on the audience. I'm in my own space with the gear, which requires a lot of attention. One friend described me and the VJs I perform with as "monitor junkies." You really need to be with your rig. This has become automatic for me—I reach for certain knobs before I even consciously know it. In my subconscious, I feel where I'm going to go next, and then it happens. It's very primal, like getting into a pre-cognitive state. You're doing high-level thinking in order to operate all this complex equipment, but it's also primal, because it's all about how you feel and how you're reacting. It's my drug. I don't need drugs—I have mixing.

Also, you aren't center stage, like a traditional performer would be. But everyone is looking at what you're producing, reacting to your creative decisions. You're the Wizard of Oz—you're the man behind the curtain! It's a fabulous medium, truly unique, and I love it. As soon as I got into it, I knew right away, boom, this is it. I knew I would continue with VJing, whether it was just in my underwear at home or professionally, which is how I've ended up.

It was hard to become paid for doing this. Fortunately, I've created a niche for myself and my work, and hopefully I can continue. But the idea of the VJ still isn't widely understood. People are like, "What—you work for MTV?"

I would love to see some celebrity become interested in mixing and start performing. Some supermodel or actress or famous artist or whoever could come out, sit in with us, mix, and really get into it, champion our cause. Because it's just so fun, even if you're beginning. There is nothing hotter than going to a venue and throwing it down. You're performing, learning on your feet, finding out what does and doesn't work. It's a rush.

PS: It's accessible, too. I think there are a lot of kids out there who have laptops, and live at home with parents who have home theater projectors. They've got all the equipment you need to start with.

MU: Absolutely—it's perfect for that. Seventy-five-dollar software, and there's also tons of free software. There's cheap DV cameras to run around and shoot some of your own content. Even if they end up using their school's projector, schools have plenty of projectors. It's absolutely a grab-on-and-make-your-own medium, and it starts out at a fairly low price point. I would love to see it boom. I would love to teach courses in how to VJ.

Honestly, it is a bit frightening because I'm good at what I do, and I would hate to lose my Saturday night gig to somebody else. But even if it spreads and becomes popular, there will still always be the cream of the crop, and I would love to be able to test my work against a real population of artists.

More people would also bring equipment prices down. If ninety people are buying mixers and VJ software, the prices will stay the same, but if 900 or 9,000 start wanting them, the companies will be able to lower prices, grant sponsorships, and generally expand on what they do. Right now it's a very boutique, niche kind of industry.

PS: If it becomes popular, sure, you don't want to lose your Saturday night. But it's a live medium for a live audience, so there's plenty of room for people to be doing this in every city.

MU: And in venues that range from nightclubs to concert halls. Theater is also embracing live video—several Broadway and off-Broadway productions use it right now. It's cheap, portable, beautiful, and fully customizable. If you build a set, that's your set, unless you rebuild or repaint it. And you can only do so much with lighting. But with video, it's limitless.

This summer I'm performing in a dance festival on Broadway, and I'm in talks with an opera company to create visuals for their upcoming show in the fall. I'm excited about it; it's totally experimental.

Live video is a great way to play with different ideas, and there's such a spectrum of expression. For example, my friend Missy Galore emphasizes the political aspects. Other friends play with the deeply programmer side. No two VJs here in New York City are doing the same thing, and there's quite a group of us. And I'm sure that our aesthetic is completely different from San Francisco, L.A., London, Milan, Rome, Toronto, Sydney, or any other places that have VJ scenes. I don't think you'll find any two VJs who replicate each other in any way.

BILL COTTMAN ■ ■ ■ ■

Bill Cottman began making photographs in 1969. During the past few years, he has been performing improvisationally with his images, collaborating with his friends J. Otis Powell!, a writer, and Rene Ford, a musician. The trio has performed at numerous venues in the Minneapolis-St. Paul area.

PS: How did you get into performance photography?

BC: Technically, it was probably in the early '70s, when my friend John Watts and I did a slide show synched to "American Woman" by The Guess Who. We had a Kodak carousel projector, and we were running slides of women that we'd photographed—but they couldn't go fast enough for the music. It was only much later that I began exploring the idea of performing with photographs more seriously.

PS: That was real proto-VJ stuff!

BC: Well, I've always experimented. I originally got caught up in technology when I was a kid, sitting on the back steps, trying to light up a light bulb with a battery. My next-door neighbor saw me, came over, and said, "You've got to have a complete circuit." So he got a pair of scissors, touched the bottom of the battery with one side, put the bulb on top, and then touched the side of the bulb with the other. Complete circuit, the bulb lights, and I've just discovered electricity!

In high school, I wanted to be a commercial artist, but they guided us toward very practical careers like being doctors, lawyers, and teachers. This is in Salisbury, Maryland, which had about 35,000 people at the time. The school system was still segregated, and I was in one of the last classes at Salisbury High School, which was the all-black school in town. So I graduated in 1962 and attended Howard University studying Electrical Engineering—but still with this desire to be an artist.

I never actually picked up a camera seriously until after I'd graduated from college and I was working at Sperry-Univac in St. Paul, Minnesota. Around 1968, my next-door neighbor Ben Craven took me to a meeting of the local camera club, at the Hallie Q. Brown community center. I began taking pictures, and photography has been leading me to discoveries ever since.

I soon learned about Edward Weston, Ansel Adams, and other old masters who shot spectacular places and produced these tremendously beautiful prints. Meanwhile, I was trying to create photographs that looked like paintings, thinking that this would establish me as an artist. I followed all the rules of composition—still-lifes with the bowl of fruit, the bottle of wine, the easel, drapery on the table. The whole bit.

Then I discovered street photographers like Garry Winogrand, Lee Friedlander, and Robert Frank—artists who were photographing the social landscape. The pictures were casual, not formal; their method was in their choice of subjects. But they mainly portrayed white America, and when they did photograph black America, it often felt like there was some kind of study going on. There was always this distance, like they were producing an ethnography.

Finally I learned about African-American photographers who portrayed black people in a more personal, connected way. They became my greatest influences —James VanDerZee, Roy DeCarava, Chester Higgins, Jr., Anthony Barboza, Ming Smith Murray—it's a long list that stretches back to the Harlem Renaissance. With my exposure to this work, I had a breakthrough. I realized that I did not have to travel around the world to find spectacular places to shoot photographs, because I can take them in own my living room, neighborhood, or city. And, more importantly, these photographs would have more significance for me because they're telling my story. Before this, I wasn't asking the Why of photography as much as the How: How can I make pictures that look like Edward Weston's or Garry Winogrand's? But now I knew the Why: I am telling my story. And I'm not a spectacular, extraordinary person, so I know that the only person who's going to turn their lens on me and my family is me.

PS: That's great!

BC: I didn't understand all of this at the time, but with the benefit of hindsight I looked back and saw the path that I have walked in my photography. I have now claimed it as being my Why, and I'm moving forward with that insight, and working intently. Today, I'm very clear on why I'm doing what I am doing.

So, I was working at Sperry-Univac until 1971, and near the end of that I was getting bored. I remember calling up the Personnel department and asking them if they had any jobs in computer-generated graphics. "What??" They had no idea what I was talking about.

I worked at Rosemont Engineering, PAKO Corporation and Honeywell after that. I left Honeywell in 1997, then managed a non-profit foundation for about three years. During this time, in 1998, I had an exhibition called "Looking Backward, Moving Forward" at the Minneapolis gallery Homewood Studios. It was essentially a retrospective—although I feel presumptuous using that word, since I'm not well-known. In order to choose the seventy pieces to show, I went through all my contact sheets and searched for clues about what I was doing, patterns. What kept coming up were images of my family and of reflective surfaces—and recognizing this really clarified things for me.

Reflective surfaces are my personal metaphor for how to move forward while looking backward—because it's dangerous to charge ahead while you're physically facing the other way. Reflective surfaces and my own reflection appear frequently in my photographs, allowing me to move forward safely, so to speak, while bringing with me all of my experiences, everything that makes me who I am.

At the end of 1999, I retired completely from what I call wage work, and in 2001, I applied for a one-year fellowship in photography with the McKnight Foundation. While I was working on my proposal, I asked six friends to act as commentators for me, to bounce ideas off of and give me some real, candid feedback. I told them that I wanted to develop a proposal that captures what I do and where I want to take it, rather than tailoring it for McKnight. That's the philosophy I use with everything that I'm doing now; since I'm not trying to make a living at this, I don't worry about marketing. I respect my audience, but they're not whom I'm working for.

I was selected to be one of four McKnight fellows for the year 2002, and at the end of the year, I presented a gallery exhibition and gave a talk to summarize my work. So I wanted to flesh it out in a coherent way, and the shape I arrived at was to focus the exhibition around the four women in my life: My mother Evelyn, my mother-in-law Patricia, my wife Beverly, and our daughter Kenna. Two of them are now no longer living; Evelyn died in January of this year, and Patricia died last March.

Patricia and I had a wonderful relationship, one that destroys that whole myth of son-in-law, mother-in-law. We hosted a radio show together on KFAI Community Radio, "Mostly Jazz, with Pat Walton and Her Dear Son-in-Law Bill." When Patricia got sick, I went to the station alone, and during the last hour of each show I'd call in to her apartment, and we broadcasted live with her on the phone.

Anyway, about three-quarters of the way through my McKnight year, I commissioned my friend, the writer J. Otis Powell!, to develop text for the exhibition—he's one of the people who had commented on the proposal. I asked him if he could write biographical pieces to present with the photographs, and he said he couldn't do that because he didn't have that kind of access to the women's lives. But he was interested in creating text that speaks to issues of freedom, identity and responsibility in the lives of black women in America. I'd email him a few images, and he would email back a few lines. And that's how we developed the fourteen sequences for my McKnight Fellowship exhibition, FOUR WOMEN: stories of Freedom, Identity & Responsibility.

Now, here's where the performance aspect comes back in, and why I'm interested in VJ software. With the McKnight show, the collaboration between me and J. Otis was really beginning to cook. So at the end of the year, instead of the usual dry artist talk, we decided to do a performance based on four of the sequences, Across Two Lines, Old Soul, Fashionable, and Immortality. I created jpeg files of all the photos and projected them from my a laptop using a slideshow program. Onstage, J. Otis performed his text while I triggered the photos and did some transitions—real elementary stuff. I even misfired a couple times. But people clearly connected to it, and we have continued to perform this way. Recently a musician, composer friend, Rene Ford has entered the collaboration.

PS: So you're looking for a VJ application, or whatever application, that lets you choose and show photographs, control the timing, and that's it—no whizzy effects, but responsive enough so you can follow any cues, or the mood of the room.

BC: That's it. Most VJ content doesn't interest me—the flashing lights and swirling and pulsating images. What interests me is technology that enables me to recollect and rearrange images, transitions, and timing in response to the moods in the room. J. Otis and Rene are capable of working in a very improvisational way.

I think that just about anything that I buy will be overkill for what I want to do, but that's the nature of technology. It's so easy to add features that you get feature, feature, feature, and function, function, function. Any actual benefit is up to the user.

I could do more, like mix in some live camera. And that's all slick and cool—but again, the question is Why? What would that add to my story? Showing you as an audience member, does that add something to my story? If I don't have an answer to that question, I won't do it. I'm not going to add something just because it's technically possible.

PS: That makes total sense—I wish more artists felt that way. What other performances have you done?

BC: Just last month we did a show at the Minnesota Center of Photography called "one plus one is ONE." I designed it a little differently. Rene and J. Otis both wanted to see the images more clearly, so we all stood in the back, behind the audience. I gave J. Otis the remote, so he could control the duration of each sequence. Meanwhile, Rene got to choose which sequence we were going to do, and I brought all the images. Everyone was leading in some way, and it was as spontaneous as it could be.

There is democracy in the way J. Otis and I collaborate. At different times we parallel, converge, diverge, and intersect. I used to feel that our collaboration was best when we intersected, but J. Otis has broadened my thinking to realize value at all points of our collaboration.

Rene and I along with seven other artists are creating a production, with Pangaea World Theater, called *2704: Seven Generations into the Future.* The show takes place in a classroom in the year 2704. The actors onstage are teachers and the audience members are the students, and they're being taught the only lesson you ever need to learn, which is how to be human.

PS: It's a hard lesson, though.

BC: Right now, we are collecting our own stories and creating visuals. We want to project them forward in time and retell them in 2704, preserving these important artifacts from our own time so that future beings retain the value of humanity.

MARK CONIGLIO ▓ ▓ ▓ ▓

Composer, media artist, and technologist Mark Coniglio co-founded the dance company Troika Ranch with Dawn Stoppiello in 1994. He is also the developer of the popular real-time video application Isadora, which came out of his performance work.

PS: What initially drew you to video?

MC: It started with the first major interactive piece that my collaborator Dawn Stoppiello and I made, *In Plane*, which was about a competition between a live performer and a recorded image of her. This was back in 1994, long before you could do any kind of meaningful real-time video processing on a regular computer. So we burned all of the video ahead of time onto laserdisc and controlled the laserdisc player via serial port. Dawn wore the MidiDancer system, which uses a set of flexion sensors to measure the straightness or bent-ness of up to eight points on the body. The sensors transmit wirelessly, so that as you bend your elbows, knees, hips, and wrists, that position information goes to a nearby computer, which can then take the data and use it to do whatever.

PS: Is MidiDancer an off-the-shelf product?

MC: No, it's something I created myself, so I believe I was the first to do this for dance. I hacked it out of toy radio-control car transmitters which I'd bought at Radio Shack—but MidiDancer has come a long way since, and is far more sophisticated now.

All the music in *In Plane* was generated by Dawn's motions, so she functioned as the musician as well as the dancer. Her movement information also controlled the recall of the clips from laserdisc along with the speed of their playback, which was one of the few things that device let you manipulate in real time. Remember, this was ten years ago.

Ever since then, our work has included some aspect of video. After *In Plane*, we did another couple of pieces that used laserdisc imagery, but as an integral element along with the dancing, rather than having the dancer control it.

We have a theory that describes the four basic roles video can fulfill in a live performance. You can use video as a character, where it has an equivalent presence on the stage as a performer. It can also create an environment, a world for the performer to be in. You can use it as cinema, which happens when all performers leave the stage and the audience watches the video just as they would a film. And the final way we use video is as lighting, projecting images directly on the bodies of the performers or onto things—using the video as a light source, as opposed to as an image source per se.

In our early pieces, the video functioned as both character and environment, but it was only barely interactive. Then, around 1999, I was first introduced to Image/ine, the video-processing software for the Mac. I was fascinated by its ability to control video in real time and do things to it, so we used it in a piece called *The Chemical Wedding of Christian Rosenkreutz*. This had some basic image manipulations, nothing really that extensive, which were controlled by the MidiDancer.

I didn't love Image/ine's user interface, though. It was all table-based, and it really made me crazy. We teach a lot, at universities and at our own Troika Ranch workshops, and our students had a hard time learning it—especially since we were also teaching them another piece of software, Interactor, which I created with my mentor Morton Subotnick. Sometimes we wouldn't get anything done artistically because we were spending the whole time working on the programs. So that's why I created Isadora®. I wanted a tool that was well-integrated and easy to learn, and could do exactly the things we wanted for our performance work. That way, users could devote their time to making the artwork rather than figuring out the software.

Part of what's interesting about Isadora is that I didn't only write it as a programmer. I'm originally trained as a composer; I went to CalArts and studied with that fellow I mentioned, Morton Subotnick, who's a pioneer of electronic music. But I was also programming for money when I was sixteen, and was always good at it. So I have both of those skills, engineering and art. With the Isadora program, I believe that an artistic sensibility comes through, and that's why a lot of artists are attracted to using it.

PS: It's interesting that in *In Plane*, the performer and image compete with each other. Do you think that combining the two like that gives opportunities for addressing media issues?

MC: In 1994 it did, maybe. That was pre-dot-com explosion, and the Internet was on the rise. There were lots of questions in the air back then about what technology meant in terms of our own being and our bodies. People were discovering that they could have multiple screen names and could construct different personalities depending on whom they were communicating with, behind the façade of electronic text. So we built a narrative that asked which is better, the virtual Dawn or the real Dawn? The virtual Dawn can do all this beautiful stuff that the real Dawn can't do. It can move in slow motion, which is very seductive. It can freeze in mid air. It never tires. But it's this two-dimensional image. Meanwhile, the real, living, breathing Dawn may sweat, get tired, and eventually die, but she does things that the image can never do. The piece's title comes from the notion that the two-dimensional image of Dawn was forever trapped in the plane of this projection surface. One additional technical element that served this narrative was that the projector traveled back and forth along a twenty-four-foot track under computer control—so the image of Dawn could move laterally across the stage.

Back then, people were thinking about those issues. But we know more now and have more experience. It's been explored a lot. So at this point, I'd like to see how the technology becomes unimportant. Originally, it was an enormous step for us to manipulate video live, rather than just playing a tape during a performance. Now, because it's so easy, it doesn't have an importance in and of itself—and that's the natural progression.

There's a story I like to tell during workshops. There's an absolutely radical new technology invented by this woman, who became a superstar in Europe. She gave performances that focused on this technology, and audiences were just blown away—they had never seen anything like it. Well, the person I'm talking about is Loie Fuller and this was in 1896. She was using slide projectors, and she invented gels—colored glass that goes in front of stage lights. Seeing these colors was a spectacular experience at the time, but today none of us walks into a theater and even blinks at the fact that there's a colored gel in front of a light. This doesn't mean that people can't do beautiful things with it, but the light itself doesn't get that kind of attention.

The "new media" stuff isn't quite like gel, but it's getting there. Today, when you show an image onstage and manipulate it digitally, it has a kind of texture that we recognize as being digital. As soon as you do this, some people think, "Well, okay—this has something to do with technology, and she's being manipulated." So, because this technology is still relatively new, our problem is how can we include it in a piece and not make it about the technology? Soon this will no longer be an issue we have to think about. No one's going to care that it's digital, or feel that digital-ness has some kind of narrative associated with it. It'll just be, what does this imagery mean to me? How does it relate to what's going on onstage? How does it further the story?

PS: What other general directions do you see for video in the performing arts?

MC: Well, there's one thing I believe—have no idea if others will consider this important, but I do, and only time will bear me out. I feel that the thing we love about digital is that it can be endlessly duplicated. We can make copies, send it around, and it never loses any quality. But for live performance, this fixed quality is a problem, because the media is always the same.

Live performance is a bit of an old-fashioned notion in a society where everything is recorded and broadcast and distributed. But what gives life to performance is that it's *not* the same every night. That's why I feel that every element of a performance should be live, in one way or another. We put sensors on the dancer's body or in the space, and somehow the organic nature of what the performers do has a direct impact on the way the digital media are presented. Maybe you're working with recorded imagery, but you aren't just running clips. You're manipulating them real-time, and the final result will never be quite the same—just as the dancers will never dance in quite the same way.

I think that permeating the entire environment with this changeability will keep live performance alive in the future. That's the one unique property it has that film and television lack—anything can happen.

PS: It also brings the audience together into that time and place. They're the only people who are experiencing the same things you are.

MC: That's another reason it's sort of an antiquated notion. Dance especially, I can safely say, is the least efficient art form. You've got to rent a space, hire a crew, rehearse over and over and over—there are so many things about it that are so completely inefficient. And yet when the audience comes together with those performers, you're a small community sitting together in a dark room and sharing something. And I find that to be something that's rather important.

So I hope that the work we're doing will influence the way others use technology in live performances. Because now, most choreographers and theater directors who use video are just treating it like a fancy tape recorder, playing canned clips. It's still fixed, still dead. And I'd like to see it go beyond that, become something that's a little more living.

JOHN HUMPHRIES ▪ ▪ ▪ ▪

At the time of this interview, John Humphries was the product manager for the V-4 mixer and other pieces of video hardware at Edirol USA. He has since gone on to co-found a consultancy for the club industry.

PS: What have you been doing at Edirol?

JH: I'm basically known as the "club guy." I've been in sales for about a dozen years and also used to be a DJ. So a lot of what I do now is go into new areas, uncharted clubs, set up the gear for the night, and then do a performance to show off what our stuff is capable of. I love it because I get to be an artist and a VJ and also be a sales manager—it's a really good balance.

PS: That sounds amazingly fun—I'm jealous!

JH: Well, it's a lot of work though. I also handle corporate clients and churches, so I have plenty of eighteen-hour days. For our video product line, I saw that we needed to develop a community and promote the awareness of the whole scene. So that's where my focus has been—doing events, helping local VJs borrow gear if they need it, showing up to different parties with a rig.

PS: Hardware companies like Edirol, Pioneer, and Koss make products for VJs, but it surprises me that no digital projector manufacturer seems to have clued into the VJ market, even though VJ is completely dependent on projectors. The field doesn't have much differentiation, and I think one of them could step up and become the Absolut Vodka of the field—the cool, artsy brand.

JH: Right now, we still just have to get the promoters and the club owners to see that there should be a budget for VJs and for live video. Most of them think that looping a DVD looks just as good as a live guy, and until you get in there and show them, they won't know the difference. Also, if the infrastructure isn't there for that dynamic, immersive look, if the club's only got maybe a couple of plasmas or just plain TVs, they have to step up and add projection, which is a big investment for them.

Club hardware is interesting—different places match different equipment. Now we mainly have ultra-lounges and superclubs and not a lot in between, only a few mid-sized clubs. Pioneer is coming out with the X1 DVD deck, which is a pretty impressive piece, but I see it mainly going into the ultra-lounges and Indian casino kinds of clubs, where they want to just run and mix music videos. But the cool thing there is, that will lay the infrastructure. It'll install projectors into some new places.

One thing that really excites people now is live camera. It pulls them into the video, gets them looking at the screens and interacting. I'm seeing a lot of VJs interested in mixing live camera. Edirol just launched a mini low-light camera, actually.

PS: And it underscores that it's live, not just something playing in the background.

JH: Yeah, it's wide open. I've seen so many different levels of VJs. One guy I work with lives in Arizona, out in a trailer park near a landfill, and he goes around and mixes music videos at Indian casinos. He's a cool guy, and he is a VJ in his own way, but he's not rendering his own 3D animations, shooting his own clips, and all that. Other people I've seen just mix movies, throw them all together—and it looks great.

Edirol is giving people non-linear, almost intuitive control of vast amounts of content, at broadcast quality. The two pieces that I think have revolutionized live video control are the V-4 mixer and the DV7-PR, which is a touchscreen-controlled content playback box. With the 'PR, instead of shuffling DVDs, a touchscreen accesses vast numbers of clips. With two touchscreens and a V-4 in the middle, it's kind of like your two turntables and a mixer—you've got random access to infinite material, you can control the speed, video scratch. Also, each piece has MIDI control, so anyone onstage can interface their instrument to make the video react to what they're doing. Or you can hook into a lighting control system that sends MIDI triggers, like Whole Hog PC.

In the lighting world, the Catalyst from High End Systems is really interesting. They have a Quicktime content server that feeds a moving projector head, with keystoning and effects built in. So it's just like you're moving a standard spotlight, but it's a video image shooting around on the walls—it's an amazing effect.

Our gear fits right in the middle of theirs. The V-4 can take input from the Catalyst content server, mix it with input from the DV7-PR, and send it out to the DL-1—that's the moving projector head. It's interesting. All these companies are trying to do their own thing, and you've got complete confusion over what's going to become the standard. So Edirol and Roland are trying to build reference tools that are easy to learn and super stable. Our system's not based on Windows or Mac; it's a BeOS base platform with hardware and software that's been engineered to work together, with our own video cards based on Roland chipsets.

With Edirol installed as basic infrastructure in the clubs, the inputs are there and ready so a mobile VJ can just show up with their laptop and plug in. Applications like Motion Dive, ArKaos, and Resolume are cool because anyone with a laptop can bring what they've got and throw it down. Feed that into a V-4 mixer, add in some live camera or a DVD, and you've got a really sick little show.

Then clubs can start building their own custom video libraries and work with local artists to develop and support that content. Just like bars define themselves by the music on the jukebox, a club can develop its own visual personality—but instead of having to rely on standard titles from a distributor, the content actually comes from the local community.

PS: I'd heard that Edirol started out doing video mixers for churches.

JH: Not really, but churches have been a very strong market for us. Also, there are a couple of people in our management team with ties to religious organizations, and they've done heavy promotion into some of the bigger Christian rock tours. That's not my bag, but it's all good.

Churches are basically nightclubs these days. You've got intelligent lighting, you've got sound, you've got video—it's all the same stuff. Designers and installers will put together the exact same package for a titty bar as they will for a church.

GEORGE STADNIK ■ ■ ■ ■

Lumia artist and inventor George Stadnik is working to restore one of Thomas Wilfred's original Clavilux machines for public performance. His collaborators on The Clavilux Project are collector Eugene Epstein and Lumia artist Rudi Stern.

PS: How did the Clavilux Project get started?

GS: The original machine was acquired by Dr. Eugene Epstein from Earl Reibeck, a Lumia artist who kept a studio in the West Village for many years. After Thomas Wilfred died in 1968, Reibeck had bought the contents of Wilfred's studio from his son in West Nyack, just up the Hudson. Earl kept it all for years, but then in March 2003 the building where his studio was located was sold. He had to give up the space and move everything out or else it may have ended up in the dumpster. So Earl contacted Dr. Eugene Epstein, a major Wilfred collector in L.A.. But since Eugene was out there, and the building had to be vacated almost overnight, he contacted Rudi Stern. Rudi agreed to go get the stuff out of there and store it for him. Then Rudi contacted me to help assess the condition of the materials and write up an inventory once they were transferred to his studio in Jersey City.

Rudi went to Earl's studio with some movers on a cold wet Saturday morning, and they loaded out about twenty-eight shipping crates. The contents didn't just include one Clavilux, as we'd expected from some detective work Dr. Epstein did later in Seattle. There were actually two Claviluxes, a model F and a model G, which may have been one of the last ones that Wilfred built. There were also extra parts for other Claviluxes and Lumia projectors, glass slides Wilfred used for his theatrical work, a large volume of his publicity materials, old invoices and receipts, and other interesting bits. It was a compendium of his life and work. Even his eyeglasses and jacket were in there. We opened up these cases and made a complete inventory for Dr. Epstein, who then bought the entire lot.

PS: I'm guessing there were also tons of Wilfred's scores and notes.

GS: Actually, no. That was the damnedest thing. Rudi and I were looking for that, because if we were to restore the instrument, we wanted to know how to play it—and Wilfred's scores or notations would have helped considerably. But Dr. Epstein suggested to Rudi that Yale Library has about thirty or forty feet of Wilfred material archived, and this might include some scores. So one of the next things we need to do is to go up to Yale, but we haven't found the time yet. Based on a list that Dr. Epstein provided, Rudi and I figure that it will take several days at least to conduct a thorough search through the materials at Yale.

Rudi hired an electrician to look at the Claviluxes and assess what it would take to restore them. Considering that they've been in storage for almost forty years, they're in great shape! The electrician said that the only thing we needed to do is replace some of the wiring, which had degraded over time. We also need to replace the color gels, some of which were faded and cracked—but we could determine all the colors from the remaining pieces in the cabinets. Other than that, the instruments are intact. All the components are there, including all of the original filament light bulbs, boxes of lenses, and extra cases of original General Electric Mazda lamps from the '20s. These bulbs had exotic-looking filaments which formed some of Wilfred's imagery.

PS: He would actually shape the filaments in certain ways?

GS: There were a few custom filament lamps, but mostly they were standard lamps from the era with different filaments. Wilfred's compositions used the filament shapes as a foundation for the image, then refracted and reflected it to create variations.

PS: Are the Clavilux machines portable enough to tour with? I know that some of these instruments were installed and some were portable.

GS: Wilfred did tour with the pieces we examined, and he also built automated pieces, which were pre-programmed. The automated pieces are what Dr. Epstein has in his collection. Wilfred also created several large installations, for museums and commercial buildings, including one for Clairol's headquarters in Manhattan.

PS: This was a permanent installation?

GS: Yes, it was in the lobby of the Clairol headquarters on Park Avenue. The chairman of Clairol commissioned the piece to promote hair coloring. It had nothing to do with hair coloring, of course, but it had everything to do with color and inspiration. Recently, my wife Maxine and I have been seeking out and interviewing people who remember Wilfred—the few who are still around. We recorded one gentleman who actually worked with him on the Clairol installation. He had been Clairol's head of public relations at the time. I think the installation was there for over thirty years, but when P&G bought Clairol, they disassembled it and gave it to the Smithsonian, which currently has it in storage.

PS: I love that old skyscraper artwork from the era when so much talent went into these cathedrals of commerce.

GS: The graphic images of the time certainly communicated the notion that business and commerce were high art forms. Artists were commissioned to create attributes for brands, celebrate their almost mythical aspirations, in paint, stone, metal, and in Wilfred's case, light.

Back in Rudi's studio in Jersey City we opened up the Model F and tinkered with it. It seemed a bit chaotic at first, but it's actually amazingly precise. Wilfred was a mechanical genius—he figured out how to make numerous lenses, filaments, shadow elements, and refractive elements move around in a coordinated fashion, controlling each movement accurately and reproducibly, and all from one very flexible performance instrument.

PS: What aesthetic principles were behind his compositions? Like, how did he write them and what was he trying to convey? Did he ever explain this?

GS: Yes. Rudi and I have photocopies of Wilfred's manuscript for an unpublished book, which Dr. Epstein made from his original. It consists of a couple hundred pages, then it stops in mid-sentence. We're hoping that there might be more up at Yale. In the book, Wilfred explains that his work is inspired by primitive, visceral imagery from the dawn of time, fire, water, reflection, shadow, movement. Things that you're uncertain of what they mean, but that you react to. It's a terrific read that gives you real insight into the time, and into Wilfred's struggle to make Lumia a legitimate, recognized art form.

Wilfred also defines the projected image as a window into a larger space which extends infinitely in all dimensions. He would move elements into view, compose with them, and move them out the other side, as if the whole audience were traveling through space. The pieces were abstract and very evocative, but the frame defined a portal, rather than a surface—as it does with many abstract paintings. He created a composition called City Lights, which was very Mondrian-like.

PS: These are all without music, right?

GS: Yes, they're completely silent. Wilfred states that there's no natural relationship between tone and color, although later in the manuscript he does say that if he were to combine music and visuals, he would create the images first and then determine what accompanying sound would be generated by the image and its movement. Which is telling—it's the opposite of how, for example, SonicVision at the Hayden Planetarium was constructed. With that, the audio tracks were already laid down, and visual images were created to "illustrate" the audio.

I've met some of the people who produced SonicVision through a group called the New York Motion Graphics Association. We meet every month, and last January (2004) I gave a presentation on Wilfred, Lumia and the Clavilux restoration project. This is a very plugged-in group—many members create motion-graphics for television and commercials, and their attention span is usually about thirty frames. I showed one of my Lumia pieces that lasted for eight minutes, and nobody left the room. I was very happy about that!

One thing about Lumia is that there are a few artists out there working with it, but most of them work independently. There's no central focus—which is too bad, because it's a serious art movement that deserves attention, in part because of its influence on so much other contemporary fine art and commercial artwork.

PS: Club visuals have another problem, which is that they lack a sense of individual authorship. And that's a basic requirement for any mature art form—you have to know who's doing what, and who's borrowing what, and who's referring to what.

GS: That's what makes art…art—the context in which it's created, the context from which it comes. So I'm glad you're putting some reference points around this.

I understand that the Hirshhorn is putting together a new show about light and Lumia. The last one they did was in the 1970s. The American Museum of the Moving Image has been considering doing something on Lumia next year, which may include the Clavilux Project. MoMA has a major Wilfred Lumia in storage, but I haven't heard of any plans to exhibit it when the museum re-opens this November.

The old MoMA on 53rd Street is where I first saw Wilfred's *Opus 161*, which is the work that originally inspired me to work as a Lumia artist. I was there in October of 1968 on a field trip as an art student at Syracuse University. The piece was displayed in the lower mezzanine level, and it hit me like a lightning bolt. I knew right then that this was the direction for me to go artistically.

PS: In broad strokes, it seems that Lumia has always been high art. But later on, the psychedelic light show became more rock 'n' roll, less highbrow.

GS: Lumia stands on its own as an art form, without music, whereas with wet shows and the lighting effects you see over the past thirty years, the visuals serve the purpose of enhancing the music. Lumia is more like painting, in its purest form.

PS: So Lumia never has music? I thought it sometimes could.

GS: That's right—it's always purely visual. But it can be the starting point for other sensory experiences. For example, you could look at a piece of Lumia and feel that you're hearing music, or feel a sensation of warmth or cold, or taste a flavor—or it may even evoke the fragrance of flowers or recall a memory. It's a visual synaesthetic expression. I don't add music to the visuals I create, because I'd rather have people imagine what sounds the visual images might make, as opposed to telling them what they sound like.

PS: It's always more effective to make the mind interpret things in its own way rather than spelling it out.

GS: It's definitely more rewarding, and it makes for much better conversations afterwards, because everyone has their own sense of perception and context.

PS: One thing I've been wondering is, we've all seen flat-panel televisions get bigger and cheaper. What's going to happen when people start wanting to use the space when they aren't actively watching? What should a "screen saver" look like for a large area in a living room?

GS: I've been working on that exact problem, as have others, such as D.R. Bailey. The trick is to define the medium so that people understand it as a form in its own right, so that they don't see some visual effects and then assume that a Lumia piece is trying to be a Hollywood movie.

For example, Wilfred was very strict in what he proposed as the boundaries of his art form. He wanted Lumia to stay true to his original ideas about motion and color changes, timing and pacing, intensity, and things like that. Elsewhere, people are creating visuals that follow different rules—VJs have an aesthetic that they're developing, and motion graphics people have aesthetics for their purposes. Conveying the idea that the wall-mounted flat-panel screen is its own unique medium will eventually establish a context within which the art form can evolve and take its legitimate place among other recognized art forms.

BENTON-C BAINBRIDGE ■ ■ ■ ■
(WITH ANNOTATIONS BY WALTER WRIGHT)

Benton-C Bainbridge has "played" movies in real time for over two decades, making live audiovisuals with musicians, dancers, actors and visual artists around the world. Video synthesizer pioneer Walter Wright contributed annotations to the first part of this interview.

PS: How did you get interested in video?

BCB: What first triggered it was watching *The Electric Company* when I was about six. That show had a huge impact on me. I watched some of it again recently, for the first time as an adult, and realized that their whole aesthetic was video synthesis, video art. It had a handmade quality to it, at least by today's standards.

They had this one routine with animated words—a word starts off completely distorted and illegible, spinning around in this geometric, spin-art pattern, black against a solid, brightly-colored background. At the same time, you hear this agitated synthesizer sound matching the movement on the screen. Then the pattern slowly unravels and the sound settles down. Finally you hear a steady tone, the word unfolds, "basketball" or whatever, and you hear twenty kids yell out "basketball!" As a kid, I couldn't picture the technology that was used to make this, but I did recognize that there was some relationship between the sound and the image, and there was a live-ness to it that really appealed to me.

Years later I learned that Walter Wright, a live video artist whom I've performed with many times since meeting him in 1998, used to work on *The Electric Company* as an animator—and he was actually the one who came up with the synchronous audiovisual word routine. They used a device called a Scanimate to move the images around, and Walter had the idea to take the same control tones that were controlling the Scanimate video, and feed them into a synthesizer to generate audio. In analog synthesis, that's a useful trick, because our eyes respond to a very different frequency range than our ears do. We'll use one source signal to influence both the visuals and the sound in parallel, rather than deriving one from the other. So I would say that Walter Wright was really my first influence.

WW: *I worked for Dolphin Productions, a division of Computer Image Corporation, the developers of the Scanimate video animation system. On Sunday afternoons I had the studio to myself. One of my first experiments was to re-scan and reanimate bad sci-fi movies from Channel 9. I took the control signals used to animate the video image directly out of the console and mixed* these with the movie soundtrack. It was actually a couple of years later that the idea of controlling sound and video synthesis with the same control voltage sources was fully realized at the Experimental TV Center, by David Jones and Rich Brewster.

PS: How does the Scanimate work?

BCB: It's one of a few devices that take a conventional CRT, a TV vacuum tube, and give you custom control of how the electron beam scans. So in a sense, it's somewhere between a television, which scans regular rows, and an oscilloscope, where the beam draws patterns directly. These two different methods of making an image are the analog equivalent of bitmap versus vector graphics. Devices like the Scanimate or the Rutt/Etra Video Synthesizer can do both. You can strip the control information off of a video source, the parts of the signal that we don't see directly, and use them for something else, or warp them and recombine them with the original, which causes the visible part of the picture to distort in different ways.

WW: *The Scanimate used a special high-resolution tube. The control information remains with the signal, but instead of triggering a standard raster pattern—line by line and left to right from top to bottom of the screen—the Scanimate system allowed the animator to control the position, size and shape of the raster. Basically, Scanimate was an analog computer system that allowed the animator to program effects over time, using voltage-controlled oscillators, ramp generators, and mixers to modify the raster. The raster was divided vertically into five segments, and each segment could be controlled separately. Using the large commutator panel, the animator set the initial position, final position, size, and intensity for each segment. A ramp generator then faded from the initial to the final values. Additional modules and a patch bay allowed the animator to set timing and to further modulate these values.*

BCB: I recommend going online and searching on Scanimate. There's this early Scanimate artist in Tennessee, David Sieg, who sells a DVD compilation of Scanimate archival video. Watching this DVD makes me feel that contemporary visuals are revisiting a lot of aesthetic concerns from the '70s—it isn't all so "new" and "unprecedented." Even conventional television back then was riddled with synchronous synthesized audio-visuals that came from analog machines like the Scanimate, which dominated broadcast TV special effects for a little while.

WW: *I checked the David Sieg disc out—interesting. I remember seeing this material while working at Dolphin. The unique development at Dolphin was to use the system in real time as a visual instrument. Ed Emshwiller's* Thermogenesis *and* Scapemates *were both animated in real time in Dolphin's* *studio. I generated a number of real-time tapes which I showed at the Kitchen. Woody and Steina Vasulka have an example of the notation system I developed for the Scanimate.*

At the same time as I was at Dolphin and the Kitchen, Nam June Paik and Shuya Abe were building video synthesizers they designed called the Paik-Abe Video Synthesizer or PAVS. The first was up in Boston, at WGBH, and the second was at the Experimental TV Center, where Paik was the first artist-in-residence. They built several more after that, including one for WNET. I took the artist residency at ETC right after Paik, so I moved from NYC up to Binghamton and started working on the PAVS. I modified my notation system to fit the device, and then took it on the road to perform live at schools, galleries and public access centers, often with playing along with musicians.

After Dave Jones developed his voltage-controlled colorizer, I also took this on the road and used it live with Paul Bley and Sun Ra at Axis In Soho in the early '70s. They released the video along with the album, and this may have been the first commercial music video. I also used the Jones Colorizer with Synergy, a multimedia performance group which included Gary Hill and me on sound and video synths, and Sarah Cook performing dance.

PS: That *Electric Company* animation seems like a good metaphor for learning to read. You're extracting this particular sound, this word, from the chaos of lines and forms that you see on the page before you've learned to read. Maybe reading is a form of synaesthesia—that's what we experience when our eyes see marks on a page and then our brain hears them internally as words.

WW: *Check out Ernst Cassirer,* Language and Myth.

BCB: I need to think about that. I don't know the science of how we interpret written language, but for me, I'm definitely more cognizant of the sounds in my head when I'm reading a foreign language rather than English. But *The Electric Company* was certainly trying to teach us to read phonetically—it's not like they were trying to turn their audience of early '70s kids into video artists.

In another routine, they show the first letter of a word while you hear the corresponding phoneme. Then you'd see and hear the next group of letters, and then they'd put the two together. They'd go "fff"—"uck"—"fuck." One live video group I performed with in the early '90s, 77 Hz, did a piece that was based on that exact routine. We typed the text live into a character generator application on the Amiga.

I grew up very limited in what television I was allowed to watch, which may be why I can't stand almost all of the TV that is on now. I just don't buy any of it. My roommate can't believe how much television annoys me, but I find it headache-inducing and paranoia-inducing. Things that people take for granted, like commercial breaks or even credits, seem absurd to me. Credits have no place on the screen; it's just meta-data that should be kept separate.

If someone announced between every music track we listened to, "The guitar was played by George Harrison," and so on, we would go crazy—so why do we accept it on TV? When *Apocalypse Now* first came out, of course, Coppola didn't have any credits on it. Instead, he distributed a printed program.

At the moment, the only television I like is on HBO, and I think *Six Feet Under* is the best series I've ever seen. I don't know anybody at that network, so I don't know their strategy, but every step they take seems to be a conscious decision to reach audiences that haven't been served by conventional TV.

The vast majority of what is on television is propaganda of one sort or another. Sure, *The Electric Company* was also propaganda, but what it was instilling in young minds was the English language, and incidentally a joy of looking at shapes and colors moving around abstractly. What I took away from it as a kid was a whole set of expectations about what an image on a monitor should and could look like. That's what I miss in TV, and that's why I do what I do in art.

It's not that I'm "retro," and I'm not interested in re-hashing, but I am interested in the idea of a cinema that isn't driven by storytelling in the conventional sense. It's been a whole, rich area of exploration which we seem to forget about once every generation, but I have a feeling that this time around it's going to endure, because of what's happening with display technologies, access to video production tools, and all that.

PS: Are you talking about mostly abstract visuals or representation or...?

BCB: My personal interest is all of the above. I don't mind narrative; in fact, I love a good narrative, even a Hollywood formula. Anything is valid as long as you do it right. If the message that's being delivered makes me think, entertains me, makes me laugh or cry, gives me a place to forget, or whatever—then I'm interested.

With abstract visuals, we're seeing things now that were unthinkable five years ago. I think this is because a wide audience is being introduced to audio-synchronous abstraction through their computers' music visualization apps. For example, my dad didn't understand my abstract video for a long time. But now that he can listen to Kenny G with a plug-in and watch matching patterns on his screen, he really gets what I'm doing. To me it's just common sense that people enjoy watching abstraction, and seeing an interaction between sound and image that isn't necessarily dictated by telling a story.

As displays become brighter, bigger, and flatter, the image becomes environmental, allowing the video to color a room's ambience rather than just deliver information. Today's media is undergoing a metamorphosis as new displays beg for beautiful pictures to fill them. So we're now seeing companies offering footage of tropical fish aquariums and slideshows of impressionist paintings for all these hi-def screens. This same market will demand new and fresher content, and visualists are the natural providers.

PS: I recently read a speech by William Gibson where he said that cinema began when prehistoric people sat in circles around the fire, looked into the flames, and told stories about what they saw.

BCB: Yeah, that's exactly it. And now that video tools have become so accessible, a lot of people can control the fire, use it to conjure up the images they want to see—whether they're Paris Hilton or blobs moving on the screen.

When I first met Bill Etra, the co-inventor of the Rutt/Etra video synthesizer, he said to me, "Video won't be popularly accepted as an art form until the tools are as accessible as a pen and paper." We're a long way from that, but widespread, firsthand experience with moviemaking is happening now. Anyone can appreciate music because we've all at least clapped or banged on a drum. Not everyone can be a Vladimir Horowitz or Jimi Hendrix, but if you've ever strummed a guitar, the experience gives you deeper access to what Hendrix accomplished. You'll listen and think, "Wow—what is that sound? It sounds like seagulls, and he made that sound with a guitar!" Cinema has had higher barriers, but that's breaking down now, and as a result more people have a deeper appreciation of the moving image. At some point, almost everyone will have at least conversant knowledge about how moving images can be conjured up.

PS: John Humphries told me that Edirol has been working with the Boys and Girls Clubs of Southern California, setting up a studio for kids to learn video mixing in after school. He said they pick it up immediately. When he goes into bars and clubs, he needs to spend a long time explaining the equipment, but this is completely unnecessary with the kids. They know what the slider does, and everything else.

BCB: Yeah—the quickest study ever of my work was a nine-year-old girl I sat next to on an airplane in 2000, while flying from New York to California. I had my laptop open and was looking at some abstract video that I had synthesized, some squiggles and blobs and colorful shapes moving around. This girl next to me watched me for a little while and then said, "Hey Mister—what are you doing? What is that?" I told her this is some video I made. She seemed interested, so I kept talking through it. She pointed at one clip and asked, "How did you make this one?" So I gave her a brief explanation like, "well, I used oscillations, raw electronic signals that go up and down in voltage." And she said "Wow!" Then she pointed to a few different shapes, and was like, "How is that one made?" So I said, that one is made with an oscilloscope, which is an instrument that reads these oscillations, the increases and decreases in voltage, and that makes squiggly lines like these, or these other round, squiggly patterns here—things that look like drawings. Then she pointed at a blob and said, "What about this?" I said, "That is made by taking an oscillation and directly turning that into video by adding the frame around the video, and the other parts that make up a video signal."

PS: And she knew that the blob must have been made in a different way than the things she had pointed to before.

BCB: Yes, absolutely. But then what really startled me is, I laid out the four basic techniques that I used: oscilloscope patterns, turning pure electronic signals into video, video switcher effects, and video feedback. I showed her an example of video feedback. And then she said to me, "Hmm—well, it seems to me that video feedback is very important to your technique, because I also see it here, here, here, here, and here." And she pointed to all the other places where I had used video feedback. And I thought, "Oh my god!"

Meanwhile, her fifteen-year-old brother was sitting one more seat over, and he didn't have her level of understanding. There's something about nine-year-olds. Probably a child psychologist can tell me why, but I've found that they can understand the work on an abstract, formal level without having to be told what it's about, and they have very acute perceptions about what the content of the work is, and how to follow its progression. Obviously the Children's Television Workshop, in producing *The Electric Company*, did their research on how that age group thinks.

I've done live abstract video for a while, and like many others in the field, I never thought that there would be much interest in what I do. But with people who are about nineteen or younger, what I'm finding nowadays is that, even if they don't especially like what I do, they at least understand what it's about, and they don't have to be told why they should look at it. It's interesting. When I watched abstract visuals as a kid, I was just consuming it—but today, when a kid encounters real-time, abstract visuals, they know they're probably not too many steps away from being able to create some themselves, or at least influence them by selecting some preset parameters. This sets up very different expectations surrounding media. When you watch nine-year-old kids cutting and pasting HTML to change the backgrounds of their web pages, you know that we can look forward to new types of media that will cater to their expectations.

PS: I'm looking forward to it!

BCB: Yeah, me too.

One thing I see happening now is that VJing is a global phenomenon. Everywhere in the world that I've performed over the past few years (other than in Nicaragua, which is still developing) I always meet someone who comes up and says, "I'm a VJ too," or else I meet a VJ in a club. The gear is pretty ubiquitous, and even if you can't afford the latest and greatest, you can pick up stuff that's two years old from someone who's upgrading. There's a tremendous pool of tools that people worldwide are picking up and using to make cinema.

PS: I think it's a folk art—a self-taught, do-it-yourself form of collage. People create it with things that they find and put together themselves, which gives it a folk-art texture. And it hasn't been institutionalized yet.

BCB: Live video is definitely a field where everybody has gone off and learned it on their own. That doesn't mean they didn't learn from other people, and there are some good books and online resources. But basically, unlike the video produced within the studio system, there's a bit of the hacker in putting it together. As often as not, you're capitalizing on raw experimentation and things going wrong. Like, "Gee—no one said I could plug this cable into that place, but when I did, it produced something that I like and haven't seen before, so I'm gonna go ahead and use that."

But patterns are emerging in the ways people perform—stylistic sub-subcultures within the subculture, just like you see in the DJ world. For example, many people are adamant about effects on one side or the other. Some people say, "I don't like effects; they're cheap. I want to deal with montage, manipulate images in a pure, Eisensteinian sense, but in real time." But others get deeply into the algorithm side, the programming and the effects. And it's interesting how important physical locale still is. Different regions spawn different schools of thought. In London, a lot of VJs don't use any effects unless they mimic classic optical film techniques, whereas San Francisco is very synthesis-oriented, with flashy psychedelics or brainy computer stuff. VJs in Berlin, meanwhile, seem to favor a minimalist aesthetic.

I myself used to be really pure about my ideas. I had a long list of rules of things I wouldn't do in my videos. Like, I only used color effects with primary or secondary colors, or I'd use something monochrome or simple like a sepia. Also, I restricted myself to doing everything live. Nothing was pre-generated. In those days, I was generally following some purist notion at one point or another. But then at a performance event called "Ongolia" in Williamsburg, Brooklyn, about five years ago, I was talking with Bill Etra, going on and on about some idea that I was convinced was absolutely sacrosanct. He was listening to me, and he just rolled his eyes and said, "Benton, don't be a purist." I thought about it, and he was right. Now I'm not so dogmatic, although I definitely still lean toward keeping things live. And I'm still adamant about keeping the content, the "data," separate from the title and credit info, the "metadata," in my own videos.

PS: Well, there's nothing wrong with going through a blue-green period. Artists routinely limit themselves, and these self-imposed boundaries evolve over time as their interests change.

BCB: I agree—and doing this allows you to become really sensitive about the thing that you're interested in, really focus in on it and hone it. Abigail Child, who also makes film and video, called me a "maximal minimalist." I don't know exactly what she meant by that, but I like it. I can relate to it—that all-or-nothing sense. I always try to keep in mind what I want to convey and be ruthless about not doing things that don't enhance that one main idea. Like, if I want people to concentrate on a line and follow it along as it dances, unravels, or coalesces into recognizable imagery, then introducing color might get in the way of the central focus.

But for me, thanks to a combination of getting bored and lightening up a little bit, I've come to the point now where I think that literally anything can be a successful approach. You just have to do it well, put care and love into it, and you'll make something powerful and moving.

PS: How did you first get involved with analog video synthesizers?

BCB: Well, I knew from a young age that I wanted to be involved with moving pictures, although at first I thought it was going to be monster movies. And I was exposed to video technology pretty early. Like, my friend's family had a 3/4-inch VCR, which was originally supposed to be a consumer format, and they would record the Monty Python shows. Meanwhile, my school also had some video equipment. But the first technology that I could buy, own, work with a lot myself was 8mm and Super 8 film.

Many over-30's who work in video remember their first film experiences: how they shot it, then sent it off to the lab, and when it came back it wasn't what they expected. And that's what led them to video. That's my case, too. I was also taking piano lessons at the time, and it was obvious to me that if I practiced the piano I could hear it instantly and refine what I was doing. When I messed around with tape recorders and reel-to-reels, those worked the same way—it wasn't like having to wait for the film lab.

But even when I was making films as a fourteen-year-old, I gravitated towards real-time techniques. Sure, I played with stop-motion animation, but in most of my early movies, I wanted to figure out how to make things happen live, and I was upset that I couldn't get real-time feedback, like I could with a piano or tape recorder.

In 1989 I did a residency at Experimental Television Center in Owego, New York, and that's where I encountered a whole studio of gear designed to do what I'd been imagining in my head, like have total control of a moving image. ETC confirmed many ideas that I'd had about the possibilities of cinema, and it also introduced me to the whole history. They have an entire library of video works. But during that time people were under the sway of a limited understanding of Postmodernism, and a lot of stupid things were said about video art. One writer argued that *all* video art is ultimately about television, because that's how we most commonly experience video. At that time I was a twenty-year-old kid who grew up watching very little television, but had spent a lot of time looking at monitors—playing video games, getting flight information, working on a personal computer, and checking out security cameras. So I knew that wasn't true for me and many others of my generation.

ETC is the only institution in America that has been dedicated, since its founding, to encouraging video artists to build their own studios and gear. That sounds trivial now, but it was once a radical idea, back when artists had to rent time at commercial studios and rely on engineers. Professional, broadcast-style video suites cost in the upper five figures back then. ETC had its own equipment, generally on the less-expensive side, and they helped artists build their own studios and put stuff together themselves.

They had some video synthesizers there, mostly built by David Jones, who has been a major influence on how I think about moviemaking. He's still active at ETC, and if you see an art installation somewhere that has multiple synchronized channels from DVD, he's the guy who designed the controller. He's been developing video technology for video art for a very long time now.

PS: I'm imagining that these synthesizers are video equivalents of classic audio synths like the Pro-One or Minimoog—using electronic, non-digital electronic circuitry.

BCB: They had both analog and digital solutions. I know that some people fetishize analog now, but people like Bill Etra and David Jones, who have been designing this stuff for a long time, have spent as much or more time working on digital solutions than on analog. To them, each approach just has its own qualities, and they're confused about why so many people are obsessed with analog.

This year, I reached the conclusion that there's no important difference between analog and digital. A few years ago, during the peak of the whole dot-com thing, everybody seemed to conclude that digital was automatically better. But what really matters to me is whether or not something is electronic. I mean, what distinguishes video from film? They're both cinema, right? What differentiates the two is that video can give real-time feedback. Digital video has actually been a step backward in this regard, because despite what the press releases say about saving time, if you work with DV on a computer, you'll have to spend a lot of time rendering—even on the very fastest machines out now. What is significant is that in electronic cinema, you have real-time feedback. You turn a knob, press a button, or move a fader, and you see its effect immediately.

A lot of people have put thought into what electronics mean, like Marshall McLuhan, Nam June Paik, John Cage, Maryanne Amacher—endless people have put thought into this.

All my work is about this real-time aspect, both when I perform and when I make a studio piece with no one else there. It's me and an instrument or some set of tools, and I'm working with it live. I turn a knob and I see a certain thing happening, and because it responds to me, I can respond back to it. It's sort of a dance, just like with someone who's playing a musical instrument.

PS: Or like Jackson Pollock painting. And then the painting itself is just the record of the interaction.

BCB: Exactly. I do pre-shoot material now, because if I want to perform a piece that's about a certain place, that's how I can present it, because I'm not a good 3-D modeler. As I said, I used to be very pure, and during the '90s my collaborators and I in The Poool and NNeng used prerecorded material only very rarely in our shows, as roll-ins. Now other people, such as Sue Costabile, are pursuing this idea with live camera work that's often fed through some real-time image processing, and again we're seeing performances based entirely on video feedback. However, I feel that I've already satisfied that live-purist urge for myself. Now I love to work with video that I've shot.

As I see it, presenting movies live, in a way that reacts to the audience, is in the tradition of the traveling troubadour. When a troubadour was in one town, they'd learn about the place and the local people. Then they'd carry that all to the next town and use it to amaze, amuse, scare shitless, and send into spasms of laughter the people there. The way I can do that kind of thing today is by pointing my video camera around wherever I am, capturing something, and then bringing that material to the next town on the tour.

HENRY WARWICK ■ ■ ▨ ▨

Henry Warwick organized the San Francisco Performance Cinema Symposium in 2003.

PS: You've emphasized the importance of narrative in all forms of performance, because storytelling...

HW: That's the essence!

PS: Yes, that's how the brain works.

HW: The reason I came up with Performance Cinema is that the term "VJ" is tied into the DJ aesthetic of pastiche—gluing things together that are not normally related. The DJ's purpose is to keep a party going, and you don't need narrative to have a really good dance party.

Most VJs reinforce this lack of flow in terms of ideas. They just throw stuff together, and there doesn't have to be any brain behind it. Like, they'll take swishy-looking images, then mix in some home movies of somebody's pets, combine it with George W. Bush, throw in some traffic images and clips from *Koyannisqatsi*, and that's it—they're done. It's easy to do, and it might look cool for about ten minutes, but it's not telling me anything. I mean, it's kind of "political" because of the *Koyannisqatsi* and Bush images, but it's not a studied idea, you're not really getting a point across. There's no narrative.

There doesn't always have to be a specific point, but there might be some kind of resonant logic behind what you're looking at. Otherwise it's like, well, I've seen this a thousand times.

PS: Many people go to clubs, see the video on the screen, and don't even realize that somebody's performing it live. And I think that's a failure of the VJ, to come across as so disconnected.

HW: I talk about that in terms of the placement of the artist in relation to the audience. That's a whole issue of cathexis.

PS: What's cathexis?

HW: It's a psychological term that I glommed from Lacan. I don't actually agree with most of Lacan. I think that, like Freud, whom he draws from, he was a good mythologist, a good storyteller, but not a scientist. He never made predictions and collected empirical evidence. He fails Popper's criterion of falsifiability.

But Freud and Lacan do have useful insights. One of the ones I've pulled is the idea of cathexis, which is the emotional or psychic projection that you invest in someone else's presence. We do this all the time; you're doing it to me and I'm doing it to you. Audiences do the same thing, but there's a question of where they focus their cathectic power. When you go to the movies, it's focused on the screen. For example, at some big tearjerker movie, you're completely captivated by what's up there. It's brilliant storytelling, great acting, the editing is pulling you right along. You're being manipulated and you love it, and you go right into the story.

PS: Like, early on, you see the main character do something nice, and it makes you think, "Wow—I care about this person! What's going to happen to them?"

HW: Right. That's the kind of cathexis you give to a movie. But with live work, I pull ideas more from music because, frankly, you're never going to get thousands of people to sit together and listen to a CD. A performer's body becomes the locus of cathexis as they create sounds. The same dynamic governs live visuals; the performance cinematic artist or VJ plays between the screen on the one hand, and the audient on the other. When you perform, the audient (singular) invests its emotional energy into what's ahead of them through *you*. When everybody does it collectively, it actually feels like a wall, or a wave.

So there are different places you can perform from. There's onstage with the image, like Laurie Anderson. She's in front of her movies, and she's talking to the audience. Tommy Becker did that at the Performance Cinema Symposium; he put himself right onstage with the imagery, and people invested in his body directly. Then you have somebody who's much cooler, like Greg Bowman. He performed from the front of the hall off to the side. It was classic VJ. You could watch him work, twiddling knobs and pressing buttons. But realistically, you can't put much emotion into twisting a dial.

PS: Still, it's important that they're up there. Like, if someone came in and asked you what's going on, you'd point out, "That person over there is creating the stuff that's being projected here."

HW: Yes, and that makes it a live experience, takes it from the diachronic into the synchronic. That's a big difference. Movies are diachronic; they exist outside of time. And although you might bring different things to them at different times, they don't change. Performance cinema is synchronic. The video that's flying out comes from someone's actions at that time, which makes everyone invest in that particular moment.

PS: That's one thing I like about the medium. It's like a gift to the present moment that connects everyone that you're with, rather than broadcasting remotely to people you don't know who aren't even necessarily paying attention.

HW: When the performer connects, it becomes very intimate, like a concert. I've been a musician for a jillion years, and in my experience some audiences are good, and other times you have a bunch of dumbasses who aren't paying attention and aren't grooving on it. There are multiple ways to approach that. You can just say "fuck you" and turn everything up to eleven. But maybe they're serious about being there and just aren't involved because they can't quite understand your playing. In that case, the better thing to do is give cathexis to the audience, reach out to them, and try to build up a feedback cycle.

PS: So, you pay attention to what catches their interest, and amplify that back to them.

HW: Basically. It's kind of psychic, how it works—although I'm such a materialist that I hate using that term. There are probably cues that involve the acoustics of the place, the body language of the people, the background noise level. It's a weird vibe that a good performer cues into.

Robert Fripp, the guitar player from King Crimson, writes extensively in his online tour diaries about audience-performer relationships. He's such a stickler about it that he doesn't want any photography, video, or tape recording at his shows. He wants you to pay attention and be completely present in the moment. A lot of people are put off by this because he's coming out of the rock genre and trying to establish the dynamic you find in classical or jazz, but I understand where he's coming from. I saw King Crimson at the Fillmore a couple of years ago, and they had the audience in the palms of their hands. They played brilliantly; they were giving to the audience, and the audience was giving back. It was this massive cathectic feedback loop.

PS: I think that live audience events are necessary for societies to define themselves. Audience members get cues from each other and collectively decide how it's appropriate to respond to things. Like, I remember when I first saw *There's Something About Mary*. Early on, I felt that people were hesitant to laugh because there was this un-PC material, but the early-laughers prevailed, and everyone wound up loving it. Stories can test whether you'll laugh or cry, be sympathetic or judgmental, and when you have a bunch of people following along together, they discover the prevailing sentiments and where the lines are drawn.

HW: A similar thing on the flip side is, my wife went to see *The Butterfly Effect* with a friend who does trailer checks—she sees movies for free if she records on a special notepad the trailers that are shown. It's for the advertisers. Anyway, they said the movie was so bad that the audience didn't know when to laugh. Something stupid would happen, and you'd hear a titter go across the audience, although it wasn't meant to be funny. Any cinema performer who inserts himself in front of the audience has to deal with all of these things directly.

Just to finish up with the logical positions, a performer can also work from behind the audience or in a projectionist booth. In that case, the audience is totally focused on the screen, and any clues that it's live must come from the imagery itself.

In dance clubs, the VJ takes cues from the DJ, which automatically puts them onstage or just offstage. But in that setting, the cathexis is not on the screen or even primarily on the DJ. Instead, it's spread out and moving around as part of the mating ritual, which puts it in a totally different category of human organization than a sit-down performance.

In the early 1990s, VJs were automatically important because the equipment was so expensive—especially projectors. That was the last peak of VJ, in terms of fame and fortune. Back then, VJs or video artists were listed at the same level as the musicians and DJs, or at least they got second billing. Then technology made everything faster and cheaper, and suddenly anybody could VJ, at least superficially. Now, VJs don't even get credit half the time, and they certainly don't get paid much. They're just there to make flashy stuff on the screen. And I think they have only themselves to blame, for having accepted a secondary role as handmaidens to the music.

PS: But in a place where dancing is the main focus, won't the music always be more important?

HW: Bingo. That's why VJ is doomed, so long as it's carried by the dance scene. To evolve, the form needs to break away and expand into other branches of performance cinema.

It's not going to be easy. First of all, there's the whole economic issue. The club VJ currently has industrial backing from DJ equipment manufacturers, but performance cinema does not. Another thing is, you have to get people into a space where they're willing to pay attention to something long enough to get involved with it. That's hard to do, especially for a form that's unfamiliar to most people. There's an important political issue here as well: the right to assembly. This right has no meaning when people don't get together, when everybody is atomized into their suburban bunkers.

Another issue is more technical: performers need the ability to control the audio. They don't currently have this because most of the live video mixing tools are designed for the DJ/VJ scenario, which divorces the VJ from the sound. None of the major VJ software applications I know of give you significant control over audio production. Sometimes they take audio in, but only for triggering or eye candy "visualizations" that are dictated by the music. From the other end, almost all software for mixing audio clips can't handle video very well, if at all—certainly not in the sense that a VJ or live cinema artist requires.

Tool-providers are giving the tool-users what they want, and right now a large number of users just want to make goofy shit that flies around on the screen at a party. So we're limited until performance cinema can rear its ugly head and tell developers that we'd like to control both video and audio in a comprehensive, coordinated, and synchronized way. I've been in touch with many of the major developers who are in the middle of this. They are all doing amazing work, but it seems to me that they spend a lot of time optimizing their software for live video processing, not live audio/video arrangement and direction.

Due to processor bandwidth constraints, the VJ applications I know too often play on the same thing: photo jpeg compressed clips at low resolutions (like 320 x 240) and low frame counts (usually 15 fps or less), that you trigger live from a keyboard or from MIDI events, then process through various filters. Technically, the interesting stuff right now is all the different filter algorithms, so that's where much of the development effort is going. But I don't find that terribly important, because we already have a lot of wild-looking filters. The real problem, which toolmakers can help address, is making art that counts, art that means something when I look at it.

PETER METTLER ■ ■ ■ ■

Filmmaker and sometime VJ Peter Mettler melds intuitive processes with drama, essay, experiment, and documentation to create films that elude categorization—meditations on our world, rooted in personal experience. His most recent films include the documentaries Picture of Light *(1994) and* Gambling, Gods and LSD *(2002)*

PS: How did you get interested in live video mixing?

PM: It grew naturally out of the associative and improvisational way that I make films. I like to mix like an alchemist, juxtaposing elements that you wouldn't expect to find together, prompting the viewer to respond associatively. I constructed my last film, *Gambling, Gods and LSD*, through responding to situations and people I encountered during the filming and traveling process. It was organized by themes, as opposed to a script or predetermined structure. Then I edited chronologically, maintaining the original relationships of the unfolding experience I was recording. Often, when I chose to film something, it was done as an intuition or an exploration, without yet understanding it intellectually or how it would function within the finished film. Sometimes it felt obvious that I had just filmed something important, but its meaning only emerged in the editing stage.

Editing *Gambling, Gods* took three years—literally day and night for three years. The first cut was fifty-five hours long, with a very wide spread of materials and scenes. We ultimately reduced it down to three hours, and at the tail end of that process, I was in a strange kind of mode. There was all this material, which I knew in detail, and I began entertaining the possibility of working with it spontaneously in an improvised way, like a performing musician might work with sound. I've always tried to inject spontaneity into my films, but it's difficult. I mean, I can improvise with the camera, but improvising in the actual editing of a theatrical film is another cup of tea.

Coincidentally, at that time, I was asked if I had any ideas for a presentation at the 2002 Swiss National Exposition that would pertain to expanded documentary. I'd always wanted to work with a musician on image-sound improvisation, so I proposed a performance with Fred Frith, who is a master improviser—he's currently a teacher in residence at Mills College, and he's collaborated with many great musicians and performers, including John Zorn, Derek Bailey, and Bill Laswell. Fred and I had already worked together a few times on sound elements for my films, so we understood each other fairly well.

We got the commission and then had about two months to assemble what we needed. I'd never mixed images before and didn't even know what a video mixer was. My past experiences of editing had always been on celluloid. But I did some research and gathered the basic hardware and practiced to do video mixing through multiple channels.

So, that was my first attempt. I worked from about six simultaneous video sources, including much unused material from *Gambling, Gods and LSD*. At one point we also ran a 35mm film projector, showing part of the final version of the film.

It was a blast—so from that point on, I've tried to do as much video mixing as possible with different types of live musicians, and in the club scene as well. There's a huge annual techno music event in Zurich called "Street Parade," and I performed there for six hours straight. That was the first long stretch of mixing I'd ever done, and it became a kind of transcendent experience, without drugs.

I come at this very differently than most of the VJs I've met. Many of them have a computer background, and they work with small snippets of images, loops, and animations, manipulating them with sophisticated software. They are often like beautiful abstract moving paintings, working in cycles, and their creation mystifies me. I bring with me the conditioning of a filmmaker, a film editor's process—I'm used to working with photographed rather than rendered sources, and spending long amounts of time building musical, narrative and thematic structures over a timeline. Performing improvisationally, however, means giving up contemplation time and reacting instantly with my editorial instincts.

I'll typically have up to seven video inputs. Most of it's MiniDV, and some of it's DVD or VHS. Maybe 50% will be my own stuff, with the rest taken from varied sources: a bank instructional video, finished films by other people, whether experimental or classical, documentaries from other cultures, sports events—anything goes. Preview monitors let me see what's currently coming through the pipeline. It's important to me that there's some randomness to what's running through the machines, that it isn't calculated. Sometimes I'll know what's generally coming up on a tape, but the specific constellation of imagery that appears moment by moment is out of my control. I really like that aspect of it, that you're forced to react, forced to make quick judgments. It's all trial and error, reacting and recontextualizing what's currently coming through the input channels.

Meanwhile, the videos' sound channels are available via an audio mixer, and I can also selectively add in extra sound sources—I record a lot of wild sound material as well. So in the end, I'm dealing with up to fifteen audio and visual channels. When I perform with musicians, my sound goes into their sound mix board, and they have the opportunity to manipulate it or not. So it comes out as a mix of what they're doing and what I'm doing, and we're responding to each other the whole way through.

PS: The chance juxtapositions make me think of a psychology experiment I once learned about. There's a part of the brain which constantly builds connections between things—it bridges gaps, generates rationalizations and expectations. The experimenters took subjects and put them to sleep, but somehow kept this part awake. Then they showed series of randomly-chosen items, like, say, a toothbrush and a dog. The subjects would all immediately say something like, "OK, it's a toothbrush and a dog because dogs have hair and hair needs to be brushed." Improvising with visuals must tap into that mental organ a lot. When you're deciding what you want show next, are you trying to express certain things, solve any problems, make any cases, or have some particular effect?

PM: Editing film as a filmmaker involves an ongoing process of analyzing what you're doing, and part of what excites me about improv is that you don't have time to think about the Why. I may have a whole theory, derived from years of film experience, about how a particular image or structure might trigger particular meanings, but when I see a poodle and a tree on the monitors, I really don't have time to think about why they might go together. Some decisions may come from a theoretical, analytical part of my mind and others from direct experiences or aesthetic biases, but most are simply reactions without a lot of time to consider. And many things just happen as a matter of course, by chance. That's what I like about it—it's all happening too fast for the rational part of the brain to completely deal with it.

PS: It sounds sort of like an oracle.

PM: Exactly—part of the process I used in making *Gambling, Gods* I dubbed "Teledivinitry." The term refers to sensing or divining currents of meaning through the use of technology. Live mixing is a bit like going into a technological trance, letting things unfold and emerge while reacting to the things which are coming at you. I record the mixes on tape, because there's no way I can keep track of all that's happening. In reviewing it, I can start to see the embedded narratives and surprising juxtapositions. There is a logic within that is very different from anything the rational structuring mind would have come up with. I find that exercising associative perception like this can give you a finer appreciation of the relationships between things. Perhaps this different perspective has something to do with how an oracle works.

PS: Maybe the Tarot was the VJing of its era—you've got all these familiar images with strong associations, you arrange them, and your mind does things with that. The cards jog the mind into seeing and understanding new things.

PM: Recontextualizing gives a new perspective. Take anything out of its familiar framework and put it against something else, and you've freed it of its locked-in meaning and freed yourself of your normal response. You break it open. When I perform for an audience that's watching rather than dancing, I get a lot of feedback, and the range of what people say is much more unpredictable than when I show a film. It's radically subjective. Some people say, I saw this, had this experience, or read it this way, and tell me that it's great that I put that together. And I tell them, I didn't put that together—*you* put that together. That I find really exciting.

But performing in clubs is also exciting because it's a live social group of people who are engaging with each other and also engaging with the music and visuals on some level—they're at least aware of it. And it goes for a long time. There's a shared journey through the night that only exists in the context of that time and place. It's a one-time experience. The room is feeding the mix, the mix is feeding it back to the room. It really is live in the purest sense of the word. Even if you're using reproduced material, you're giving that little twist, that particular emotion that suits the "vibe"—the same way the DJs do.

I'd like to develop that experience. I've been planning a show in Toronto incorporating a gamelan orchestra, a cello player, live electronic beat performance, live video mixing, and a lighting designer. All these elements are to run through an eight-hour, coordinated sequence of phases, bringing different players into the foreground, creating different scenes throughout the night. One of the new things I'd like to try there is working with text. We'd project a set of questions, and people would write their answers on slips of paper and pass them in so that we could mix them into the imagery. This would create another channel for audience feedback, based on text.

PS: Like making one big conversation.

PM: Or a poem.

I've always felt at home making films and music, and when I came to do this live mixing, I imagined it as an audiovisual film-like journey with expanded dimensions, a spontaneous film that applies only to the particular evening or installation. It has the potential to go beyond certain limitations of conventional filmmaking. Such events have the potential to bring in an aspect of collective ritual and interactivity, something that's missing from most typical modern moving-image entertainment.

The way we go to see films today has become rather cold and isolating. One often has to walk through a shopping mall, and be subjected to watching trailers and advertising. It's become an overtly consumer experience. You rarely interact with people in the theatre, and after you leave, you're back in the shopping mall. I prefer showing films in a context where people can stay afterwards and talk or dance or share their experience, where ideas can be shared, whether it's a fun or constructive forum. For example, an event could begin with a sit-down presentation, then the environment could change, taking the audience into a different more social dynamic—a whole evening experience that could feed different parts of your perception and your intellect and sense of community. A few of us did a multimedia concert in Switzerland which began with a live musician and very somber, very slow, extended images. The evening progressed through three different DJs, and by the end, six hours later, it was intense techno with fast, dense, multilayered imagery, some of which was adapted from the earlier images. The whole evening had the sense of a composition to it, and the energy and activities of the audience was an integral part. That's a simple variation—the possibilities are endless.

PS: There aren't many places where people go to experience some culture together and then stay and discuss it afterwards. Church is the only example I can think of.

PM: Maybe the response only involves being in each others' presence and talking about other things, but it's a better option than the isolation of a mall parking lot. Rave culture is interesting in this way. People come together, all ages, all types—there's a lot of crossover. They share in a kind of ritualized active emotional experience driven by music. Sometimes it's a party experience, sometimes it's art, or even a political statement. There's an interaction being produced which combines everybody together, and often it isn't centered around or focused on performers as stars. Sometimes you don't even know who the DJ is, and you're usually not concerned with what track they're playing. People are most interested in collectively creating a heightened state of celebration.

PS: It rejects celebrity culture.

PM: And with the image mix, it is possible to take some of the commercial imagery that you're inundated with and give it new life, taking it into your own hands, gaining control over that which tries to control you. Sampling and recontextualizing. Maybe that's just a feeling of the VJ, but I think it has that feeling in the room as well.

PS: So, do you think you'll pursue live video over filmmaking?

PM: No, it'll probably be both. I certainly like the immediate possibilities of mixing, but linear time-line cinema film is still something I'm very involved with. Filmmaking as a process, and as presentation, has been a vital part of an ongoing exploration to provoke more understanding about who we are, physically and metaphysically. I think the two practices together can inform each other well. Mixing is a realm of open experimentation for me right now, and it's free of all the financial and institutional encumbrances of filmmaking. But there is nothing like the cinema experience of a darkened room and a beautifully constructed journey through a dreamlike reality.

PS: On television, I'd like to see a wider range of live event coverage enhanced by improvised video mixing. Like, *Monday Night Football* shows instant replays, "chalkboard" play diagrams, and archive footage, but what about speeches and interviews? I'd love to see a candidate debate annotated live by a commentator like Jon Stewart—or even just a good fact-checker.

PM: At the Visions du Reel festival about a year ago, I did a live-mix presentation that incorporated interviews with the festival's director, Jean Perret. The day before the show, Jean and I had videotaped each other having a conversation. For the show, Martin Schutz, a musician, and I performed from behind a translucent screen. For the first part of the show, we could not be seen. People had been watching regular films on this same screen for days, so they weren't expecting anything live. But as we performed from behind the screen, slowly at a certain point the lights came up on us, and the audience could see us through the screen. We were actually inside the projected frame of the images that I was mixing, and they could recognize the sound coming from Martin's instruments. That was a revelatory, powerful thing for the audience: to suddenly realize that the film they were watching was actually being created on the spot. So next I took the two interview tapes of Jean and mixed them out of sync on two different channels: one being his camera perspective of me, and the other my perspective of him. You'd hear him talk and hear me talk, and you'd see the images over each other, with time delays in the sound and other images superimposed as well. It created quite a strange kind of emotional response as Jean expressed what drove him to create this documentary festival dealing with "visions of reality." The audience eventually started applauding him as the director of the festival. It was a special kind of space/time/reality/recording relationship that would be hard to get any other way.

JAY SMITH ■ ■ ■ ■

Video performer Jay Smith is the president of Livid Performance Technology, makers of Union software and the Viditar and Tactic video instruments.

PS: How did you get involved in video performance?

JS: Back in college, studying fine arts, I got interested in video control. So I built interactive installations as art pieces, some of which involved playground equipment, actually. For one interactive environment, I hooked up motion detectors to oversized swings that were big enough to make adults seem like kids when they sat on them. Then I surrounded the swings with video screens and set them up so that the movements of people swinging controlled different aspects of the video.

That was fun, but they were fine arts installations, which was ultimately limiting, I think. People who aren't up on the arts could certainly appreciate the pieces, but it's hard to get most people out to visit an art installation to begin with.

Meanwhile, I also wanted to control the video directly, as a performer. A couple of friends of mine were the singer and guitarist in the band Sinch (which I later joined) and so the three of us began collaborating on some multimedia performances, as a side project. We did all-electronic shows, music and video, with no instruments except for a synthesizer.

Through that, I became interested of the notion of a multimedia rock star, a video performer who reaches people the same way that a lead vocalist or guitarist does. When you consider the way bands like Radiohead and Tool perform, they're not just playing music. As I see it, they're basically doing art shows, but they're also reaching millions of people. I think that's really interesting.

This led me to start designing the Viditar, which is a video instrument that looks like an electric guitar, but it lets you trigger and control video clips. So, after years of experimentation and patent writing—

PS: Wow—you got patents on it! Did you ever study electrical engineering?

JS: Not formally. Everything I've learned has been from reading books. I don't have the patience to be an engineer, or at least go to engineering school—but I do have the patience to teach myself what I need.

Anyway, I eventually finished building the Viditar and developing the software for it, and then joined Sinch to play visuals. We signed a record deal with Roadrunner—that's a label under Island Def Jam, part of the Universal Music Group. We put out a record and went on tour with Stone Sour and Chevelle. Through that, we wound up playing with all kinds of groups—P.O.D., Rob

Zombie, all these crazy shows. It was cool because we got to reach a totally different set of people with this obscure art form, and they all got it. They appreciated it completely. Sixty thousand people watching, and no one needed an Artist's Statement like you have to write for an art show.

With VJing, hardware has been a real problem. With a DJ you've got mixers, you've got turntables, and everything's designed for its function. But with VJing, people are using bastardized controllers, like triggering clips with a musical keyboard. You see someone performing like that onstage with a band, and you'd think they're playing keyboards rather than visuals—which blows. People just miss the whole point.

Other times, VJs just sit behind their computers, and as far as the audience can tell, they could be typing an email or playing a DVD. They don't see any connection between the performer and the visuals. But the live aspect is essential—the visuals almost come secondary to the fact that it's live. So that's why I created the Viditar.

When I was first building the Viditar, I wasn't thinking about selling it; I just wanted to perform with it myself. Since then, a lot of people have asked if they could buy one, but I think that for most of them it would be a big leap from sitting behind a laptop or an Oxygen 8 keyboard to holding a video guitar in front onstage. So, about a year ago, I started creating another video controller, the Tactic, as a sort of gateway instrument. It shares some patents with the Viditar, and it's also a handmade wooden instrument, but it goes on a keyboard stand. It's got an LCD in the center, and on the left-hand side there are thirty-six buttons for triggering clips. On the right, there are six sliders and six knobs for pre-settable effects, and the cross-fader is in the center. There are also sliders for scrub, speed, and volume, and at the top you can switch image banks, so you can carry over four thousand video clips.

I left the Viditar in prototype while I spent my time developing the Tactic, which has now gone into production. Meanwhile, a lot of people we talked to wanted to use the Tactic's software to do other things, like control art installations. So we decided, okay, let's modify the software to make it more versatile, and sell that as well. That's how we created Union. We hadn't originally intended on selling the Tactic software separately, but there was an obvious demand. So now we're selling the Tactic and Union. Union you can buy online, but we can only build about six Tactics per month. They're custom-made, like an original Les Paul or Moog synthesizer.

There hasn't been any good software for VJing that you can just open up and start messing with. Tools like ArKaos are interesting, but I don't think they're versatile enough. Meanwhile, there are also applications like VDMX, but I think that's just too complicated for most people, and actually learning to program in Max/MSP is even harder. People's creativity should become the driving force behind the medium, not technical expertise.

So I wanted to make Union easy for beginners, but with advanced capabilities and flexible enough to use in different ways. I'm personally more interested in performance art and multimedia performance, but it's also got beat-matching for VJs, and you can automate stuff for installations. For example, you can have it play music files or a CD and automate effects to the beat. You can also hook up all sorts of crazy MIDI controllers.

Adam Gates from the band Primus uses Union software. They want all of their video to be live and reactive, and tailored to the venue. Primus does something really cool in their shows—they project onto these huge weather balloons. Union lets you do masking with PICT files, so they put a round mask on top of all the video, and it fits onto these floating balloons. It's a beautiful effect.

At the other end of the spectrum, I got a call from Hilary Duff's manager a while ago, and he was interested in the Tactic. So now Hilary Duff, this teeny-bopper idol, is touring with a VJ who's playing a Tactic console onstage. Their budgets are far bigger than anything I can imagine—they have three thirty-foot video screens. It's amazing.

PS: Do you know what kind of clips they're showing?

JS: Yes—I actually created the whole show and then hired someone good to go on the tour and perform the content.

PS: So, what did they ask for? That sounds like an interesting problem, coming up with the right visuals for a performer like that.

JS: My own stuff tends to be pretty dark and in-your-face—I use provocative imagery and do a lot of social commentary. And obviously you can't do that when you're dealing with eight-year-olds who are out to see Hilary Duff. That's not what they're there for.

But at the same time, I didn't want to just show patterns—I wanted to get the kids thinking. So I created material that played off of the lyrics, to engage them with the meaning there and add some depth to it. The songs were real pop-type stuff, singing about rain and love and things like that. The clips are designed to work with a lot of live feeds, because you can do feeds with Union, so there's a lot of her singing live mixed in with imagery based on what the song is about. Obviously, it has to be bright and interesting and cool to look at, but I tried to make it convey some content rather than just using patterns and shapes. A lot of VJs love that abstract, 3-D rendering stuff, but I actually think it sucks.

PS: Yeah, there's not a lot there. With electronica, there's no text to follow, whereas with even a bubblegum song, there is some meaning you can work off of.

JS: Exactly. Not that there's anything wrong with eye candy. In a club environment, it's great. You don't want to be too artsy in a dance club because people just won't get it. You have to at least allude to the idea that they can get it. But if it's too obscure, it won't make sense, and no one will pay attention.

That's a problem with being a VJ in a club. You're in the background, and everyone's dancing and not paying attention. It's not an audience atmosphere. People are partying, drinking, having fun, and they're not trying to absorb what's being created around them.

I'm in a different boat from a lot of the people who perform live video. When I started, I didn't know anything about VJs and wasn't into electronic music. I'm oblivious to the club scene, raves, and all that stuff. I came to this from a rock point of view, a punk point of view. So I've learned a lot and have opened up to alternative markets for this, because I think it can stretch beyond the club DJ music scene. I see it like a new punk movement, which can cross over many different formats.

Everything is becoming so cheap now, which is great. A lot more people have the tools, the gear. You used to need tens of thousands of dollars to do this, but now you can get started for a couple hundred bucks. The problem is, the documentation is horrible. There are very few references, so you need to be deeply into the scene in order to know what's possible and to learn how to do it. So I'm glad you're writing this book. Hopefully it'll help people understand video performance better.

PS: I'm really hoping to interest the talented, creative people out there who don't happen to live in cities like New York or San Francisco which have established VJ scenes. A lot of them have laptops and projectors already, maybe from dad's home theater. They can shoot stuff with digital cameras and camcorders and create or download whatever they want. I would love to see more people use this creative power that they already have access to.

JS: That's essentially what I hope to help bring to this industry: the idea that to do this stuff, you don't need to be a technical genius or learn how to write software. You just need to run some software on your mom's computer, shoot some clips, and start messing around.

Sinch tours around the country. We play big metropolitan areas, obviously, but we'll also play the middle of Minnesota, the middle of Iowa. All I have is a projector, my laptop, and my Viditar. It's pretty low-budget. But one thing that I find really fulfilling is that I'm taking this experimental art form to these kids who have never even heard of anything like this, and it inspires them. Sometimes we'll do autographs after a show, and most people will be lined up wanting to talk to me about the instrument—all these heavy metal kids, or goth kids with black makeup, wearing all black clothes, saying, "I wanna do this— how do you do this?" It just blows me away.

Another interesting thing is, the singer in Sinch does artist-in-residency in some elementary schools in the Northeast here, and he's had me come into his classes for a day to show them what I do and work with them. The second- and third-graders immediately get what I'm doing because visuals and technical knowledge are just part of their culture, part of their world. It's amazing—they're like, "Yeah—you press a button and it plays a movie, and then you mix them together. I want one for Christmas."

PS: When you're first showing people live video, do you get a sense of what they want to do with it, or how they imagine using it themselves?

JS: It's funny, I don't get many technical questions; they tend to be conceptual questions. A lot of rock bands go, "This is great—we have these videos we've been shooting for years on the road, and we'd love to have someone play them to the music." Honestly, there's only so much a band can say by jumping around on a stage, and this adds another way to reach people. Singers are especially drawn to having a Viditarist, so that what they're saying can be represented visually.

PS: I think that one of the reasons the typical four-piece rock band works is that the roles fit different personality types, and it makes sense to me that singers would be most interested in the Viditar. They're the ones who convey the representational part of the band's content, which is something you can do with both lyrics and visuals.

JS: True, but it also takes attention away from them, which is interesting. Singers are known for their egos, and they get the most attention, but this gets the audience looking at the screen instead of them and the other band members.

PS: But if the singers are good sports, they can get a live camera and point it at their bandmates and give everyone a close-up, if they want.

JS: Exactly. Also, my relationship with the band isn't like I'm the lighting guy. They don't say, here's the music, now create some visuals to it. I'm a member of the band who has a different kind of instrument. We all rehearse together, four days a week, and we write the songs and the visuals at the same time. It's a multimedia band, not just a musical band. And that appeals to a lot of people, kids especially, who don't sing or play an instrument but who understand music conceptually and can think visually.

Sometimes we'll rehearse our songs, and then we'll just jam for a while and come up with new ideas, both musically and visually. The band dynamic is interesting. The drummer might have an idea for the guitarist, and that will give the guitarist an idea for something visual. So then I'm like, why don't you guys try playing this, and meanwhile I'll do this. We're trying to create in this new medium. It doesn't even have a name. Rock-media, rock-multimedia—I don't know what the hell it's called. But it's more than just music, and it's exciting.

PS: Sounds like total fun.

JS: Yeah, it is fun.

YUSEI HORIUCHI ■ ■ ■ ■

Yusei Horiuchi founded the performance group Lab Type Zero and has performed live video throughout the U.S. and Japan.

PS: What's your background in VJing?

YH: I started towards the end of my undergrad years at Carnegie Mellon in Pittsburgh. I majored in fine arts and had been doing hard-gear sculptures with wires and bare television tubes, and creating video content to go with. Then, in late 1998, a friend of mine was organizing a warehouse party, and she asked me if I wanted to do an installation for it. I said yes, but when we visited the place later, I saw that it was this dirty warehouse with a huge amount of empty wall space. So I thought, I'm just gonna project something, which I'd never done before and wanted to try. I figured that I'd make a couple hours worth of source and just play it back, but then I asked her how long she thought the party would go on. She said it would probably be more than six hours, so I thought, why don't I just mix it live along with the music? Not only as entertainment for the audience, but to give me something to do for all that time.

So, that was my start. I rented equipment from school: five VHS decks, some thirteen-inch monitors, a projector, and this huge mixer. It was broadcasting gear; I didn't know about smaller mixers at the time. The projector was a three-lens Barco that was really tough to move around.

Three hundred people came to that party, and one of them was this woman named Kaye. She happened to be an old-school raver, and everyone knew her in the local scene. She danced with those light-saber flashlight things that people use to direct traffic. Anyway, Kaye really liked it, so she came over and said, you should continue this visual stuff—I've never seen it before. She knew a lot of organizers in the area, and she gave me a bunch of phone numbers and told me that if I want to play more parties, I should just give these people a call.

I went back home and forgot about it for a few days, but then found the piece of paper again. I didn't want to call everybody, so I just picked one, and luckily he turned out to be one of the biggest organizers in town. So I played at one of his parties the following weekend, and that had around six hundred people.

Some friends of mine wanted to perform video too, so the five of us started doing it together. We had different interests, which was good—film, graphic design, photography, computer graphics. Things started picking up after that, and we got a lot of calls from around the tri-state Pittsburgh area: Pennsylvania, Ohio, and West Virginia.

PS: What was your source material?

YH: I used everything back then. I would make my own stuff and also sample a lot from movies, anime, television. I used a lot of Discovery Channel—I'd sample that and change the colors, make a tape with different shots that loop for about three seconds. I also borrowed videos from school and rented them from stores. I wasn't using a computer; it was all on VHS, and it took days to make a tape of good source material. The tapes all had different themes, like Nature, Space, Psychedelic. To do a show back then, we carried all those videos and VHS decks and stuff—it was terrible. Eventually, we made over five hundred tapes, which I actually still have. These days, though, I don't take anyone else's work. I use only original material.

At the beginning of 2000, we played at the Winter Music Conference. That's a week-long conference in Miami Beach that's open to the public, with parties and new bands playing everywhere—it's like South by Southwest. You have to be invited there; you can't just go and play. But one of the promoters we'd worked for in Pittsburgh recommended us to an organizer of the conference, so they called up and offered to fly us out. The event is fun for students and artists, but recording companies and booking agents also go there to scout. So right after we performed, the very same night, we got an agent from a company called GREY MultiMedia. After that, we got a lot of shows through them, although that agency no longer exists now.

But then, in June, 2000, *Time* magazine came out with that big cover story on Ecstasy and raves. Remember that issue? That had an enormous effect on the scene, killing a lot of raves. Right after that article came out, we were booked for a two-day beach party in North Carolina, an enormous party with twenty or thirty thousand people. When we were setting up our gear, a television reporter came over to interview us. Next thing we know, we're on the local news channel and people are starting to attack us: "So, there's gonna be a lot of drug dealers here? This is some kind of psycho party?" We had been performing legitimately, for organizers who always made sure to obtain permission in advance from the city or whatever other authority—because with over one thousand people, you need to notify the police department, hire paramedics, and file all kinds of paperwork. But after that *Time* article came out, it became a lot harder to get any go-ahead from city governments to use large spaces, indoor or outdoor, for dance parties.

In the wake of the *Time* article, I was faced with a dilemma: Do I want to continue this, or are the parties just going to die out? I had a show booked that weekend, and as I was preparing for it, I kept wondering about the future. But then, at that show, I saw this one kid who was dancing while watching my screen all night long. I thought it was cool that he seemed so connected to what I was doing, so I went over to talk with him. He gestured to me that he was deaf, and I was like, whoa—but then I started writing questions to him on my notepad. He explained that he couldn't hear the music, but he could feel the beat and figure out what kind of music it was by watching the visuals. So I thought, this is really beautiful! Everybody can enjoy a rave, and I'm going to continue doing this.

As the rave scene was dying out, I moved back to New York. That's where I spent most of my time growing up, after my family moved from Japan. Parties started moving more into clubs and daytime events, which would typically run from noon to midnight. I got a job at a club called Exit, on West 56th Street between 11th and 12th—it's one of the biggest clubs in the city, and they drew around eight thousand people every weekend. Dave, the owner of Exit, seemed to have a lot of mysterious, high-level business connections, and he paid well and spent a lot of money on equipment and everything else. Like, back then, you didn't see many plasma screens because they cost over ten thousand dollars each. But Exit had fifteen big forty-five-inch plasmas arranged on a wall that hung over the main floor, in an open atrium that was four stories high. You could move this video wall up and down with a winch from the fourth floor to the ground floor and back. Another thing is, every three months, Exit completely changed the look of its interior. They would gut it, put in all new walls, lights, and decorations, and it would suddenly have a "Miami" or "Ultra-Lounge" theme. Most clubs don't have the resources to do that, especially small clubs. Still, a club is always going to be a club—it's not like putting a rave on in some new location outside.

Then September 11th came, and the party scene died out completely. There was nothing we could do about it, so a lot of us DJs and VJs just laid low for a while. More DJs got into recording, because it was hard to find work and they still wanted to make music. They loved talking about what they were doing, and I picked up a lot of good ideas from them. The way DJs think, the way they compose their music, has definitely influenced me in the way I compose my visuals. There's really no difference between VJs and DJs. We all do the same thing and use the same kinds of equipment. The only difference is whether it's audio or visual.

But now, after three years, things are finally picking up again. I've been performing at the Winter Music Conference every year since 2000, and right before this year's conference I got picked up by another agency, Premiere Artists Group, who represent a lot of prominent DJs, including Mixmaster Mike, DJ Spooky, and DJ Qbert. I'm actually the first visualist on their roster. Soon after that, I moved here to San Francisco. Premiere is based in this area, and there's a big VJ scene here as well.

With my old booking agent, I did a lot of nonstop six-hour shows. But when I went over to Premiere, I told them I wouldn't do those anymore—instead, I wanted to play my sets alongside a DJ for the same amount of time, ninety minutes or two hours or whatever, and get equal billing. Or, if some major DJ is doing a four-hour set, I'll work the same slot. For a little while, this reduced the number of bookings I got, but I think it also earned more respect for me and for the visual side.

125

PS: Where would you like to take VJing in the future?

YH: There's a lot of things I want to do, and luckily, I've been able to get some companies to sponsor me in order to help out, including Motion Dive, ArKaos, Edirol, ESDJCo, and hopefully Alienware.

The first thing is, I think it's important to really establish a VJ market in the U.S. A lot of people are working independently, and I'd like to unite all those people, make them aware of each other, and start to develop categories like the ones DJs have—you know, the way there are house DJs, trance DJs, jungle DJs, hip-hop DJs, and so on. Right now, I do pretty much every style of music, and that's great, in a way, because I'm still learning new techniques. But eventually I'd like to specialize, so that I can concentrate on the kind of music that inspires me, rather than having to create visuals for some style of music that I would never listen to.

Another thing: I want to help standardize the gear so that VJs can compete. DJ competitions are possible because they all use the same standard setup, two turntables and a mixer. But right now, in the VJ world, everyone uses different rigs—so how can you compare people's pure skills? It isn't a level playing field. Most VJs do use mixers and laptops though, so I think those components can become standardized. That's why I'm now working with Edirol's marketing department, and am also trying to promote Motion Dive software in the U.S.

PS: I remember talking with Grant Davis and Michael O'Rourke about how at SIGGRAPH a couple of years ago, they organized a VJ competition, and it became very athletic, actually. It was a tournament with multiple elimination rounds, and they talked to the VJs throughout. The VJs were all really "on," but they had different strategies. One explained that he was going to conserve his energy for later rounds and not show all of his clips at the beginning. Others did well at first, but when they got called back for the next round, they didn't have anything left. There was this whole competitive narrative which made it interesting to see unfold.

We speculated about doing a TV show like *Iron Chef*—that's that cooking show where they unveil a feature ingredient and then chefs compete to prepare an entire meal, from appetizers to dessert, where each dish contains and honors the ingredient. So, we were thinking, why not have a sort of "Iron VJ," that's based around stories that everyone knows, like *Little Red Riding Hood*? VJs would compete by telling the same story improvisationally in their own way, using what they have. That way, you really see their different approaches.

YH: Exactly—that's just the kind of thing we need. In Japan, there's a late-night television show produced by Takkyu Ishino that's all live VJ/DJ performances. It's not that long, maybe half an hour, and at the end of the show they bring the performers out and introduce them. It's a great show; a lot of people watch it. I think that's what we need here. MTV should really do more live, performance-oriented programming—it would be a natural for them. And it would also be great for VJs, who can only go so far only performing locally.

PS: What's the VJ scene like in Japan?

YH: It's definitely more advanced there than it is here. VJing took off there in 1999, when Tomoyasu Hirano published a book called *VJ 2000*. He's an interesting person—he had started out as an engineer at a company called Third Stage, which made software for theatrical lighting and visual effects. Later, he founded an offshoot called Digital Stage, which produced visualization and effects software for interior design and architecture showrooms. Digital Stage was also developing Motion Dive, for live video performance, and that's what prompted Hirano to commission the book *VJ 2000*. He knew that VJing was going to become an important new genre.

The book starts off by explaining how to VJ, what kind of mixer to use, what kind of computer, what kind of software—including Motion Dive, of course. It talks about how to make sources, following easy, step-by-step instructions: shoot your footage, bring it into Premiere, and so on. It also discusses more technical stuff, like compression rates, what compression you should use. It's basically how-to, "VJ For Dummies" kind of stuff. That's the first part of the book, anyway. The second part of *VJ 2000* talks about who's in the VJ scene right now.

PS: Wow—that sounds exactly like my book!

YH: Yeah, but that's great, I think. That's what you need to do. The second part of the book just covered some VJs that Hirano happened to know and like, but because of that book, those VJs are now the most famous VJs in Japan!

So a book is really important. One of the reasons *VJ 2000* was so successful, I think, is because Japan is a single-race nation, and everyone follows the same thing. Once the influential people start reading a book, then it's like, you should read that book as well, so you can become successful as well.

PS: It seems like a big motivation for coming out with *VJ 2000* was to promote sales of Motion Dive software.

YH: Yes. Mr. Hirano is a pretty smart guy, very sharp. He knows when to invest money and when not to. After *VJ 2000*, Motion Dive became the most popular VJ software in the country, and it still is. There were other VJ applications out before, but they were too hardcore, too difficult to use. One of them in particular, M7, was really good; it came out in 1998. M7 had everything—you could mix with it, it took MIDI inputs, just like with ArKaos. But it came out too early. They should have waited and come out with M7 after Motion Dive and *VJ 2000* were released, because then many more people would have known what it was and how to use it.

PS: Who in Japan is most interested in VJing?

YH: In the mainstream, the most in-demand VJ is Naohiro Ukawa. He's a professor at the Kyoto University of Art and Design, but he also performs. Ukawa became famous by collaborating on a four-hour mix performance with Takkyu Ishino, who's one of the biggest techno DJs and producers in Japan. He's the guy who produces that late-night DJ/VJ television show.

PS: But in terms of non-famous people, who's buying and learning Motion Dive, for example?

YH: Actually, I don't know if I should say this, but someone at Digital Stage told me that two-thirds of the people who buy Motion Dive software are not VJs—they're businessmen who use it to run presentations. I think this shows a cultural difference with the U.S. Here in the States, everybody is good at standing in front of a group and giving a presentation, because that's always the first step to doing business. Japan follows a different protocol—if you want to propose something, you write a fifty-page proposal and give it to the people you want to present to, without ever talking to them. After that, if they like it, then you can meet and present to them. So presentation is a second step, not very common.

But that's changing now, and presentations are becoming popular at some companies. As a result, Motion Dive became a smash hit among younger businessmen, thirty to forty years old, who are comfortable with high-tech and want to show off a bit. PowerPoint lets you do a lot these days, and it's getting better and better, but it's still nothing like Motion Dive, where you can enter text live, mix images and video in real time, play music, synchronize visuals to the beat, and so on. At Digital Stage, they're trying to push presentation as a business tool, and they see VJ and presentation as essentially the same thing.

PS: Interesting—yeah, if you think about all the various places where people perform in front of groups, in the broadest sense, offices might be the most common.

YH: I've heard the same kind of thing from Edirol. A lot of their mixers aren't used by VJs or lighting people in clubs; they're actually used in churches. I was surprised when they told me that, but it makes a lot of sense. Churches have sound systems and big walls; they're great places for live video. But I don't think it would work for a temple or shrine—that's another cultural difference. It would go against the mentality to use technology like that in a shrine. There's no right or wrong either way, but it is a difference.

PS: I agree. It's interesting how the Mormon Church, for example, is very video-oriented, and they show a lot of videos in church. But other religions have the perspective that religion is about words rather than images, so video doesn't fit in.

Anyway, what about the underground side of VJing in Japan? Is it, like, mostly guys in their twenties or thirties, or are kids into it, or older people?

YH: It tends to be people around my age—I'm 28. I'm sure a lot of older people are into VJing as well, but I just don't know about it. Also, a lot of girls are doing it now, which is a really good sign.

But VJing in Japan has actually been stuck at the same level now for a while. A lot of people started doing it after *VJ 2000* came out, but it's tapered off since. There are only a few top VJs in Japan, all sponsored by Motion Dive. They all know each other, and some of them told me that they're getting bored. Yes, they're established, which is nice, but there's no new competition coming up, so they feel stuck in this field that isn't going anywhere right now. And they're stuck in Japan, a small island, because that's the only country that has an established VJ scene now.

Even in Japan, many clubs still treat the laser and lighting people as more important than the VJ, and VJs still play behind the stage, out of sight. Sometimes they're completely isolated from the audience, working from a little room in the back. Some geek kid who's really into visuals will know that there's a big-time VJ performing back there, but most people at the club aren't even aware of who's playing what.

So my dream is to establish a VJ market in the U.S., which ArKaos, Motion Dive and Edirol want to do as well, and also bring the VJ scene in Japan up to the next level, make it more dynamic.

PS: How would you do that?

YH: One thing is, there's a company based here in San Francisco called ESDJCo, for "Extra-Strength DJ Co." They've been making clothing and accessories for DJs since 1993. They're established here in the States, and they just got a distributor for Europe, a big distributor in the UK. Now I'm working with them to find a distributor in Japan, to open up that market, and also to design and launch a new line of products specifically for VJs.

One of the things that we've never had, even in Japan, is clothing specifically for VJs. Like, if you're wearing ESDJCo, people can tell that you're probably a DJ. It's just like, you can look at someone's outfit and tell, oh, she's into hip-hop, or he's into skateboarding. That kind of thing is important to people, and I think it's one of the reasons that the DJ, hip-hop, and skater scenes made it so big.

So I was always looking for a clothing company for VJs, but nothing really clicked until I came across ESDJCo. Because they concentrate on DJ stuff, there's a lot of crossover. I asked Sam Staton, the president, if he would sponsor me if, every time I performed, I wore his clothes. He said yes, but then later I was thinking, this is all DJ gear. So I told him, if you're interested, I'd like to design shirts and jackets and gear, like laptop colors, that are especially for VJs, not DJs. So he called me back and said yeah, let's do it. We've been working on it, and next year, ESDJCo will be spinning off a new company to launch a line called "VJ." The name might change, though, so if you have any good ideas, let me know. We're doing design and final sketches right now.

I've even been thinking of putting together a VJ package, like if you buy an Edirol V-4 mixer, it comes bundled with a copy of Motion Dive software and a VJ t-shirt. I used to listen to a lot of heavy metal, and Metallica had this great boxed set where you got all their CDs, plus bonus photos and artwork and a Metallica t-shirt. It's the same idea.

PS: That's an interesting design problem, coming up with clothing and accessories for VJs. What kind of look do you think would suit a VJ?

YH: Like, the t-shirts? That's a good question. Right now, we're still brainstorming. There are a couple of designs that I'm doing right now which I can send to you once they're approved. Some of the graphics are technical-looking, with goggles and machinery. But the first thing is, before any clothing, we have to set standards for basic VJ accessories. When I come into a club, I want a space ready for a VJ that's right next to the DJ booth, and the laptop that's loaded with VJ software and clips should have a distinctive color and a recognizable VJ symbol on it.

Another company I've gotten sponsorship from recently is Alienware. They make ultra-fast, high-power laptops for hardcore gamers. They're a smart company, and they take the gaming market very seriously. Their newest laptop actually lets you change the video card, so you can upgrade without having to buy a whole new system. Alienware's graphics are faster than any other laptops', which is essential for gaming, but it also makes them fantastic for VJing.

The laptop question is interesting. Most of the VJs I know, I'd say 90%, use Apple computers. That's understandable, but I personally think Alienware is better, not just for its speed, but also because of the cooling system. That's one of the main problems in laptop design, keeping the processors cool enough. The Titanium series PowerBook looks sleek, but the heat sink really isn't that great, and after a while, those can overheat pretty easily. That's especially bad for VJs because it's not like we're playing in some air-conditioned room—we're in some pretty extreme environments with crowds of people sweating and drinking beers. Alienware has five cooling systems, and they can handle very intense use. Even the little AC adapter on the power cable has its own fan.

Alienware is a small company, though. All the VJs in Japan want to get Alienware, but they don't sell it there. They still don't make one with Japanese version of Windows and a Japanese keyboard. I asked them if they were interested, and they said they definitely were planning on opening up a market there some day, but because they are so small, they're still just establishing themselves in Canada, right next door.

I use Apple too, but I'm getting tired of them. One accessory I want to make for the VJ line, though, is an auxiliary cooling system for PowerBook. They have those now, made of aluminum, with a fan.

When I first approached Alienware, they turned me down, because they didn't understand what VJing is. But I got a call later from Melvin in the sponsorship department there who said that he just talked to his boss, and this is exactly the kind of thing they've been looking for as a next step. Melvin himself is into techno music, and he went to the Premiere Artists site and saw that all of his favorite DJs are on their roster—so he was really psyched. Opening up the VJ market is really good for Alienware, I think. I mean, gaming is cool, but you also need more active people who aren't just playing at home.

PS: I don't even think there's that much of a difference between VJing and gaming.

YH: Yes, it's the same, they're the same thing!

I don't think Apple will ever sponsor me, though. They don't tend to sponsor stuff unless it's educational, or else it's going someplace like the MoMA, some very established institution. Another goal of mine is to bring VJing to the fine arts level, both in Japan and the U.S. It isn't right for the Metropolitan, but I think it's good material for places like the MoMA and the Guggenheim. What we're doing is pop art, pop culture, like Andy Warhol.

I'm currently working on a proposal for a museum in Japan. I've done a lot of gallery stuff and have found that it doesn't go anywhere. You may get some local interest, but that's it, and a lot of times, they won't even have the money. A museum, on the other hand, takes care of everything—the installation fees and everything else. And you get more credit than you do with a gallery. Since I'm in San Francisco, there's the SFMOMA. I haven't done anything yet, but I'm researching right now whom I should talk to.

PS: One good person to contact might be Kathleen Forde—I don't know if you've run across her. She's an independent curator, and I did a great interview with her. She has curated several video series at the SFMOMA, where she used to work, and she also recently put together an exhibit that's going to tour internationally, called *"What Sound Does A Color Make?"* It's about synaesthesia, the recent history of video art, and art that combines sound with visuals and vice-versa. She's definitely an arts-insider type who's also very into the VJ scene and clued into live video performance.

YH: Well, I think we're qualified to show at SFMOMA. I do believe that the field has advanced since Nam June Paik. Of course he took the first step, which is awesome. But museums have this tendency to keep bringing the old people back. It's understandable, but after a point, I mean, come on! It's time for them to open their doors a little. What we do is informed by and works within the same tradition as the video that they show. Some of the stuff you see there, it's like, what *is* this—?

PS: I definitely think that there's been a disconnect between the quality of the video coming from VJs and commercial motion-graphics people, as compared to the work you typically see in museums; I've gone to major museums and seen video installations that I just thought were silly and obvious. Maybe if I knew more about it, if I were more up on what all the other high-art video artists were doing, then I would be able to recognize that, yes, this does have a niche, and it is very clever how this artist has found a way to answer everyone else's work. But as a less-educated person, I often just don't think it's very interesting.

YH: I would rather bring what we do to a museum as-is, but I understand that from their point of view, they might want it to come across as more fine-artsy. In which case, we can tweak our video to conform to a museum look.

PS: Well, I actually think it's their turn to learn and adjust what they're doing a little bit. I understand from talking to Kathleen that it's been a real struggle for her within the museum community to convince people to take VJ-influenced video art seriously. But she seems to be succeeding, which is really nice.

YH: We have to educate people. And it's exciting to be in the early stages, because whatever we do will help set the standard. How many times in life do you have the opportunity to define a standard? Usually you follow someone else's system and do the best you can within it, and sometimes you can change it a little bit. A lot of people say it's impossible with VJ, but I think there's a lot of potential. That's why I'm trying to drag others along, like clothing companies. Five years ago, when I first started, It would never have occurred to me that I would get involved with designing clothing.

PS: I'd never thought of it either until you told me, but you're right—it makes perfect sense as another way of defining a genre. Basically, I want to do the exact same thing as you do. I haven't performed yet as a VJ, but I'm approaching the topic more from a technology journalist point of view, like the way I did at *Wired*—what's the outside view, and if you want to get involved, where can you go. But like you, I have the feeling that many people are doing interesting stuff here, and it just hasn't been mapped out yet.

YH: Also, I think we use the technology in the right way. When I was in grad school, I was working on VR, virtual reality, in the Entertainment Technology Center—that's a new school at CMU, a joint program between Computer Science and Fine Arts. But they're a private school, so they have to get funding, and a lot of it came from the military—especially once the recession hit. I guess you can make a lot of money working with the war people, but, for myself, that's not how I want to do it. I don't want to sound corny, but that's how I feel.

PS: I totally understand. Right after college I went to work for a defense contractor, writing Artificial Intelligence software. I'm basically a lefty, pacifist guy, and the experience really challenged me and caused me to revise my assessment of my own personal integrity. The job had everything going for it otherwise— the problems were interesting and important, and we had a lot of creative freedom. But ultimately, what I was working on was not my cup of tea.

YH: At the same time, we do need a military. And that's where a lot of this technology originally comes from. Lasers used to be for military and research use only, and now party kids shoot them through the air just because it looks cool. And that's the way it should be. These things, the lasers, lights, and video, can make people happy and also create a lot of business. There are no boundaries right now to where it all might go. You can feel it, sense it.

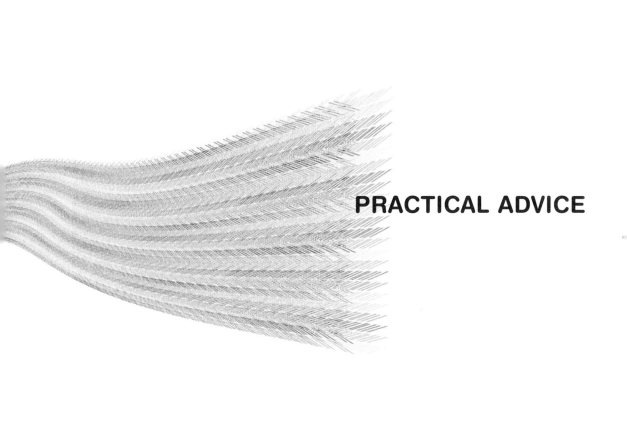

PRACTICAL ADVICE

KITCHEN BASICS ■ ■ ■ ■

THEORY

VJing is simple in principle, and it can also be simple in practice. Like any-one else, VJs take inputs and produce output. But in the VJ's case, inputs are mainly visual, and these may include (but are not limited to) anything they've ever shot with a camera, recorded from television, rendered with software, played on DVD, downloaded from the Internet, or scanned from the pages of a book or magazine.

Some of these sources resonate instantly as part of our shared visual alphabet of cultural meaning: familiar news clips, movie scenes, landmarks, artworks, logos, celebrities, symbols, and even words and phrases. Others carry a more limited or personal significance, while others are simply inter-esting—aesthetically, intellectually, emotionally, or whatever.

As a VJ, you collect these inputs and then perform with them by combin-ing them in any way, optionally adding visual effects. The results are usually projected large on a screen or wall for the enjoyment of a group. All of this can be done with just an ordinary laptop, free software, and a digital projec-tor—or you can do it with forty thousand dollars' worth of professional video equipment, and work with a broader palette and more responsive tools at higher resolutions.

VJ tools fall into three general categories: video hardware, optical hard-ware, and software. The distinctions between these aren't always clear, and you can mix components however you like—that's what it's all about.

KNOW YOUR INGREDIENTS

So, you want to be a VJ? As they say in the traditional language of media manipulators, Mazel Tov! When you're a VJ, the world is your palette. Species such as ours, who receive most of their information via their eyes and enjoy advanced cultures and technology, create lots of great visuals and visual tools to play with. This section offers quick notes on some of the main sources VJs use, in approximate descending order of how much respect they earn in the VJ community, rightly or wrongly.

Original source, captured or rendered

True auteurs will only use material that they created. The pinnacle is video or images that they shot themselves or created using professional animation software. Extra points if they wrote the software themselves. More extra points if it actually looks good.

Old film

Okay—the statement above isn't strictly true. There is another class of auteurs, usually more politically inclined, who use appropriated materials *only*, so long as they're appropriated from proper sources. The more difficult the material is to obtain, the more credit is deserved. The best is old film, which may be lifted from dumpsters, rescued from schools, or bought at swap meets, on Ebay, or through film-collector publications such as Big Reel.

Live renderings

It's hard to look away from swirling, synthesized eye candy that's dancing to the music or otherwise reacting to, feeding back, and amplifying the goings-on. Some impressive examples come from custom synthesizers built on software platforms such as Max/MSP + Jitter, PD + Gem, or EyesWeb.

Another class of application, including Matinee, Machinimation, and UnrealEd, piggybacks off of the game engine software which underlies most recent-vintage computer games. Games use these "engines" to translate high-level scripts of what's happening in the world—who's running and shooting where—into the corresponding animation onscreen. These engines are what allow multiple people to play *Quake* online despite limited bandwidth. The applications feed scripts into these engines directly, without your having to play the game, making you the puppet-master within a fully-realized world of eye-catching characters and environments. These applications are also used to create machinima, a growing, low-budget form of moviemaking based on existing game worlds.

Live captures

It's easy to mix with live video; just hook up a camera. And it's always appreciated. People love to see themselves onscreen.

VJ DVDs and other non-Hollywood commercial DVDs

Independent VJ DVD publishers, such as LightRhythm Visuals, and forward-looking record labels, such as Asphodel, publish DVDs that are dedicated to VJ visuals. Mixing with these means you aren't using all-original or rare material—but it does mean you are supporting a nascent industry that's filled with good people who are trying to make a go of something new and interesting. Besides, most of the visuals are absolutely spectacular.

Obscure and discontinued Hollywood products

Lots of great old material will never see the light of DVD, whether it's your own old home movies, old TV shows, or obscure cult-appeal films from companies like Something Weird Video or Super Happy Fun—these companies sell movies on VHS or unremastered, custom-burned DVD. Mining these sometimes-intentionally "lost" movies isn't just fun—it also fulfills the VJ's holy duty to remind the public of the full range of cultural history, including films like *Skidoo* (1968), a vivid, brain-addled feature which studios would rather keep in the can.

Books and magazines

Countless great stills that no one else has—at least, not in projectable format—are sitting on your bookshelf, and in your local library and bookstores.

Games

In an abstract sense, playing a computer game and VJing are similar activities. Taking a friend on a sightseeing tour of a game title that you know is just another type of real-time video performance—and the visuals can be amazing. Many game titles have a "demo-record" feature which plays games back, and Capcom's *Auto Modellista* driving game expands this feature into "VJ mode," which lets you apply effects to the recorded games. Naturally, you can also record any game video directly off the video-outs, or just play it live in performance. Meanwhile, VJs also use rendering software based on game engines, as discussed above, to perform puppetry within game worlds.

PowerPoint and other non-VJ applications

The business-oriented presentation application PowerPoint has been mocked for years, banned from influential technology conferences like DEMO, and pummeled by design guru Edward R. Tufte. And for good reason, although some of the ire may stem from resentment left over from high school that today's power geeks felt for all the popular kids who later went on to work in PowerPoint-addicted sales departments.

Be that as it may, musician and artist David Byrne began using PowerPoint as an artistic medium a few years ago—as a joke, at first, but it eventually led him to produce several gallery and museum pieces, as well as a multimedia book/DVD package, *Envisioning Emotional Epistemological Information*. Which just goes to show that you can make art out of anything. And perhaps the breakthrough act of seeing new possibilities for something that's been overlooked, as Byrne did with PowerPoint and Tarantino did with Travolta, is the greatest artistic contribution of all.

Television

Shows, news, commercials—it's all up for grabs, especially if you have TiVo or equivalent.

Internet

Anything downloadable online is also up for grabs, from corporate videos to the latest hilarious piece of Photoshoppery that's been making the rounds through word-of-email. One great source is the Prelinger Archives, which serves public-domain video conversions of ephemera such as old commercials and educational and instructional films. The Audiovisualizers site runs a free, membership-based loops server that's dedicated to collecting and sharing original clips for use by VJs. Meanwhile, for the most visually amazing material, check out the online portfolios of motion-graphics hotshots working the commercial world, like Lynn Fox and the World Domination Design Group (WDDG).

If you haven't bothered to prepare any material in advance, you can still perform using live broadband and mix with stills and clips downloaded on-the-fly from sources like Google Image Search. You'll need to do some fast alt-tabbing between apps, and you never know what you'll get, but maybe you're feeling lucky.

Meanwhile, it shouldn't be long before standard VJ apps will be able to accept video streamed over the internet from news networks and other sources. This will open up a world of possibilities for commentary which we can now only dream about.

Movies, and clips ripped therefrom

You can always mix with clips from commercial movies or the DVDs themselves. Some VJs look down on this, but honestly, this material is beautifully produced—great resolution, great lighting and everything else—and more resonant than almost anything you could put together yourself. You want to communicate? Movie scenes are among the most widely-understood words in our cultural vocabulary.

For unabashed bottom-feeders, *The Bare Facts Video Guide* catalogs a wide variety of films on video, indexing the exact points where famous actors and actresses appear nude. Each scene (or brief flash) is listed with its timecode, a description, and a rating of how "good" it is. Earlier versions of *The Bare Facts* listed both actors and actresses, but in more recent editions, the book's author has focused exclusively on actresses.

Koyannisqatsi and *Baraka*

These two films overflow with sumptuous visuals, but you should also know that they're also beginner-VJ clichés. Usage: "He isn't just some bozo who throws *Koyannisqatsi* up there and goes to get a beer."

RIGS ■ ■ ▦ ▒

NO MATTER WHAT EQUIPMENT you use, your basic modus as a VJ is to immerse yourself in possibilities of what to show next or how to change what you're showing. But there is a fundamental distinction regarding where you want to focus your attention, what you want to interact with most immediately in order to control what you're showing. If you're telling your laptop what you want to show next, then you're software-based (AKA laptop-based). If your top-level control comes through a video switch or mixer, then you're hardware-based. And if you're operating in the physical world, managing an array of slides, liquids, and other unencoded, transparent objects, then you're optical-based, you hippie.

Unlike in the DJ world, which has standardized around the setup of two Technics 1200's and a mixer, the set of equipment a VJ uses (their "rig" or "kit"), differs widely among VJs. But the distinction between software-, hardware-, and optical-based approaches does dictate the basic configuration. Here are examples of some typical software, hardware, and optical rigs. The details about what everything does will be covered in detail later, so don't worry if it isn't all immediately clear.

SOFTWARE-BASED RIGS

Bare-Bones Laptop

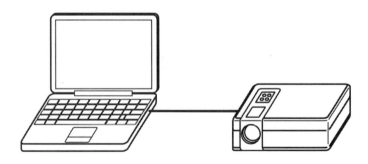

This software-based approach is simplicity itself, just a laptop running free or inexpensive software hooked up to a digital projector. The easiest thing to do here is to run an "eye candy" or "visualizer" application or plug-in (such as G-Force, MilkDrop, or R2/Extreme) which generates dazzling visuals synchronized to any music that's playing on your laptop, from either the file system or a CD. Instant party! Just let it run. You don't have to do anything, and it looks amazing. If you haven't already tried out some of this software, this one easy suggestion alone is worth the price of this book.

Some eye candy applications also let you tweak settings, enter banner text, and otherwise exercise live control over the visuals. But if you really want to be the VJ and perform your own material, you should run a VJ application. Very roughly and with much overlap, these can be divided into two categories: video mixers such as ArKaos, which let you play, mix, and apply effects to video clips stored in your file system, and video synthesizers such as Videodelic, which synthesize video based on live inputs from the VJ and other sources. Maybe it's a mistake to even draw this distinction, since many applications from each category perform functions of the other. When a VJ changes a parameter to make everything look more orange, you can consider it either tweaking an effect or playing an instrument.

When you run a VJ application on a laptop, your laptop screen and projector screen need to show different things—the laptop screen shows the application interface with all of its controls, screens, and clip images, while the projector is the stage, showing only the output that you want to present.

Some laptops have dual monitor support, and some don't, which means that their video output is always the exact same thing as what's appearing on the main screen, a "mirror." Meanwhile, some VJ software can run two screens at once—one for the app and one as the stage—and some can't. If your laptop and VJ software both support dual displays, you can configure the software to designate the projector as the "stage," sending your full-screen mixed video to it, while you use the laptop screen for the application interface.

But if your hardware or software can't handle two different screens at once, you need to put a scan converter between your laptop and the projector. Then you follow the old VJ trick of zooming the scan converter output onto the VJ application's Preview window, which usually appears as a rectangle in the middle of the upper half of the interface. That way, your laptop screen shows the entire interface, while the projector image is zoomed in on only what you want everyone else to see.

Effects

You can apply video effects using both software and hardware. With software effects, someone simply had to write the code, whereas with hardware, people had to write the code, design it into a chip, fabricate the chip, and design and manufacture hardware that makes use of it—a far more expensive process. The result is that hardware effects are faster and cleaner, and they don't crash—but you'll find more variety with software effects. That's where the engineers can really go nuts. In the world of software effects, there's a further distinction between the ones created through a computer's operating system and the ones which access graphics hardware directly via OpenGL, a platform-independent low-level graphics language. The latter category is faster, and all VJ application developers are encouraged to use OpenGL.

Effects offered by VJ applications can be as simple as producing a negative image or as complex as making the source video look like it was painted by Vincent van Gogh. Popular effects include hue, brightness, and contrast changes; mirror, kaleidoscope, and other coordinate transformations; blurs; edge detection; pixelation; trails, delays, and feedback effects; texture overlays and virtual lenses, and text overlays.

Two standard, useful effects that you'll find in both VJ software and video mixing hardware are chroma-key and luma-key. In each case, one image is designated as the top layer, in front, while the other image is the background, the bottom layer. With chroma-keying, you set designate a specific color, most often bright blue or green, and wherever this color appears in the front-layer image, that area becomes "transparent," revealing the bottom layer in back. The film technique of bluescreening is based on the same idea. Chroma-keying works in a similar way, but with a brightness threshold instead of a specific color. For example, if you set a low luma key for a bright image in front, you'll see most the front image, with the background image only peeking through where the front image contains shadows or other dark areas. In practice, luma-keying often looks messy and isn't used as frequently as chroma-keying.

Some software-based effects trace their lineage back to the "transfer modes" functionality in Adobe Photoshop and Adobe After Effects. Transfer modes blend two images or video streams together by applying arithmetic formulas, pixel by pixel, over the sources, producing a combined result. In VJ software, only the simplest formulas can be calculated fast enough to keep up with real-time video. However, it is hoped that in the future, video-processing hardware developers will encode into hard silicon more of the wide range of popular transfer-mode effects that are already familiar to software users. Hint, hint.

Laptop with Input Devices

MIDI Controller

In performance, VJs constantly trigger clips and change numerical settings. Unfortunately, a laptop's physical interface can complicate both of these tasks. A typical GUI for clip-triggering software shows a menu of thumbnails that represent each clip. You start a clip running (typically, it will loop repeatedly until you trigger the next one) in one of two ways: you either click on it, which requires you to find the cursor and move it over to the thumbnail, or else you hit the key on the keyboard that the clip is assigned to, which means having to read or remember whether the clip you want has been assigned to the Q key, the W key, and so on.

Meanwhile, most VJ applications associate the numerical settings that control colors, filters, playback speeds, and other effects settings with knobs, sliders, and other onscreen controls. You change these settings onscreen by clicking and dragging on the little pictures of knobs, or else by entering values directly with the keyboard.

Working through the laptop's screen and keyboard like this may seem easy enough, but in the heat of the performance moment, having to mouse around onscreen and worry about hitting the right keys can interrupt your flow—especially if you're trying to play in sync with fast music.

To make things easier, many laptop-based VJs trigger clips and change numerical settings via external controller hardware. Lighting-control standards such as DMX, used in professional lighting and theatrical equipment, are the most relevant to VJing, but controllers based on the MIDI standard ("Musical Instrument Digital Interface") are cheaper and more portable, so that's the standard that VJs adopted. This is why you see many VJs using piano-style keyboards, even though they aren't playing music.

The MIDI language defines two types of abstract objects which are handy for VJs: Note and Continuous Controller (or CC). VJ software assigns notes to clips and maps continuous controller values to knobs and sliders. This allows the MIDI device to trigger a clip when you play a note and adjust a value when you turn a control knob. Within the VJ application, you build layouts that map keyboard keys to different clips and define a Parameter Control Interface, which associates the knobs or slider controls on your hardware, each of which has a unique MIDI controller number, to the visual effects parameters of your choice.

The most popular MIDI controller for VJing is the Oxygen 8 keyboard from M-Audio, which offers two octaves' worth of keys, to support twenty-five clips per layout, and eight assignable CC knobs for twiddling visual effects settings. The Oxygen 8 is also easily portable, costs less than $200, and has a USB port, so it plugs directly into a laptop without requiring a USB-MIDI interface.

If you have a tablet computer or a laptop with a touchscreen, you don't need a separate controller for triggering because you can just click the clips directly onscreen. This is the best interface of all, much better than having to deal with a piano keyboard. In this case, it's still nice to have an external MIDI device just to control the CC values. There are several good pieces of hardware for this purpose, including the Doepfer Pocket Control, a small box with sixteen MIDI control knobs. For this and other MIDI devices which lack USB (which is most of them), you would connect it to your laptop via a MIDI-PC interface dongle, such as the M-Audio Uno or Edirol UM-1X.

In theory, you could use any type of MIDI controller to trigger clips, not just piano keyboards. MIDI violins, flutes, accordions, guitars, etc. are all fair game. There's little technical justification for doing this unless you're actually playing music and the video clips you're using have a specific relationship to the musical notes. But even if not, it might still work well in performance, provided your audience doesn't have too many smarty-pants types.

Game Controller

Standard gaming accessories such as joysticks, gamepads, driving wheels, and FPS (first-person shooter) controllers provide another way of enhancing the laptop VJ interface. These devices don't speak MIDI, but they'll work as your mouse, and you can also map the buttons to specific keys on the keyboard, for fast clip triggering, video-game style. Of course, these toys constitute a mini-industry of their own, and dozens of manufacturers are competing over which ones work better and look cooler, so as a rule these controllers are not expensive, they work very well until they break, and they offer ample opportunity for personal expression through consumer choice.

Webcam or Camcorder

Another popular accessory for laptop rigs (and hardware-based rigs as well) is a webcam. These let you mix live camera into your performance, which crowds typically love. The best ones connect via Firewire, which is faster than USB.

You can also add a live feed using most camcorders, which (unlike a web-cam) can also be zoomed and panned, by you or by someone else. Webcams are the cheaper and more portable of the two, but you may already have access to a camcorder—especially if friends of yours or you yourself have recently had children.

Scratching

Some VJ software lets you scratch video clips—that is, run them forward and backward following your hand motions using only the mouse or trackpad. You do this in the Preferences by assigning the mouse's horizontal and vertical positions to MIDI controller numbers, typically 7 and 8. Associate one of these to a clip's position or speed, and you're scratching with the mouse.

As above, however, adding auxiliary hardware gives you an interface that feels and works better. You can scratch with any MIDI knob or slider by assigning playback position or speed to the corresponding continuous controller value. For more precision you can use a jog/shuttle controller, which is a common piece of equipment in video editing studios. These let you navigate clips more easily via a jog wheel: a large, recessed knob with an indentation for your fingertip. For real turntable action you can use Ms. Pinky or the EJ MIDI Turntable, which convert standard turntables into video controllers.

HARDWARE-BASED RIGS

Limitations of Laptops

As powerful as laptops are, the demands of VJing can still bring them to their knees. VJ software running by itself is best suited (as of this writing) to handling clips under 10 MB in size, at resolutions of 320 x 240 or lower. If you try playing and mixing with larger files at higher resolutions, your computer will balk, stutter, or lock up entirely—all of which are considered undesirable in a live performance setting.

If you're working at a full-screen resolution such as 720 x 480, you need to divide the labor, at least until laptops can walk and chew gum at the same time. A laptop will play full-screen video files smoothly from the file system (using an MPEG-4 player, for example, or DV Codec Out in Final Cut or Premiere), but the real-time decoding required for playback doesn't leave room for mixing or applying effects. This means you'll need to send the video to a second laptop for mixing with a VJ application that takes video in. You'll connect the player laptop to the mixer laptop via a USB video capture device such as Belkin's USB Video Bus 2.

A laptop will also produce high-definition video when it's simply playing a DVD, but even then, it's the most expensive and least reliable DVD player you'll ever use. If you just need something to play DVDs, you're better off with a cheap DVD player.

OLD-SCHOOL HARDWARE

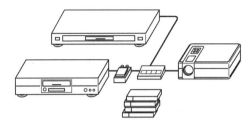

This is where the hardware approach comes in. At its most basic, it relies on DVDs and VHS tapes and a simple video switch you can get at Radio Shack. Like the VJs (and DJs) of yore, you perform by selecting and swapping in from your stacks of discs and tapes, mixing it up by switching back and forth between your input sources. This old-school approach relies on your unique content rather than rapid-fire transitions or effects. What gets you invited or hired for the night is your personal library of fascinating and obscure video material—stuff which everyone loves but no one else has (hence the importance of forgotten VHS tapes). You are a VJ; you are what you play.

And actually, you *can* apply real-time effects to your video using this approach. Put an old guitar effects pedal, like a fuzz box, between one of your video sources and the switch, with simple RCA to 1/4-inch (TS) plug adapters on either side. It's designed to distort audio, but it will distort video as well. It isn't a sophisticated effect—usually just a burst of semi-transparent static— but it offers a nice punctuation mark that fits the rig's down-and-dirty, no-nonsense aesthetic.

MIXER-BASED

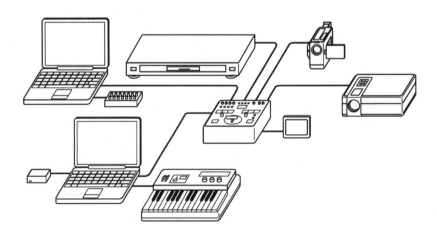

Higher-end hardware rigs center around a mixer rather than a simple switch, letting you fade, mix, and apply effects to high-resolution video with the speed and sure feel of dedicated video equipment. A popular choice is the Edirol V-4, which takes four analog video input channels, plus MIDI-in for synchronizing transitions and effects to the beat of music coming from a DJ or other source.

Based on a four-channel mixer, this setup dedicates one channel to a live camcorder (with analog out) and another one to a DVD player. A third input connects to a laptop that generates swirly visuals by running an off-the-shelf video synthesizer application such as Videodelic, or else a custom instrument built on a software platform such as Max/MSP using Jitter. These visuals can also synch to music via MIDI input or incorporate other video inputs, and settings are tweaked via another dedicated MIDI controller, as with the laptop setup above. The fourth channel comes from another laptop, which is dedicated to clips, triggering them via an application such as Vidvox Grid, which simply plays clips for output to other devices, rather than also performing as a video mixer as with all-in-one VJ applications.

Connected via Firewire port to the clips laptop is an external hard disk drive (HDD) which contains additional video files. The clips stored on the laptop's own internal drive are public-domain and original video files that the VJ can legally perform anywhere, while the ones stored on the detachable HDD are proprietary—scenes from movies, television news footage, commercials, and other intellectual property, in either raw form or modified in an entertaining fashion, that were originally recorded off the air, archived from TiVo, or ripped from DVDs. With this arrangement, the VJ can either take or leave behind a library of video content that's legal to perform with in some places and illegal in others. This is discussed further in the Legal Issues chapter.

Mixers like the V-4 also have a preview jack, which allows you to plug in a monitor to display the video that's coming into each of the channels, switching around among them by hitting corresponding buttons. Any video display will work as a preview monitor; it needn't be high quality (or even color). One favorite is the five-inch LCD display from Reactor Car Audio, which is small, easily portable, and can be set up on a bit of table space behind or next to the mixer.

MULTIPLE STATIONS

For big fun in larger venues, you can send identical source video streams through multiple VJ stations and let the VJs project onto multiple screens. The basic pieces of hardware that enable this are distribution amplifiers and matrix routers. A distribution amplifier the opposite of the switch device described above. Instead of taking multiple video inputs and outputting one of them, it takes one input stream and duplicates it over several outputs. Matrix routers combine the functions of switches and distribution amplifiers, allowing you to route any inputs to any outputs.

As shown in the diagram, you can use distribution amplifiers and matrix routers (along with plenty of coaxial cables, extension cords, plastic cable ties, and duct tape) to chain VJ stations and projectors together like Tinkertoys. Setups like these let VJs work simultaneously off of the same sources, use each others' output as their own source input, and otherwise fill the room with an all-encompassing, multi-screen visual jam session.

OPTICAL RIGS

Psychedelic

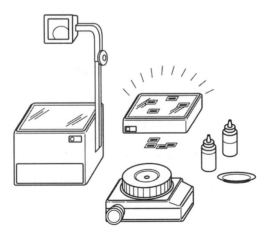

Most VJs focus on electronic inputs and outputs, but there's a wealth of beautiful techniques that require only optical equipment, much of which can be found cheaply second-hand. Furthermore, the effects have far higher resolution than any video. Next to a regular television image, the sharpness and clarity of a brightly backlit, churning sea of bubbles is breathtaking. Rather than calculating pixels, these classic psychedelic light-show techniques use the ubiquitous, infinitely-parallel processing power of the universe itself as it continuously iterates the laws of optics and physical reality. You might be able to simulate these effects with a computer—but unless you're doing it for research rather than aesthetics, why bother?

All of these visuals begin with the old-fashioned overhead projector. Schools have been getting rid of them, so they're easy to find second-hand, although they are still being manufactured.

In the usual practice, "liquids," also known as "wet shows," are based on loose mixtures of mineral oil and water, or mineral oil and glycerine, one or both of which have been dyed with food coloring. You perform by pressing and kneading the liquids between two watch glasses or Petri dishes on the stage of the projector. But anything goes, of course; you can stir and tilt the liquids, squirt in new colors, blow bubbles with a straw, run little chemistry experiments, or whatever else. Just make sure to keep a bucket, a small siphon, towels, and fresh liquid ingredients nearby so you can clean up and start anew, because if you manipulate one set of colors for an extended period of time, they can get muddy (and tiresome). The shallow glass dishes are extremely prone to tipping and sloshing, especially in the heat of performance, so you should siphon them out and wipe them clean, rather than expect to convey them over to the bucket without spilling oily dyes all over.

Another classic psychedelic effect on the overhead is moiré patterns, which you project by moving overlapping transparencies printed with black-and-white op-art designs. Dover Publications has a few books you can copy these from. For a real time trip, shine them on go-go dancers wearing black-and-white swirl mini-dresses, available for cheap from the Halloween store.

For all of these effects, you can also dispense with the overhead projector and substitute a webcam attached to a stand, pointed down at a light table which functions as the stage. The webcam's output feeds into a digital projector, either directly or indirectly. Going digital this way loses the original, stunning resolution of your light-show patterns, but it means you can pipe them into laptops, mixers, or other devices for some "old meets new" action.

There are many other great optical effects—crystal slides with rotating polarizing filters, projection kaleidoscopes, oil projectors, strobes, and of course the association-rich mirror ball. These can range from homemade, psychedelic-era contraptions to the high-end professional nightclub lighting equipment that they evolved into as the psychedelic era gave way to disco in the 1970s. For DIY designs, visit the Rainbow Prism Atomic Lightshow website. You can find low-end, living-room light show gear from companies like Johnson-Smith and professional lighting from American DJ. Note that the search term "professional lighting" also includes things like bubble machines, smoke machines, and fog machines, all of which add to the atmosphere.

Film

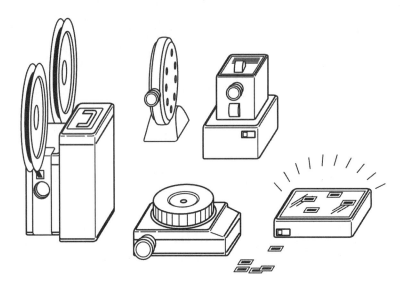

Traditional film, slide, and filmstrip projectors offer a representational counterpart to the high-res, low-tech abstraction of liquids. These devices are pretty self-explanatory; you just run them normally using the most interesting films or slides you can. But there are two simple, traditional modifications you can make to create that classic light-show atmosphere. One is to find interesting three- to four-foot sections of 16mm film and splice them together end to end, creating loops that repeat continuously when projected. Another is to interrupt the beam of any projector with a rotating color wheel. This adds an elusively shimmering color-shift effect to any image—and to the entire room, if it's dark.

STANDARDS AND CONVERSIONS ■ ■ ■ ■

VJS TYPICALLY SPEND A LOT OF TIME hooking equipment up and taking it back apart; the oft-heard lament is that they're always the first to arrive and the last to leave. Furthermore, they need to know what's compatible before they can start hooking things up, and in a world of evolving and competing standards, this means having to keep track of a lot of specific details about standards and formats. In broad terms, there are two types of video standards: video transfer (or display) standards and storage or file standards.

Video transfer standards define how video information travels between pieces of equipment, for example, how it's sent to a monitor that decodes the signal and renders it onscreen. This category of standard includes composite video and VGA, which are analog, and DVI (Digital Visual Interface) and HDMI (High Definition Multimedia Interface), which are digital.

Storage standards define how video information is stored, including tape formats such as VHS (analog) and MiniDV (digital), DVD (digital), and video file formats such as Quicktime and MPEG-4, all of which are digital.

Other distinctions cross-cut these two categories: whether a standard is analog or digital, and whether it was designed for television, computer displays, or both. These distinctions are discussed more fully below.

Analog vs. Digital

At the most basic level, humans can only experience video and audio as analog information, while computers must store and process them in digital formats. As a result, any computer video that a person is working on or performing with requires conversions from analog to digital and back. And because software only operates within the digital world, any analog/digital conversions must ultimately be performed by a piece of hardware (or, theoretically, at the level of only the most basic, machine-level software or firmware). These pieces of hardware constitute a boundary between the physical analog world and the digital.

Wires can carry either digital or analog signal, based on their current or voltage level. Similarly, magnetic media (tape) can carry either digital or analog information, based on the varying level of magnetism over their physical surface. Optical fiber can also carry either digital or analog, but no one uses it for analog. Optical media read by laser (CD, DVD), hard drives, flash cards, and other computer-accessory media can only carry digital. (Note: if you're thinking "duh" right now, please bear with.)

Until fairly recently, the signal carried through all wires and cables in audio/video equipment was analog. This makes sense, since analog voltage is what's ultimately needed to drive a speaker or a video display, and analog signal is what comes from microphones and the CCDs inside video cameras (this is why, in a pinch, ordinary headphones make usable microphones). Today, however, more devices send audiovisual signal through cables, such as data cables (USB, Firewire) and digital video cables (DVI, HDMI), in digital form.

Digital cable formats have high throughput and the signal doesn't degrade—two of the usual advantages of digital. As a result, analog signals are sensitive to cable quality—materials, thickness, shielding—while all digital cables built to standard will work equally well. In addition, digital signal can be encrypted, and this issue may become even more important in the future, if the consumer electronics industry develops new standards designed to further prevent access to content, as hypothesized in the Predictions and Reflections chapter.

Television vs. Computer

The final major distinction among video standards is whether they were originally designed to carry signal to television screens or to computer monitors—as if it matters. File this one in the always-annoying "legacy" category.

Analog TV standards, such as composite and S-video, use round plugs, in the music equipment tradition. Meanwhile, computer display standards such as VGA and its kin (SVGA, XGA, etc.), which are also analog, tend to use the flat, multiple-pin style of connectors that are better suited to the edges of circuit boards. In addition, computers also transmit and receive video via general-purpose data I/O standards such as USB and Firewire, which have characteristic flat-connector cables of their own.

Newer, digital video standards such as DVI and HDMI represent a wise convergence between television and computer standards engineering and are used in display devices designed for living rooms, offices, and playrooms alike.

TRANSFER STANDARDS AND HARDWARE COMPATIBILITY

By their nature, transfer standards have always been coupled with standards for the cables that carry them, and over the past couple of decades, a "plug-and-play" design revolution has dictated that any new transfer standard should correspond to a new set of physical standards for cables, connectors, and ports. These combined standards are crucial to video because they determine how you hook everything up. As a result of this design convention, consumer electronics have increasing numbers of funny-shaped ports along the sides or in back, each with their own distinctive icons: USB, Firewire, S-video, DVI, HDMI, and so on.

Ideally, this means that if you can physically plug in the cable, the devices you're using support the underlying standard, and so hooking up component systems has become increasingly like playing with the matching peg-and-hole toy in kindergarten. This is convenient and great when manufacturers and software driver developers hold up their ends of the bargain—which is most but not all of the time. Furthermore, additional complications arise with popular standards that predate plug-and-play, such as the many different flavors of component video and VGA variants which use identical physical cables.

With so many video standards, having to convert between them is almost inevitable. When in doubt, you can fall back to one standard in particular: *composite video running over coaxial cable*. This is the lingua franca of video hardware, an old format that's compatible with almost all video equipment, and a lot of computer equipment as well. A more complete discussion of composite video and coaxial cable follows the video conversion chart below.

Video Format Conversion Chart

Video devices need to be using the same standard, speaking the same language, when you connect them together. If they aren't, you need to find some means of translation, which can range from a two-dollar adapter to thousand-dollar professional studio equipment. There's an entire industry devoted to cables and converters that translate from one format to another. The chart below lists what you need to perform these conversions. Following the chart are more detailed discussions of each format, the general classes of equipment (adapter, cable, bridge, box, deck), and where you can find it.

Video Formats

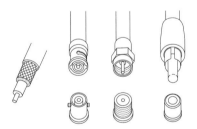

Composite (cable: coaxial; connectors: BNC, F-type, RCA)

Composite video, which runs over one circuit (two wires), is the wired equivalent of an analog broadcast television signal carried over a single channel or frequency. Therefore, it's a composite of all the different components of video—all brightness and color information is combined into a single signal. Because so much information is loaded through these wires, they're usually configured as a coaxial cable, so-called because the wires share the same axis, with one inside of the other. This geometry eliminates interference that

FROM \ TO	Composite (coaxial cable)	YC (S-Video cable)	VGA, SVGA, XGA, etc. (HD15 cable)	Component (3x or 4x coaxial cables, or HD15)	DVI (DVI cable)	ADC (ADC cable)	HDMI (HDMI cable)	Firewire (Firewire cable)
Composite (coaxial cable)	Cable ¢+, depending on quality	Any old VCR ¢-¢¢, or cable adapter or small box ¢¢-$$	Small box "scan converter" $$ or editing system $$$$$	Small box "decoder" $$$-$$$$ or editing system $$$$$	Small box $$$$ or editing system $$$$$	Editing system $$$$$	HDMI receiver $$$$ or editing system $$$$$	Camcorder with analog pass-through $$$$ (if you can't borrow or don't already have) or converter box $$$$ or editing system $$$$$
YC (S-Video cable)	Fair results with adapter or cable ¢¢, better quality with small box $$	Cable ¢+; for long distances, use 2x coaxial with splitters at each end	Small box "scan converter" $$ or editing system $$$$$	Small box "decoder" $$$-$$$$ or editing system $$$$$	Small box $$$$ or editing system $$$$$	Editing system $$$$$	HDMI receiver $$$$ or editing system $$$$$	Camcorder with analog pass-through $$$$ (if you can't borrow or don't already have) or converter box $$$$ or editing system $$$$$
VGA, SVGA, XGA, etc. (HD15 cable)	Small box "scan converter" $$, but most devices and cards have composite out	Small box "scan converter" $$, but many devices and cards have S-Video out	Cable ¢¢-$$, depending on length and quality	Small box $$ or editing system $$$$$	Small box $$$-$$$$ or editing system $$$$$	Small box $$$ or editing system $$$$$	Use HD15 to DVI with DVI to HDMI cable, or editing system $$$$$	Multifunction box or deck with Firewire out $$$$$ or editing system $$$$$
Component (3x or 4x coaxial cables, or HD15)	Small box "encoder" $$$$ or editing system	Small box "encoder" $$$$ or editing system $$$$$	Small box $$-$$$$ or editing system $$$$$	Cable ¢-$$; for long distances, use 5x coaxial with breakout cables at each end	Multifunction deck $$$$$	Editing system $$$$$	Use Component to DVI with DVI to HDMI cable, or editing system $$$$$	Multifunction box or deck with Firewire out $$$$$ or editing system $$$$$
DVI (DVI cable)	Small box ¢¢	Small box ¢¢	Small box $$$$ (adapter ¢¢ OK for DVI-A and DVI-I) or editing system $$$$$	Converter deck $$$$$ (adapter ¢¢ OK for DVI-A and DVI-I) or editing system $$$$$	Cable ¢¢-$$$ depending on length	Cable or small box $$	Cable $	Multifunction box or deck with Firewire out $$$$$ or editing system $$$$$
ADC (ADC cable)	Bridge ¢¢	Bridge ¢¢	Bridge ¢¢	Editing system $$$$$	Bridge ¢¢	Cable $	Use ADC to DVI with DVI to HDMI cable, or editing system $$$$$	Editing system $$$$$
HDMI (HDMI cable)	HDMI receiver $$$$-$$$$$ or editing system $$$$$	HDMI receiver $$$$-$$$$$ or editing system $$$$$	HDMI receiver $$$$-$$$$$ or multifunction deck $$$$$ or editing system $$$$$	HDMI receiver $$$$-$$$$$ or multifunction deck $$$$$ or editing system $$$$$	Cable $-$$	Use HDMI to DVI with DVI to ADC adapter, or editing system $$$$$	Cable $-$$$ depending on length	Use HDMI to DVI with DVI to Firewire, or editing system $$$$$
Firewire (Firewire cable)	Converter box $$$$ or editing system $$$$$	Converter box $$$$ or editing system $$$$$	Editing system $$$$$	Converter box $$$$ or editing system $$$$$	Converter box $$$$$ or editing system $$$$$	Editing system $$$$$	Converter box $$$$$ or editing system $$$$$	Cable ¢¢-$

Conversion type

Analog	
A to D	
D to A	
Digital	

Price Key

¢	$<9
¢¢	$10–29
$	$30–79
$$	$80–199
$$$	$200–349
$$$$	$350–499
$$$$$	$500+

would result if the two wires simply ran next to each other, and were therefore subjected to each others' changing electromagnetic fields. Coaxial cable, which is built to specifications with names like "R59U" and "RG6," is layered like a baseball. A solid core wire in the middle is surrounded by a layer of plastic shielding. Surrounding the plastic is the second wire, a flexible mesh tube, which is itself surrounded by an outer shielding layer and a coating. These are the television cables that reach through the walls of countless houses, and while home theater aficionados may sniff at the format, it has provided clear pictures (at NTSC resolution, anyway) for decades.

But even the simple world of composite/coaxial is complicated by three different connectors commonly used on the ends of coaxial cable: BNC, F-Type, and RCA. BNC, common on professional video gear, has a small twist-lock mechanism. F-Type, found in security-industry and consumer equipment, uses screw threads or (more cheaply) a sleeve that slides over the screw threads. RCA, also used in consumer equipment, is a format that was originally designed for audio. RCA video cables look the same as stereo cables, but by convention the connectors are colored yellow, and the cable itself is built to different specifications. (Using an audio cable to carry composite video signal is not recommended, even when it plugs right in, since it won't have the proper resistance of 75 ohms.)

In spite of these different hardware formats, any coaxial cable carrying composite video can hook up to any style of port with the aid of small, inexpensive adapters that convert BNC, F-Type, and RCA plugs into each other. Many VJs have little sewing-kit boxes filled with these.

Y/C (AKA S-Video; cable and connector: S-Video, AKA Y/C)

This analog standard improves upon composite by separating the signal into two components, luminance (brightness, or Y) and chrominance (color, or C). It's often referred to as S-Video, after the name of the cable designed to carry it, but correctness-dorks know that Y/C means the signal, and S-Video means the cable. The standard was developed in the 1970s alongside the advent of S-VHS or Super-VHS, so people also sometimes (incorrectly) refer to Y/C and S-Video as S-VHS. S-Video cables use round, four-pin connectors, and they're susceptible to interference, so for long distances it's advisable to carry Y/C over two coaxial cables, splitting and reassembling the channels with a breakout cable at each end. S-Video jacks are featured on many computers, camcorders, game consoles, and home theater components.

VGA, SVGA, XGA, etc. (cable and connector: HD15, AKA D-Sub, 15-pin, RGBHV)

VGA (Video Graphics Array) and its extensions are analog standards for PC monitors, all of which run over a fifteen-pin connector. This format assigns different pairs of pins to red, green, and blue components of the video image, as well as dedicated pins for horizontal and vertical synchronization and other information. This means that HD15 is a handy cable standard for carrying multiple parallel connections that are *not* VGA-compatible, such as various component video formats (described below). Some equipment uses HD15 cables in this way, an arrangement referred to as "component over HD15," "RGBHV over HD15" or some such phrase. This should not be confused with VGA or SVGA.

Marketing departments have defined an alphabet soup of VGA-based terms for different picture resolutions, including VGA (640 x 480), SVGA (800 x 600), XGA (1024 x 768), and SXGA (1280 x 1024). With any two pieces of video equipment, you can never assume intercompatibility at these different resolutions, and the picture you get by hooking up a player or driver to a display will generally fall back to the lower of the best resolutions that each device is capable of. For this reason, grouping all of the VGA standards together into one row and column in the chart above is a bit of an oversimplification, and an entire sub-field of scan converters is dedicated to down- and up-converting among the different resolutions that occupy this category alone.

Component video (standards: YUV AKA Y/Pb/Pr, RGB, RGBS, RGBHV; cable: multiple coaxials or HD15)

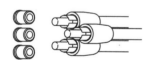

As with the VGA family, component video refers to a set of standards, but the situation here is even messier. Most component video is analog and splits the signal into three parts, which are carried over three separate cables. The simplest standard that people call "component video" is RGB, where three coaxial cables correspond to the red, green, and blue components of the picture, carrying pixel-by-pixel brightness information for each color separately. But RGB wastes bandwidth, because our eyes are far more sensitive to small differences in overall brightness than they are to small differences in color.

Enter YUV, also known as Y/Pb/Pr, which dedicates one channel entirely (Y) to overall brightness, or the black-and-white image. The two other channels carry color information, compressed via a simple arithmetic formula based on the blue minus Y and red minus Y values. For all three channels, weighting factors are multiplied in to balance out how bright the different primary colors appear to our eyes. The display device reconstitutes the three component values back into the original red, green, and blue values, using simple analog circuitry, with more precise overall brightness values than would have resulted without the conversions. Other component standards, such as YIQ, follow the same basic formulas as YUV, but have slightly different weights for the relative brightness factors.

YUV is a great way to carry high-definition signal and is used by a lot of professional video and home theater equipment. The practical problem is, RGB and YUV are often confused, and some pieces of hardware even label their YUV ports incorrectly as RGB. Component video jacks on the back of video equipment sold in the U.S., no matter what they're labeled, generally carry YUV, but the best strategy is to do background research, ask sellers about specific compatibility, carry what you need to try before you buy, and keep all your receipts.

Some equipment breaks video into four or five separate cables. With these, three cables carry basic red, green, and blue. The four-cable arrangement (RGBS) adds a composite synchronization pulse, while five cables (RGBHV) carry separate horizontal and vertical syncs.

As described above, some equipment uses HD15 cable to carry various flavors of component video rather than parallel coaxial cables.

DVI (cables and connectors: DVI-A, DVI-I, or DVI-I)

DVI (Digital Visual Interface) is a display standard designed as a digital-capable successor to VGA, better suited to LCD and DLP monitors and projectors, which create images using low-power, digital signals. To preserve backwards compatibility, some DVI cables carry VGA analog signals (RGBHV) alongside the digital, so you need to pay attention to which flavor of DVI and DVI connector you're working with: DVI-D supports digital, DVI-A supports analog, and DVI-I ("integrated") supports both for backwards compatibility. To accomplish this, DVI-I connectors have a whopping twenty-nine pins.

The DVI standard also optionally supports an encryption scheme known as HDCP (High-bandwidth Digital Content Protection) or DVI-CP. Many new DVD players output HDCP signal, but unfortunately there are many display devices with DVI input ports, especially projectors, that can't decode the signal, which means they can't show it. So much for plug-and-play. The company behind HDCP, Digital Content Protection, wants people to avoid this situation by purchasing DVI display devices that are "HDMI-compliant."

ADC (cable and connector: ADC)

ADC (Apple Display Connector) is a proprietary format developed for the Apple Studio Display, which streamlined connections by combining DVI-I video with power and USB. This consolidation meant that the display could be connected to the computer using only one cable rather than requiring a separate power cord, and a USB mouse could connect to the display, rather than to the computer. Classic Apple streamlining. But Apple's newer Cinema Displays use regular DVI ports.

HDMI (cable and connector: HDMI)

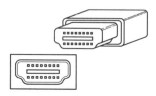

HDMI (High Definition Multimedia Interface) is a digital-only standard for HDTV and home theater that combines audio and video. Like DVI-D and DVI-I, it optionally supports HDCP encryption.

Firewire (AKA i.Link, 1394, IEEE 1394, Firewire 400; cable: Firewire; connectors: Firewire Type 1, Firewire Type 2)

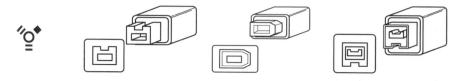

DV camcorders, high-capacity storage drives, and other devices use Firewire to transmit video data in real time, or transfer it faster than real time. Running at a maximum speed of 400 Mbps, the standard theoretically allows a DVD's worth of video data to be shipped between devices in less than fifteen seconds. Firewire was designed with video in mind, but it's actually a general data format, like USB, so it's also used for audio. Firewire cables have two styles of connector: a six-pin plug, which supplies power, and a four-pin version that does not. A related standard, Firewire 800, supports transfer speeds of up to 800 Mbps, and uses a nine-pin connector.

Webcams, still cameras, and other devices also sometimes transfer low-resolution video over USB 1.1, the 12 Mbps data format used by zillions of devices. USB ports are not common on video equipment, but standard on lap-tops—which is why VJ applications take MIDI input from the USB port.

Conversion Equipment Types

Adapter
A small, inexpensive piece that converts a plug or port into a different shape standard without changing the signal.

Cable
A connector with plugs at both ends, with the same or different formats. Cables work passively, using incoming signal power rather than requiring their own power.

A "breakout cable" takes a compound plug format such as HD15 and brings each component wire out into its own coaxial cable to be re-combined at the other end. This helps multi-wire analog signals such as S-Video or VGA run over long distances by minimizing interference between wires. Breakout cables are sold with names like "VGA to Component," but this does *not* mean the cables actually perform the signal conversion, and the manufacturer would rather you learned this lesson *after* you buy their cable. So beware: complex conversions between video formats cannot be performed by inexpensive cables.

Bridge
Also known as an "adapter cable," this is a cable with some dedicated circuitry in the middle that converts from one format to another. The circuitry is housed in a small, unobtrusive case that has no controls (well, maybe one switch, maximum) and requires no attention. These are sometimes called "dongles," although that word more often refers to small hardware devices used for security or networking.

Small box
A self-contained box of circuitry dedicated to performing conversions. Unlike adapter cables or bridges (above), they need to be plugged into their own power outlet. Also, the electronics are typically housed in a box with switches and other controls that configure the conversion, which means that they should sit on an accessible surface.

Deck
Expensive, multi-function pieces sized for rack-mounting with other equip-ment, like in a professional studio or videophile home theater system, which perform a wide range of conversions.

Editing System
Expensive, professional video editing software suites that run on high-end com-puters, usually MacOS, sometimes bundled or accessorized with additional boxes or cards for hardware conversions. These are designed to do anything.

Equipment Manufacturers and Retailers

AJA: High-end A/D video conversion boxes and cards, including the popular Kona cards and D-Series boxes.

AViD, Media100: Professional editing systems.

DVDO: HD-oriented video processing and A/D conversion decks, including the popular iScan HD+, which has composite, S-Video, component, HD15, and DVI in/outs.

Datavideo: Video converter decks, including the professional studio DAC-10, which has composite, S-Video, component, and Firewire in/outs, and converts among a variety of component formats.

Canopus: A/D video conversion boxes, including the popular ADVC-100, which has composite, S-video, and Firewire in/outs.

Panasonic: Home theater receiver SA-XR70S had HDMI in/out.

Apple, Dr. Bott: ADC bridges for composite, HD15, DVI, etc.

DVIGear: DVI conversion boxes.

Other video conversion box makers: Analog Way, Audio Authority, Extron, Gefen, Grandtec, JS Technology, Key Digital, Kramer Electronics, Rio Wave.

Analog / Digital Conversions

Digitizing video from analog sources like old VHS tapes, live television, or "archive" output from TiVo or ReplayTV DVRs ultimately means using some sort of hardware, since software can't understand analog input. Dedicated hardware encoders work inside all of the A-to-D and D-to-A devices in the chart page 154, from consumer DVD players, DVRs, and DV camcorders to costly professional video equipment. The DVD players and DVRs don't expose the codec functionality, presumably because they play commercial content, and studios would get mad. But some DV camcorders support "analog pass-through" feature which lets you connect any source to an analog input port so that the camera's internal codec can convert it to digital video output in real time. Look for this feature!

Several companies, including ATi, Adaptec, AVerMedia, Hauppauge, and Imperx, sell TV tuner and tuner/graphics cards for PCs that perform A/D conversions. These have gotten mixed reviews and don't yet offer as high quality as the types of equipment listed in the conversion chart above.

Still lower down the food chain are inexpensive hardware/software hybrid products from ADSTECH, AVerMedia, Belkin, GlobalMedia, and Pinnacle Systems, with Pinnacle being the best-known. With this type of product, an external "video-grabber" box or dongle performs a preliminary digitization of the analog video input and feeds it into your computer's USB or Firewire port. Software on your computer then takes the half-digitized video and compresses it into a standard video format. In principle, the process should work fine, but as of this writing it brings many machines to their knees, isn't always reliable, and produces results that aren't as crisp as with other methods. This is likely to change, of course, and hopefully in a few years, these products will be much better.

Converting Digital Formats

Want to convert video from digital sources, like files you've shot or created yourself, downloaded, or obtained from DVD? Commercial applications that produce video, such as Final Cut Pro, After Effects, Maya, Studio Artist, and Houdini, will typically let you export video into the format you want using the parameters you select. An important rule here, which holds for all video production, is to wait until the last possible moment to compress the video into the "delivery format"—in this case, the clip format that your VJ application uses. The pros use tools like cleaner 6 or cleaner XL from Discreet to master the video and perform this final conversion.

Among VJ applications, Quicktime is the most commonly-used clip format, so it's wise to build your collection primarily out of Quicktimes. Not surprisingly, the best software for converting video files into Quicktime format is Quicktime Pro, an inexpensive upgrade to the free Quicktime Player, available from Apple. If you want to convert files ripped from DVD, you also need the MPEG-2 Playback Component, which is another paid upgrade from Apple.

Ripping DVDs is a useful special case of file format conversion, since it opens up a wonderful world of video source material that's beautifully produced and culturally resonant, if not exactly original. There are commercial products that extract and convert DVD files, such as 321 Studios' DVDXcopy, on the PC. The procedures below explain how to create Quicktime clips from DVD using free software along with Quicktime Pro and the Quicktime MPEG-2 Playback component. Do not do this in any countries where it is illegal; it is your responsibility to comply with all local laws. (For informational purposes only.)

For the final conversion, there are free alternatives to the Quicktime upgrades. For Mac OSX, check out the versatile ffmpegX. WinXP allows several ways of encoding clips from DVD into AVI files, such as dvd2avi and vfapi (which you use together, interchanging via D2V project files). Then you can convert your AVIs to WMV files by using Windows Movie Maker, which is included with XP. Some VJ apps will handle these, but as of this writing, there's no good free way of producing the Quicktime files. Just bite the bullet and buy Quicktime Pro and the MPEG-2 Playback component. You'll be glad you did.

SmartRipper DVD-to-Quicktime recipe for PCs (WinXP):

1. Install Quicktime Pro and the MPEG-2 Playback component from Apple. Find and install an ASPI layer (Adaptec has one) and SmartRipper.

2. Insert DVD and launch SmartRipper.

3. From within SmartRipper, select the title that contains the movie (the longest one). Under the Input tab, select chapters you want to rip, (uncheck the ones you don't). Refer to the DVD's chapter list.

4. Under the Stream Processing tab, uncheck all but the video stream (and the audio stream, if you want that as well).

5. Under Target, choose a destination folder. Click Start and wait a while.

6. Find the VOB file(s) just written into your destination folder and give them meaningful names. Delete the other files.

7. From within Quicktime, open each VOB file. If you have trouble opening the file, change the file extension to MPG. Choose Export... from the File menu, and then Export: Movie to Quicktime Movie. Review compression settings under Options... tab (see below). Wait some more.

8. From within Quicktime, Open the MOV (Quicktime) file you just generated. Using the little arrows below the slider, bracket the clip you want to save; click Edit / Trim, and File / Save As... to save the clip.

9. Serve and enjoy.

OSEx DVD-to-Quicktime Recipe for Macs (OSX)

1. Install Quicktime Pro and the MPEG-2 Playback component from Apple. Find and install OSEx.

2. Insert DVD and launch OSEx.

3. From within OSEx, select the title ("Ti") that contains the movie, which will be the longest one. Uncheck the chapters ("Ch") you don't want to extract, and check Chapter under segmentation ("Seg") to specify that you want separate files for each. For format, check "Elem. Streams" if you want video only or separate audio and video, or "Prog. Streams" if you want both.

4. Uncheck the audio ("Aud") and subtitle ("Sub") tracks you don't want.

5. Click Begin, choose a destination folder, and wait a while.

6. Follow steps 6–8 in PC recipe above, substituting M2V for VOB file-type if you formatted to elementary streams.

7. Follow step 9 in PC recipe above.

Compression Settings

As is clear from the Options... settings in Quicktime, video compression and conversion is insanely complicated. Broadcast standards and file formats have different sizes, scan rates, frame rates, interlacing schemes, quality levels, and other parameters. Even within one codec, there are dozens of ways to tweak the compression. This must be a fascinating area for people who understand it, since it combines algorithms, math, and human perception. At least, it provokes religious-war arguments about which codec is best. For the rest of us, who just want to make clips that look good and work well in a VJ application, your best bet is to refer to the documentation and see what the authors of the software recommend.

Failing this, you just need to experiment with your own rig and find out what works best. The User Guide documents for Discreet's cleaner 6 application, especially Chapter 8: Encoding, available online, provide a good overview of the issues (thanks, Discreet!). Fortunately, since you'll play the clips locally on your own machine rather than distributing them online, you don't have to worry about bandwidth limitations or any "target" machines other than your own. Here are some suggestions for settings to start with:

Codec: Sorenson3, MPEG-4, or Photo-JPEG

Key frame: Key frame rate determines how frequently the compression saves the entire frame, rather than just the difference between it and the previous image. Some codecs specify a key frame at regular intervals, and with others it can vary as needed, like when a shot changes. Other codecs, such as Photo-JPEG, don't use key frames at all. If you plan on doing a lot of scratching with the clip or running it through complex effects, set the key frame rate to 1 (key frame every frame), which makes the file larger but minimizes the burden of calculation on your computer. Otherwise leave the setting blank, for variable key interval, or come up with a number that matches the clip—higher if it has lots of movement and fast cuts, lower if it's static.

Frame rate: 12–30 fps.

Size: 320 x 240 or 640 x 480, depending on your software and laptop. If your computer is really fast, try 800 x 600.

Quality: The High setting is fine. Best usually isn't worth the additional space.

AUDIO AND AUDIO CONTROL STANDARDS

Some VJ hardware and software takes plain audio input for synching or visualization. For this, however, a single audio channel can be converted around— headphone, microphone, RCA audio, and 1/4-inch jacks—with inexpensive adapters. Other VJ tools take MIDI inputs (designed specifically for music, MIDI is a bit like an electronic version of sheet music and has its own cable and connector). For hardware, this means a regular MIDI cable, whereas for software it means a MIDI-USB bridge (M-Audio makes a few) plugged into your laptop.

VIDEO STORAGE / FILE FORMAT STANDARDS

All computer video and image formats are digital, since that's the only way a computer can store information (unlike with videotape or audio tape, where the varying magnetizations can be analog representations). For best results in creating or converting video files for use in a VJ application, you should know the basics of how the file formats (AKA architectures) work.

Digital video makes a distinction between compression standards, or codecs, and file formats. Standards describe the rules and algorithms by which raw video is digitized, compressed, and decompressed—hence the term codec. Some, such as the MPEG codecs, Photo-JPEG, and H.263, are developed by independent standards organizations and published openly. Others, like Cinepak, Sorenson, and RealVideo, are proprietary schemes developed by companies. New standards are engineered to serve new technologies and needs.

For instance, MPEG1 was originally designed in 1991 to put ultra-compressed video on 700 MB CDs (VCDs) at relatively low resolutions (the compression scheme it used for the audio track, MPEG1 Layer 3, took on a life of its own as MP3 audio). MPEG2 was developed in 1994 as part of the higher-quality, 4.7 GB DVD format, and MPEG-4, a more sophisticated ultra-compression scheme than MPEG1, was published in 1998 for limited-bandwidth applications such as downloading, streaming, and teleconferencing.

Specific implementations of these compression standards can be in either hardware (a chip or chipset) or in software. Chips that perform such conversions are called encoders and decoders, or hardware codecs. Pieces of software that run the conversions are called compressors and decompressors, or software codecs.

The files containing the compressed video that these codecs produce follow a file format (also known as a container format or architecture) which is usually distinct from the compression standard. The codec writes the letter, while the file format specifies the envelope that's addressed and sent around by your computer. File formats include Quicktime, VOB, ASF, RealMedia, and DivX. In addition, the MPEG standards can work as their own file formats, so MPEG1, MPEG2, etc. are both codecs and file formats—the aerogrammes of video files.

Most file formats can contain both video and audio streams, packaged so they run together in synch. For example, Microsoft's ASF and WMF formats combine Windows Media Audio (WMA) and Windows Media Video (WMV). VOB, a format used on DVDs, contains Dolby Digital audio and MPEG2 video (which can be within a container format, but needn't be). Some container formats, like Quicktime, may hold tracks from a variety of codecs. Quicktime files can carry video compressed by MPEG, Sorenson, Cinepak, Photo-JPEG, and others.

Separating the audio and video files, which is a good way to create small, portable video clips without sound, is called demultiplexing, or demuxing. Putting them back together is called multiplexing, or muxing.

The commercial file formats Quicktime, WMF, and RealMedia are associated with the Quicktime Player, Windows Media Player, and RealOne Player, respectively. Originally, these players only played files in their own format, but thanks to people's understandable frustration, the walls are breaking down. The Quicktime Player took the early lead in becoming the most versatile of the three, which might be one reason Quicktime seems to be winning the format wars. Fortunately (but not surprisingly), Quicktime is also the favored file format for most VJ applications. As for players, the most versatile of all, beating Quicktime Player, is the free, open-source VLC player from VideoLAN.

Some VJ applications also let you trigger and mix with still pictures and Flash animations. The ones that can handle stills, in .jpg and .gif or sometimes .bmp formats, treat them like single-frame video clips. VJ applications such as Flashmixer play Flash animations only, instead of video files. These .swf files are comparatively much smaller than video, with crisp, vivid, vector-based graphics. In the meantime, an increasing number of VJ applications, including ArKaos and Resolume, can play both video and Flash animations—which is great.

HARDWARE ■ ■ ■ ■

QUICK NOTES ON SOME HARDWARE COMPONENTS VJS USE

Laptop and Tablet Computer
The determining question is Mac vs. PC. Some VJ apps can run on both platforms (see Software chapter), while others run only on one or the other. In
either case, it helps to have multiple monitor support (AKA dual-monitor support or screen spanning), which allows you to run applications on the laptop
screen while feeding video output separately to the projector or mixer.
Without this, you need a scan converter. Apple PowerBooks running OSX have
dual-monitor support standard, while iBooks and other older Macs do not,
although a popular firmware hack called Screen Spanning Doctor adds this
capability. Your VJ application sends the contents of the "stage" to the second monitor, which you configure via System Preferences / Displays.

While the VJ world is super-proportionally Mac-oriented and some of the
best VJ apps are Mac-only, there are also advantages to the right Windows
machines. No matter what, you need a laptop with fast CPU and graphics
processors and a big, fast hard drive. You'll get the best performance from a
super-powered graphics-oriented laptop, AKA a "gamer laptop," like the ones
from Alienware and VoodooPC. These machines eat high-resolution graphics
for breakfast. Meanwhile, a touchscreen, available on some PC laptops and
tablet computers, makes triggering clips much easier.

Digital Projector
This book doesn't discuss projectors much, not because they aren't important,
but because there isn't much to say about them that's specific to VJs. There are
major differences in their technology, resolution, optical geometry, features, etc.,
but they're all basically just very simple, dumb monitors. You hook them up to
any video output source, computer or television. They'll take whatever you feed
them and make it look big, bright, and great. Online, Projector Central is the
best place to read reviews and technical information and find out more.

DVD Player
Any DVD player will work, but small, portable DVD players are nicer—especially
if they have their own screens, which serve as a convenient preview monitor.
One nice but rare feature is the ability to turn off the on-screen display (OSD),

the telltale logo design that appears on your television when it's receiving signal from a DVD player that's empty. Having one of these appear in the middle of a performance while you're swapping DVDs is not considered cool. A DVD player manufacturer would please the VJ community enormously by producing a portable, skip-resistant player that goes all-black rather than showing a logo and that has a small monitor screen built in.

The Pioneer DV-F727 DVD/CD holds three hundred discs, which automatically makes it an interesting piece. Unfortunately, it lacks a couple of features that would make it an amazing VJ tool. First of all, jostling or moving the player causes the discs inside to spill all over, which limits it to permanent installations, such as rack-mounting in a booth at a club. Second, it lacks the memory capabilities that a VJ would want. Rather than being able to save and index a large number of disc/chapter/time points, letting the user arbitrarily cue up specific shots or scenes from the entire disc library, the DV-F727 can only remember how to jump to the beginnings of fifty chapters and the last five time points. But the DVJ-X1 scratching DVD player, also from Pioneer, proves that the company is clued into VJ—so perhaps we can hope for a VJ-friendly three hundred-DVD jukebox that's based on the DV-F727 chassis.

Hard Disk Drive
HDDs are a great way of storing and swapping your libraries of clips. Get Firewire, since it's faster than USB. Some drives are powered through the Firewire cable, rather than a separate power cord, but these are much more expensive and not always as fast. Better to get one with its own power cord, since you're going to be plugging lots of equipment in anyway. If you're often mobile, look for a drive that's fairly rugged. Some cheaper ones are fragile.

Switch (AKA Selector, Switcher)*
These inexpensive, passive devices accept several video inputs and route one of them to a single output. An example is the Radio Shack Model 15-1983 4-Way Audio/Video Selector Switch.

Distribution Amplifier (AKA Splitter)
Distribution amps take a single video input and amplify and duplicate the signal to several outputs, usually four or eight. Splitting the signal requires power, so distribution amplifiers, unlike switches, must be plugged in. People characterize distribution amplifiers by how many outputs they can feed: "one into four," "one into seven," etc. Video duplication houses rely on these devices for making mass-duplicates of tapes, and VJs use them to feed visuals into multiple projectors at once.

Distribution amplifiers are also sometimes referred to as "splitters," but "splitter" more often refers to a cable or small adapter that splits signal without boosting the power, so the outputs have only a fraction of the brightness of the input. These passive devices are only good to perform with if reduced brightness is part of the plan.

<u>Matrix Router</u> (AKA Router, Switcher, Matrix Switcher, Mixer)*
These combine the functions of switches and distribution amplifiers, above. They have multiple in and out jacks, and allow you to send any input to any output. Routers are characterized by how many inputs and outputs they take, so a "four by four" has four at each end, and you designate which input feeds into which output jack by throwing switches or pressing buttons on the front. For large installations or events with multiple VJs at different stations, this allows people to share inputs and outputs.

You can buy distro amps and routers new, but it's generally a better bet to find used ones on Ebay or elsewhere. As professional video studios go digital, they're unloading a lot of rock-solid analog video equipment, and matrix routers are a prime example. To their credit, old matrix routers are typically built like tanks.

<u>Mixer</u> (AKA Switcher)*
If you want fast action and high resolutions, these are essential. They take some number of input sources (the number of channels, commonly two or four), let you mix them together and apply various combinations and effects, and output analog. A preview monitor jack is a very helpful feature; it lets you see the video sources separately. Almost all mixers use analog inputs and outputs, composite and S-video, although the Videonics MXProDV also has a Firewire input for digital. Edirol's V-4 is very popular among VJs—it offers the quality and responsiveness previously associated with professional broadcast studio equipment at a price that's closer to that of older, slower mixers aimed at the wedding-videographer crowd—like the Videonics MX-1. Mixers typically also offer an array of cheesy "wipe" effects.

*Note that the terminology for video switches, switchers, routers, and mixers is often ambiguous, and depends on context or personal habit. For example, what a VJ calls a "mixer," a professional broadcast studio might call a "switcher." And the list goes on.

<u>Scan Converter</u> (AKA Video Converter, Video Scaler, Up Converter, Up-Down Converter, Transcoder)
These devices, which translate between different types of video, are less necessary than they used to be. An increasing number of components now incorporate their functionality internally, for example, projectors that take both VGA and television (composite, S-Video) inputs, and laptops that can put out S-Video in addition to VGA. The main reason remaining to use an external scan converter is to zoom your projector in on the Preview screen of your VJ application in cases where your laptop and software cannot support multiple display monitors. Lots of companies make these, including Sony, AVerMedia, Vine Micro, and Videonics (FOCUS Enhancements).

Camcorder and Camera
A full discussion of cameras and camcorders is beyond the scope of this book. As with DVD players and projectors, the VJ's needs are similar to anyone else's. But look for a camcorder that has an analog pass-through port, so you can use it to convert analog sources to DV. Canon seems to like this feature more than Sony.

Webcam
For speed, choose Firewire over USB. Some have microphones for teleconferencing, which you probably won't need. Popular choices include the iBOT, Fire-i, iREZ, and Apple iSight.

Preview Monitor
Any TV screen will work as a preview monitor, but it helps if they're small, light, and can be easily perched behind your rig. The best candidates, mini LCD screens, come in three forms: professional studio mini-screens, designed to work as preview monitors; portable game screens, which attach to game consoles to keep your kids occupied in the back seat of a car; and in-car entertainment system monitors, which have the same purpose, but are installed on seat backs. The game screens, manufactured by numerous companies, are bulkier, include dual speakers, and take batteries. The in-car screens, from Reactor Car Audio, Lilliput, and others, are simpler and nicer, but require 12V DC power, which adds back some of the clutter.

Quad Splitter (AKA Quad Processor, Video Multiplexer)
These security-industry devices tile multiple video inputs onto a single output—for example, to show multiple security camera images on one screen. VJs use them to monitor several video streams. Prices vary widely, but should be able to get new B/W for less than $150–don't need high-res, since you already know the source—just need to see what it is. Make sure it's simultaneous—the cheapest quad splitters simply rotate through video rather than dividing the screen and showing all input streams at once. Fancy multiplexers allow you to monitor up to sixteen channels at once, (or nine, eight, four, two, or one, dividing the screen in different ways).

MIDI Controller
There are entire trade conventions devoted to these things, but, as a VJ, you don't need anything complicated. For triggering, most VJ applications map to any two-octave keyboard controller. In terms of interface design, this injects a spurious and distracting association between clips and musical notes, but until the VJ world converges on a hardware triggering interface of its own, you'll get used to it.

For continuous controllers, any device with an array of knobs or sliders will work, provided that it has more controllers than the highest number of parameters that apply to effects in your software, plus a few extra reserved to control global parameters. Most effects take no more than six parameters, so a sixteen-knob controller is more than adequate.

Scratch Controller (MIDI-based and other)

You have a few options for scratching with a turntable interface. You can retrofit any turntable to control video on your computer using Ms. Pinky or the EJ MIDI Turntable. Ms. Pinky relies on a special pink vinyl disc, and you feed the turntable output into an audio interface, such as M-Audio's MobilePre USB, which is connected to your computer. The information Ms. Pinky sends is in a proprietary format, but the system is popular, and it works with Max/MSP, Livid Union, and other software.

The pricier EJ MIDI Turntable uses a barcode-like disc and an optical cartridge that attaches to your turntable's tonearm. The cartridge connects to a small interface box with that with MIDI outputs. The advantages here are that the optical needle won't skip, and the system can talk to any application that understands MIDI. Tascam's TT-M1 has a similar idea—it fits onto the side of a turntable and reads the platter's motion like an optical mouse. Unfortunately, it can only send control information to a limited number of Tascam's own CD players, rather than producing MIDI.

Another popular way to scratch is using the Mixman DM2. This two-platter device was originally released by Mattel and Thomas Dolby's Beatnik and aimed at kids, but it now has a following among DJs and VJs and is available through Digital Blue. The inexpensive DM2 plugs directly into your PC via USB (no Mac compatibility), and free DM2-to-MIDI software, available elsewhere, converts its input into MIDI for use by other applications.

You can also scratch video using a jog/shuttle controller.

Jog/shuttle Controller (AKA Jog Wheel)

These input devices center around a ring with a finger-sized indentation that lets you dial forward or backward at varying speeds. It's a good physical interface for scratching, as well as fast-forwarding or otherwise touring around through long video tracks. Popular controllers include the Shuttle Xpress and ShuttlePRO, from Contour Design.

Game Controller

This category represents a world of its own, from standard joysticks and gamepads to data gloves like the Data Glove 5 from 5DT (Fifth Dimension Technologies). They're typically USB devices that generate mouse/cursor position input, as well as keyboard shortcut inputs which you can customize.

Graphics Tablet and Tablet Controller

Tablets are the best input devices for generating fine-grained position data from precise gestures, which is nice if you're "painting" graphics or subtly tweaking effects parameters. Wacom is the leading manufacturer for these.

A newer type of hardware in this category is the STC-1000 single touch controller from Mercurial Innovations Group. The surface of this tablet uses "synthetic skin" which is sensitive to pressure as well as position, adding a Z coordinate to the standard X and Y. Aimed at musicians and other performers, the STC-100 generates MIDI output rather than acting as a mouse. Note also that it isn't as precise as a standard graphics tablet along the X and Y axes.

Miscellaneous Sensors and Input Devices

Any sensor or input device you want to rig up has the potential to add to the mix. For example, Electro-Cap International manufactures an elastic cap with embedded electrodes designed to give EEG readings. A CV-to-MIDI converter will translate varying voltages to MIDI signal. Who wants to VJ with their brainwaves?

Screen and Screen Material

Many VJs and video installation artists do amazing things with screens, and an entire book could be dedicated to creative designs that reject the tyranny of the flat rectangle. Any light-colored fabric can be rigged up to act as a projection surface with sculptural qualities. You can float stretchable fabrics in mid-air by wrapping coins in corners of the fabric, then tying pieces of string above the coins and using the strings to suspend or stretch the fabric into position. Screens can rotate, flap in the breeze, etc.

A scrim—netted, semi-transparent fabric—can literally add depth to your performance by letting you overlay projections in front of another. Stage designers have developed various types of scrim with different reflective properties and transparency levels.

Screen Goo from Goo Systems is a line of reflective acrylic paints designed to turn any wall or surface into a projection screen. One formulation enables transparent surfaces, such as Plexiglas, to display rear- or dual-direction projections.

Optical and Film Projector

Overheads: If you can't find one of these second-hand, 3M and Eiki still make them. The cheapest ones shine at a dazzling 2200 lumens. Some perspective: for the cost of one digital projector equalling the same brightness, you could buy at least ten overheads.

16mm: If not available second-hand, you haven't been looking very hard. Bell & Howell, Eiki, and Elmo make these.

Slide: If not available second-hand, Kodak, Vivitar, and others still manufacture these.

Filmstrip: If not available second-hand, good luck.

Fog Machine, Smoke Machine, Hazer

Fog machines based on water-glycol solutions are friendlier than smokers, which leave an oily residue. Among small, inexpensive units, the Antari F-80Z is a favorite. For high-volume units, check out High End Systems and Jem.

Miscellaneous Pro (read: Expensive) VJ Equipment

The DVJ-X1 from Pioneer DJ is the first-ever scratching DVD player, a great unit and a real shot in the arm for the VJ cause (although, astonishingly, it lacks MIDI-out).

The Kaoss Pad Entrancer from Korg is a audio/video effects box with a touchpad that lets you manipulate broadcast-quality video in dazzling ways with a fast, sure hardware interface.

The PowerMac-based Catalyst Pro Media Server and DL.1 Digital Light, both from High End Systems, let you project video from a moving projector head—any video you want, zooming around the room however you like.

The Hippotizer Pro from Green Hippo and the DV7-PR from Edirol are digital content servers (like the Catalyst) that let you trigger vast numbers of high-res video clips from touchscreen interfaces.

Miscellaneous Consumer Equipment

The Space Projector, from Mathmos, is a popular psychedelic oil-wheel projector.

The Baby Magic Theater from Philips projects colorful, rotating slides that are intended to lull your baby to sleep, but are also ideal for any "chill room" environment.

SOFTWARE ▪ ▪ ▪ ▪

ABOUT VJ APPLICATIONS

VJ software has exploded over the past few years. In the late 1990s, there were only a handful of VJ and visualizer applications: ArKaos, VJamm, Cthugha, and a few others. Today the Audiovisualizers.com website lists over one hundred. Some of these are personal projects, written and shared for fun, and supported in the authors' spare time, as time allows—or no longer supported at all. As one website explains, "x|GRIND is asleep. I've been fantastically busy with free-lance work and other endeavors, and can't in good conscience continue to sell x|GRIND in its perpetually beta state." Other VJ apps have more backing, with at least some engineer-hours sustainably dedicated to support, but the inter-face and manual are only in Japanese.

Fortunately, this still leaves dozens of semi-supported and well-supported apps with English language interfaces, with more coming up all the time. These are typically written and maintained by either an author with a long-term personal, professional investment in live video, or else by a forward-looking small company that's actually trying to make a go of VJ software as a viable business. More of the software is written for MacOS than for Linux/Unix or Windows machines, but there's plenty on all platforms. This is still a field of independents, and no big-name software company has yet bought or devel-oped a live video performance product (unless you count Japan's Digital Stage, makers of Motion Dive). But it seems like a natural for a company like Adobe or AViD, or even Apple.

Prices for VJ software vary widely. Many popular apps are distributed free, others as nagware (AKA annoyware), which you can download and use without paying, but until you buy a license key (usually under $25), it throws a screen in your face asking for money. Higher-end apps range from $75 to around $300, with downloadable sample installations to let you try before you buy, and unlock the full functionality by paying for a license key.

Some apps, such as Arkaos, let you get started quickly and do great stuff but stay at a fairly simple level. Others, such as Isadora and VDMX, are more serious applications which reward a steeper learning curve with greater control and flexibility. At the far end of the spectrum is Max/MSP + Jitter, a multime-dia programming language (Max/MSP) with a compatible library of video objects (Jitter), which you can learn by taking a three-credit, semester-long course at many art schools. Meanwhile, applications throughout the ease-of-use spectrum are tapping into OpenGL, a library of graphics effects, to create real-time video effects. OpenGL isn't open-source, but it's an open standard very loosely controlled by SGI, and it provides lots of fast-processing visual possibilities for live video.

There's no *Consumer Reports* for VJ software, despite the huge array of choices. So VJs tend to try and use the apps they've heard good things about and that their friends use. Some VJs generously and helpfully post individual reviews to VJCentral.com, but with so many voices and perspectives, it's hard to calibrate them against one another. The following mini-reviews compare some popular VJ applications head-to-head from a single perspective, following a uniform review format. This is a fairly superficial exploration for a couple of reasons, and is offered only as a starting point. First of all, the listing is incomplete and is based on arbitrary guesswork at time of writing, of which thirty or so English-version applications seem most popular and most likely to survive for a while. In other words, some good ones were left out (which is the overall story of this book).

More significantly, this software was tested at home with only my own hardware and clips, for just long enough to understand the general interface layout and capabilities but without gauging actual reliability under live performance conditions. This review process can be "fooled" by software that demos well, showing a good range of features and a clear interface, but frequently crashes in practice. Software like this is a VJ nightmare, and it's far better to use an application that's clunkier or less versatile, but more reliable. *Caveat VI.*

Also, different applications vary in regards to the characteristics of video files they work best with: their formats, dimensions, length, and how they were compressed. Because of this, it makes sense to collect only a small number of sample clips before trying out different applications. Then, after you've decided which app(s) you want to use, you can start ripping, shooting, synthesizing, editing, and otherwise building up a larger library of clips, saving them all out in the particular formats that your software likes.

Note also that Linux/Unix applications are not included. This is another gap, since Linux is the OS of the 21st century and the GNU Public License is one of the great political/legal documents of human history—but you Linux people are good at figuring things out on your own anyway. I apologize for the omission, but perhaps a future edition of this book will include a broader and more rigorous reviews section. Fingers crossed. Anyway, with all disclaimers now comfortably in place, here are the reviews:

VJ Application Types

Applications tend to fall into several main categories, with plenty of overlaps and exceptions here and there. The general types, listed in roughly increasing order of price and learning curve, are:

Visualization/eye candy plugins automatically generate abstract video to accompany music.

Live video players apply live inputs to affect the playback of a single video clip at a time.

Video synthesizers generate live video from user input, not based on playing clips.

Video performance tools are a catch-all category for applications that produce live video in various ways, not necessarily emphasizing either synthesized video or video clips.

Live video mixers let you trigger, mix, and run live effects on stored video clips. This is the classic style of VJ application.

Construction sets and programming environments let you build virtual video instruments by graphically linking together video sources and processes, and then perform with the instruments.

REVIEWS

Name: ArKaos VJ 3.0
From: ArKaos
What: Live video mixer
Website: *http://www.arkaos.net*
OS: Mac OSX, Win
Price: €279
Version tested: 3.0.1 for Windows
Simple, single-screen, triggering-oriented interface lets you assign clips and a wide range of effects to keys on keyboard or attached MIDI controller. User-defined "patches" assign keys to clips and effects, together or separately, and you can easily switch among different patches. Lower part of interface shows keyboard (either computer/typewriter style, or Oxygen8-style two-octave piano) with tiny thumbnails indicating clip and effect. Dual-screen capable. Easy, fast switching between "patches." Fast and responsive, and doesn't crash easily. Handles a wide range of video clip and image formats, and can also run interactive "generators" from Flash or Director files. MIDI-in control disabled in demo version. Event recorder lets you export mixes to Quicktime. Good documentation.

Name: BluffTitler DX9
From: Outerspace Software
What: Specialized app generates neato-looking titles live from text input
Website: *http://www.blufftitler.us*
OS: Win
Price: €30

Name: Flowmotion 2.5
From: Robotfunk
What: Live video mixer

Website: *http://www.robotfunk.com*
OS: Mac OSX, Win
Price: €135
Version tested: 2.0 for Windows
Channel-oriented interface simultaneously previews and runs five sources, drawn from live capture and "bank" of clips up top, letting you mix, superimpose, and change tempos using fader/slider controls. Dual-screen capable. Better suited for slowly blending live video and clips rather than fast-triggering large numbers of short sources, therefore lends itself better to relaxed, "trance"-style music than fast collage. Sleek, monochrome interface sacrifices standardness and familiarity for looks. Seems a bit flaky with long clips, and can freeze up, which gives it a "sports car" feel—touchy and unforgiving, but capable and responsive once you understand its limits.

Name: G-Force
From: SoundSpectrum
What: Visualization/eye candy music player plug-in
Website: *http://soundspectrum.com*
OS: Mac, Win
Price: Free, $10 upgrade to "Gold" version

Name: Grid2
From: Vidvox
What: Clip triggering tool
Website: *http://www.vidvox.net*
OS: Mac OSX
Price: $75
Version tested: Grid2 2.0.1
Specialized application for clip-triggering, lets you use laptop as video loop server for feeding into hardware mixer or other device. Sure and responsive, with simple, clear interface that makes maximum use of screen real estate for showing clips. Row of controls at bottom tweak speed, direction, MIDI synching, and other settings. You can scratch with slider at bottom, or by attaching ShuttlePro USB jog-wheel controller. Excellent documentation.

Name: Isadora
From: TroikaTronix
What: Live video construction set and performance tool
Website: *http://www.troikatronix.com*
OS: Mac OSX first, Win
Price: $350
Version tested: 1.0
Intuitive and very flexible interface lets you define sequences of scenes, each of which you compose via visual programming, chaining together inputs (including cursor position), outputs, and processes —like a more accessible version of Max/MSP. Scene-by-scene organization makes it well-suited to scripted performances such as storytelling, but you can also just build one scene and work off of that. In fact, Isadora comes with "Video Toy," which is a good, ready-to-use DJ-style video mixer (two screens and a fader) that's written as a single scene. Excellent documentation.

Name: Keyworx
From: Waag Society
What: Multi-user live video mixer
Website: *http://classic.keyworx.org*
OS: Mac OSX
Price: Free

Name: Max/MSP + Jitter
From: Cycling '74
What: Live audio/video programming environment and performance tool, with video toolset
Website: *http://www.cycling74.com*
OS: Mac OSX, Win
Price: $850, $59 for students (proof of current enrollment required)
Max/MSP is a full, professional programming environment for live audiovisual performance, and Jitter is a compatible library of live video objects. Max/MSP is a visual programming language which lets you connect together inputs, outputs, and processes onscreen, set parameters, and essentially build your own interface for live performance, whether it's arranged like a mixer, or any other instrument. Input and output objects can be either virtual (timers, software synthesizers) or hardware (tablets, MIDI controllers, cameras, projectors, sound equipment), with proper drivers in place. It's all the same as far as Max/MSP is concerned, and any connection that makes sense logically is possible to program and perform with. Max/MSP and Jitter constitute a small world of their own, and to use them, you have to learn them first, which takes some time. But no live performance software is more powerful. There's also dedicated developer support, a large and active user community, and excellent documentation.

Name: Meta-CC
From: Conglomco Media Conglomeration
What: Live video captioner/text crawl, can run streamed online or in live performance
Website: *http://www.meta-cc.net*
OS: Any (browser-based)
Price: Free

Name: MidiVid 1.12
From: Jason Dorie (DJ midnight) and Fred Pradel (DJ Lace)
What: Live video player
Website: *http://www.midivid.com*
OS: Win
Price: Free
Simple triggering app with good, basic effects, but I couldn't get it to work on XP; may be better suited to Win98.

Name: Modul8 V2.0
From: GarageCUBE
What: Live video mixer
Website: *http://www.garagecube.com*
OS: Mac OSX
Price: €295

Name: MilkDrop
From: Geisswerks
What: Visualizer/eye candy music player plugin
Website: *http://www.geisswerks.com*
OS: Win
Price: Free

Name: MooNSTER
From: MoDEL
What: Live video synthesizer
Website: *http://www.moonster.org*
OS: Win
Price: $60

SOFTWARE

Name: motion dive.tokyo
From: Digital Stage
What: Live video mixer
Website: *http://www.digitalstage.net/en*
OS: Mac, Win
Price: $349
Version tested: mdt trial En
Interface is laid out following the DJ metaphor, two screens on either side of a fader control. The look is pure gamer, with a dark grey cockpit style, but beneath the aggressive skin is a solid, responsive application. You assign clips to pageable grids at the bottom and apply basic effects, including a nice color-changing dial. Synchs to MIDI input. Dual-screen capable, but you need to drag main window over to second screen and then run at full-screen. Easy starter application, and demo version opens with mini tutorial.

Name: Onadime Composer
From: Onadime
What: Live video performance tool
Website: http://www.onadime.com
OS: Mac OS9
Price: $199

Name: OpenTZT (based on TransZendenT, AKA TZT)
From: OpenTZT Project
What: Open-source version of TransZendenT live video mixer
Website: *http://sourceforge.net/projects/opentzt*
OS: Win
Price: Shareware, donations gladly accepted

Name: Pilgrim R2
From: Pilgrim Visuals / Loose Goose
What: Live video mixer
Website: *http://www.pilgrim-visuals.com*
OS: Win
Price: $139

Name: PixelToy
From: LairWare
What: Live video performance tool
Website: *http://www.lairware.com/pixeltoy*
OS: Mac
Price: $20

Name: Resolume 2.0
From: Resolume
What: Live video mixer
Website: *http://www.resolume.com*
OS: Win
Price: $199
Combines triggering and channel-oriented interfaces. A 5x5 subset of the keyboard triggers clips, while three layers run concurrently, à la Flowmotion, letting you mix and apply effects to the currently-running channels. App seems easy to overload, rendering sliders somewhat unresponsive. Unique features include the ability to send different combinations of layers to multiple projectors,

and a "Chaos" mode that triggers and mixes clips and applies effects randomly, which is great for taking a break. (But hopefully, people will still notice that you're gone.)

Name: Rhythmic Circle FUSE (RC FUSE)
From: Mash Studio
What: Live video mixer
Website: *http://www.mashstudio.com*
OS: Win, Mac OS9
Price: $99 for English version, available at *http://www.audiovisualizers.com*

Name: SVi
From: Oishii
What: Live video player
Website: *http://oishii.org/svi*
OS: Win
Price: Free

Name: TouchMixer 017
From: Derivative
What: Live video synthesizer
Website: *http://www.derivativeinc.com*
OS: Win
Price: $199
The interface seems very intelligently designed and well-suited to abstract, trance-y visual creations, but unfortunately this application brought my mortal Dell Inspiron laptop to its knees. This software may work well on high-powered, gaming laptops, or it might just need to wait until computers are faster.

Name: VDMX
From: Vidvox
What: Live video mixer
Website: *http://www.vidvox.net*
OS: Mac OSX
Price: $250
Version tested: VDMXX
Clean interface provides far more depth and flexibility than most VJ apps. It abstracts a range of possible inputs, outputs, and processes (such as effects and synchronization), and lets you tie them together and apply them in arbitrary combinations using virtual buses and a virtual matrix router. The application doesn't devote screen space to a clip-thumbnails window, so you need to know your sources by filename (or supply them from someplace else, like another laptop running Grid2 or GridPro). This is the most serious and well-designed mixing application tested, but it's also the most abstract, and it takes time to learn. You can't just import a bunch of clips and start noodling around by eye. Excellent documentation.

Name: Union
From: Livid Performance Technology
What: VJ controller application
Website: *http://www.lividinstruments.com*
OS: Mac OSX
Price: $299
Like many other easy-to-learn VJ apps, Livid Union centers its interface around the DJ metaphor: two screens on either side of a mixer. But among starter apps with this format, it's the most powerful, thanks to a dizzying collection of effects, which are controllable onscreen by a bank of virtual knobs

and sliders, or offscreen by outboard hardware controllers. Union can also synch to MIDI input, and it has an Automator that lets it run by itself, like Resolume's Chaos mode, but more controllable.

Name: Videodelic
From: U & I Software
What: Live video synthesizer / performance tool
Website: *http://www.uisoftware.com*
OS: Mac OS9 (OSX version in the works)
Price: $249

Name: visualJockey R3.5
From: Visualight Studios
What: Live video mixer
Website: *http://www.visualjockey.com*
OS: Win
Price: $199
Like Isadora, this interface is more composition-oriented than other apps. You chain together sequences of clip/effect clusters with transitions in between, then play in sequence, triggering from section to section via assigned keys. There's no dual-screen support, which "goes against the visualJockey philosophy" according to documentation, because keys already give full control without any need for a second screen. Also, there's no MIDI input. This app's emphasis on scripted, sequential performance makes it intriguing, especially for storytelling, but its limiting interface seems to be designed by someone with very specific ideas about how to construct and perform live video.

Name: VJamm Pro
From: Camart
What: Live video mixer
Website: *http://www.camart.co.uk/vjamm*
OS: Win
Price: $299, original VJamm available from *http://ninjatune.net* for $10
Simple, cute application plays a limited number of video clips with sound, allowing you to maintain the beat with MIDI input. Interface is spare but responsive. No dual-screen support.

Name: WIMP (Windows Interface Manipulation Program)
From: DXLab (Victor Laskin and Alexei Shulgin)
What: App that vividly animates (messes with) a Windows desktop
Website: *http://www.wimp.ru*
OS: Win
Price: Free

Name: x |GRIND
From: Kenneth Woodruff
What: Live video synthesizer / performance tool
Website: *http://www.xgrind.com*
OS: Win, Mac OS9
Price: Unsupported shareware

Name: Zuma 3.0
From: 3dMaxMedia
What: Live video synthesizer / performance tool
Website: *http://www.3dmaxmedia.com*
OS: Win
Price: $59

LEGAL ISSUES ■ ■ ■ ■

VJS WHO APPROPRIATE COPYRIGHTED MATERIAL step into the same thicket of legal issues that the music world's rappers and rippers have struggled through for years. On the one hand, the owner of a copyrighted work such as a movie owns the exclusive rights to publicly display the work and to create derivative works. On the other hand, the legal notion of Fair Use allows limited amounts of quotation or sampling under certain circumstances, for certain purposes, and with certain underlying intents.

What courts have deemed Fair Use and infringement in the past has varied widely. Creating a parody of an entire song, for example, has been deemed legal, while sampling a short excerpt from one for non-parodic purposes has not. Thanks to the Digital Millennium Copyright Act (DMCA), fair use also varies across media. While it's clear that book reviewers may freely quote short written excerpts, you can't copy a single frame from a movie you own on DVD onto your computer without permission from the studio to decrypt the DVD.

Consumer electronics and the internet have turned copyright and intellectual property into a huge battlefield for the culture industry. Much of the relevant legislation was written decades ago and is open to wide-ranging interpretations given today's tech-driven scenarios; the newly-added DMCA hurts more than it helps. For this reason, it's impossible to make accurate general statements about what is and isn't legal—the courts need to decide these issues case by case.

Meanwhile, VJs and other artists will make their own assessments of what they can get away with. Many of them, presumably attracted to righteous civil disobedience, intentionally push the envelope—witness the "Illegal Art" exhibit that toured New York, Chicago, and San Francisco, a collection of works chosen because they violate or otherwise challenge intellectual property laws.

If the film and video industries begin seeing VJ as a more of a threat in the future, it's conceivable that they might form a body to demand fees from clubs that perform video. ASCAP has played this role on behalf of music publishers for years, offering blanket performance licenses for its catalogue of composers and enforcing compliance by sending "spies" into individual clubs and maintaining an intimidating legal department. A video equivalent sounds like a good job for the MPAA or a newly-formed collecting society.

GENERAL GUIDELINES

Amid the fuzziness of Fair Use, the Copyright Act gives us a non-exclusive four-factor test, instructing courts to examine: 1) the purpose and character of the use (non-commercial, critical, and transformative are better than commercial duplication); 2) the nature of the copyrighted work; 3) the amount and substantiality of the portion used; and 4) the effect on the market for the original. The more of these factors are on your side, the better.

There are a few general guidelines for VJs who want to use appropriated material legally without having to get permissions from the owners.

1. Don't record your performance or (worse) allow it to be broadcast.
Insert obligatory Gil-Scott Heron quote about "The Revolution" here.

2. Use short samples from multiple sources.
If you're just messing around with one movie, for example, you may be "publicly displaying a work" and "creating a derivative work," both of which actions the copyright owner has the exclusive right to do. You'll also run into fair use factor 3. Better to draw from multiple sources and create something new and clearly different (which is more interesting anyway).

3. Make sure no one profits from your performance.
Commercial use of someone else's imagery is less likely to be considered "Fair Use." (factors 1 and 4)

4. Emphasize criticism, commentary, or parody of source materials.
Amazingly enough, these rebel virtues actually help any "Fair Use" argument you might make. (factor 1)

5. Use factual and published materials.
It's also more typically "Fair Use" to lift factual and published materials, rather than imaginative and unpublished works. If you steal footage from your housemate's work-in-progress independent feature, they have ample legal justification for calling your actions "unfair," even if you don't settle the matter within the court system. (factor 2)

6. Use neglected materials that won't impact anyone's profits.
Sampling some old, obscure movie that hasn't been published on DVD and isn't making money for anyone is more likely to be deemed "Fair Use" than ripping a major new video release that's topping the charts at Blockbuster. (factor 4)

WHAT'S LEGAL WHERE

With this in mind, and all appropriate disclaimers in place, the chart below is an attempt to provide some guidance regarding what you can mix with in various settings. Row and column headings are explained below. But keep in mind that valid legal advice can only come within the context of an attorney-client relationship, from a lawyer who knows all of the specifics relevant to your individual situation. *The information here is no substitute for the advice of a licensed attorney.*

What you can VJ with, and where		Setting				
		Private	Educational	Non-commercial Public	Commercial Public	Broadcast
Sources	Original captured	OK	OK	OK	OK	OK
	Original rendered	OK	OK	Probably - check software license	Maybe - check software license	Maybe - check software license
	Public domain or Creative Commons license	OK	Setting	Probably - check source's terms of use	Maybe - check source's terms of use	Maybe - check source's terms of use
	Games	OK	Maybe - depends on intent, etc.	Maybe - check software license	Maybe - check software license	Maybe - check software license
	Commercial	OK	Maybe - depends on intent, etc.	Probably	No	No
	Copied, commercial, illegally obtained	Maybe, but ripping it in the first place was illegal	No	No	No	No
Subjects	Private individuals	OK	OK	OK	OK - with model release	OK - with model release
	Public figures	OK	OK	OK	OK	OK
	Logos	OK	OK	Maybe	No	No

Settings (Columns)

Private
Private performances take place in the home for an audience consisting mainly of friends and family, with no admission charge. In this context, you can show whatever you want, so long as it's legally obtained, without having to worry about infringing copyrights.

Educational
Copyright law recognizes special exemptions for public schools and nonprofit educational institutions, provided that the performances have an educational purpose, are performed by the instructors and pupils themselves (rather than an outside artist), take place in the regular classroom, require no admission charge or other payments, and are lawfully made. If you are not a real teacher, it would be ill-advised to claim, for legal purposes, that your VJ performances are "educational." But if you are a professional educator, you have a special opportunity to do interesting and fun video work with your students. Go for it!

Non-commercial public performances
This is when you're performing in a public place, or any place with "a substantial number of persons outside of a normal circle of a family and its acquaintances," but no one is charging admission or otherwise making any money off of your performance. This may or may not apply to settings such as the Burning Man festival, a large private event that takes place on public land. Burning Man does charge admission, but the many VJ performances there are offered free of any further charge, just like all the other performances and exhibits.

Commercial public performances
As with non-commercial public performances above, these take place in public-accessible places or else contain large numbers of people outside your immediate circle. But in addition, people are making money off the event. Restaurants and bars are commercial public performance spaces, even if they don't charge separately for the music or video being performed.

Broadcast
The performance is recorded or transmitted, available to people who aren't physically present.

Sources (Rows)

Original captured
Video that you've shot and edited yourself, on your own time, using equipment that doesn't have any strings attached (you didn't borrow it from work, where your employee contract says the footage therefore belongs to them).

Original rendered

Video that you've rendered or synthesized yourself, with same caveat about ownership as with Original captured, above.

Public domain or Creative Commons license

Video you've obtained from a source such as the Prelinger Archives, or under a Creative Commons license which authorizes some uses of the material. Public domain is material in which there is no copyright (such as expired copyright or U.S. government works). This category includes scans of illustrations from old books with expired copyrights.

Games

Video you've saved or otherwise captured from a commercial game title.

Commercial

Video from a commercial source, no matter what the medium or how it's obtained. This includes video fed directly from the output of a DVD, VCR, or other device playing a pre-recorded disc or tape that you've bought commercially. It also includes video clips that you've legally copied from a commercial source onto a hard drive or other storage medium, triggerable with VJ software, such as news footage, commercials, or movie trailers.

Copied, commercial, illegally obtained

Video clips ripped or otherwise decrypted, without the copyright owner's permission, from an encrypted commercial source to a storage medium. These are illegal. To legally VJ with lots of movie clips, you'll need to invest in a DVD jukebox. But even then, your mixer's frame buffer might be breaking the law as well, because it's constantly storing a couple of seconds' worth of unencrypted signal. So don't use any delay-based effects when the MPAA is around.

Subjects (Rows)

Private individuals

Likenesses of people that you've captured yourself via photo, video, or other means. This material is yours, but you can't use it for commercial purposes without having your subjects sign a model release. Also, you can't defame them.

Public figures

You can use any public figure's likeness that you've captured or created for some commercial purposes without obtaining a model release—that's how paparazzi and editorial cartoonists can stay afloat. But you can't use these images in advertising or otherwise imply their subjects' endorsement. You also can't defame them, but for public figures, this is harder to prove than it is with private individuals.

<u>Logos</u>
Logos like the Nike swoosh have special protection against infringement or "dilution." You can't use them to imply endorsement of the work, but can use them in documentary or critical contexts. Parodies of logos, modified so that they're clearly different from the originals, are fine.

PRECEDENTS

(Many important recent IP precedents come from music, but video will undoubtedly get its turn.)

<u>Encyclopedia Britannica Educ. Corp. v. Crooks</u>, 558 F. Supp. 1247 (W.D.N.Y. 1983)
It was illegal for the defendant to systematically make off-air copies of educational programs and distribute them as a business (but as a teacher, you might be able to make one copy to show to your own classes).

<u>Los Angeles News Service v. Tullo</u>, 973 F.2d 791 (9th Cir. 1992)
It was illegal for the defendant to take commercial footage owned by someone else, mix it into their own video productions, and sell the result without obtaining permissions.

<u>Sony Corp. of America v. Universal City Studios, Inc.</u>, 464 U.S. 417, 104 S.Ct. 774 (1984)
It's legal for Sony to manufacture and sell video recording equipment, even if consumers might use it to infringe upon copyrights in their homes.

<u>Campbell v. Acuff-Rose</u>, 510 U.S. 569, 114 S.Ct. 1164 (1994)
Because it's a parody, the 2 Live Crew song "Pretty Woman" does not infringe upon the Roy Orbison song "Oh, Pretty Woman."

<u>Teleprompter Corp. v. Columbia Broadcasting System, Inc.</u>, 415 U.S. 394 (1974)
It was legal for community antenna television (CATV) system to retransmit television broadcasts to paying subscribers because reception and retransmission does not constitute a "performance" of a copyrighted work.

<u>Bright Tunes Music Corp. v. Harrisongs Music</u>, Ltd., 420 F. Supp. 177 (S.D. N.Y. 1976)
George Harrison's song "My Sweet Lord" infringed upon the Chiffons' "He's So Fine" because they share a distinctive combination of two musical motifs (even if Harrison did not appropriate them consciously).

<u>Grand Upright Music Limited v. Warner Brothers Records, Inc.</u>, 780 F.Supp. 182 (S.D. N.Y. 1991)
Biz Markie's song "Alone Again" infringed upon Gilbert O'Sullivan's "Alone Again (Naturally)" because it contained a direct sample from O'Sullivan's recording.

LESSONS FROM FILM EDITING ▪ ▪ ▪ ▪

SINCE THE INVENTION OF CINEMA, film editors have been both discovering and influencing the ways that our brains put together and interpret visual perceptions. The resulting body of work, sometimes called "the language of film," constitutes a sort of visual and audiovisual grammar. Some of the rules of this grammar are innate, proceeding from how our eyes follow motion, assume object persistence, and interpolate, or how we automatically posit cause-and-effect. Other rules are conventions, useful and familiar, but subject to (slow) change. Sometimes it's hard to separate nature and nurture enough to know which rules are which, but they all dictate how the film editor should assemble footage in order to communicate clearly and have certain effects.

For the VJ, these rules accomplish the same things, which makes them a great resource. Knowing basic editing technique enables you to fabricate new meanings by shuffling clips around, and imply relationships and interactions between objects and people that never actually existed in the same space. Talk about a recipe for fun!

Here, then, are some film editing rules, lifted and reverse-engineered for VJ from Karel Reisz and Gavin Millar's *The Technique of Film Editing* and Daniel Arijon's *Grammar of the Film Language* (the fantastic '70s-era illustrations of which, alone, are worth the price).

Action and Reaction

There are no cuts in real life; our eyes give us a continuous stream from a single point of view. But we make sense of the world by following action and reaction, which is why cutting between the two seems so natural, and the conclusions implied by these cuts are accepted automatically by our minds, without question. Pioneer filmmakers and theorists Lev Kuleshov and V.I. Pudovkin demonstrated this with some instructive experiments on how audiences interpret sequences of shots.

In one experiment, they showed an audience an actor smiling, then a gun, and then the same actor looking terrified. To another audience, they showed the same three shots with the order reversed. The first audience saw the actor character as cowardly, while the second audience saw him as heroic. Another experiment showed an audience the same shot of an actor with a neutral expression, cut against shots of a bowl of soup, a dead woman, and a girl playing. Pudovkin reports (as quoted in Reisz, p. 31):

When we showed the three combinations to an audience which had not been let into the secret the result was terrific. The public raved about the acting of the artist. They pointed out the heavy pensiveness of his mood over the forgotten soup, were touched and moved by the deep sorrow with which he looked on the dead woman, and admired the light, happy smile with which he surveyed the girl at play. But we knew that in all three cases the face was exactly the same.

The "Kuleshov effect," as this phenomenon is called (and which puppeteers probably knew about all along), makes reaction shots a powerful device which can be used to make anyone or anything that's imbued with consciousness look like they're having a particular reaction to anything else.

Reaction shots of people's expressions are always close-ups, and they're typically short, less than two seconds (unless the subject is listening to someone, with the audio carrying over, which is unlikely in VJ). It's generally most effective to show a reaction shot first to make the audience wonder what the character is reacting to, then show the action, which explains it, and then cut back and show the reaction again, reinforcing the connection.

To imply any kind of action and reaction, physical as well as expressive, cut back and forth, interleaving the two subjects. To show a hunter shooting a bird, for example, show the hunter aiming the gun, the bird flying, the hunter shooting, and then the bird falling.

To suggest that something is being shown from a character's own point of view, interleave close-ups with shots where the camera (real or virtual) is moving or otherwise changing its view. For example, interleaving live camera captures of a grinning audience member with the fast-zooming "trip sequence" from *2001: A Space Odyssey* (1968) suggests that the audience member him- or herself is experiencing a "trip." A similar message would be conveyed by cutting in blurred, unsteady live shots of the room.

Juxtaposition
When it isn't logical or possible for two clips to be directly related in the same space, interleaving them won't imply direct relationship. But it will suggest similarity or some other connection, filled in by the viewer. For example, Pudovkin's *The End of St. Petersburg* (1927) cross-cuts shots of soldiers fighting and dying in trenches with stockbrokers rushing to the stock exchange, implying that businesses are profiting from the war. In other cases, the connection is symbolic, as when flying birds represent a prisoner's desire for freedom, or the snuffing of a candle represents a murder.

Another approach juxtaposes unrelated shots that somehow look similar, drawing a visual as well as semantic connection. This is also a favorite artsy-filmmaker way to transition between scenes. The iconic shot of the walking band of thieves in *Reservoir Dogs* (1992) can, for example, be juxtaposed with the visually similar shot of several emperor penguins waddling toward the water, from the nature documentary *Winged Migration* (2001).

Montages are a type of sequence in which there's no dialog—just quick cuts, usually set to music, showing many different shots that make some overall point. Shots are held only long enough for their content to be understood. This form is obvious VJ territory, and once the theme of the montage is established, any clips mixed in will be interpreted as somehow bearing upon the unifying theme, with possible confusing and/or amusing results.

Geometry and Motion

Audiences pay close attention, subconsciously or otherwise, to the left vs. right sides of the screen. Objects appearing on one side should stay on that same side across shots, or be shown crossing over. Otherwise it gets confusing. Similarly, if an object is shown to be moving right to left (or left to right), it should continue moving in the same general direction, or be shown to turn around. Therefore, if you show a series of clips of different objects moving in the same direction, they will seem to be the same object or at least strongly associated.

You can suggest a dialog between two entities by cutting between them, making sure that they face toward each other, in opposite directions, from their own sides of the screen. This geometry should be maintained even if they're talking on the phone. When two figures face in the same direction, it implies that they're both looking at the same thing. Cut in something else, and that's what they're both looking at.

To suggest a journey, show a figure leaving the frame, then crossing successive frames in the same direction, and finally stopping in the middle of the last frame. No matter how varied the backgrounds for each successive frame, the audience will interpret them as being close together in time. If that's not the meaning you're after, you can intersperse shots of maps or standard time indicators such as turning calendar pages or changing seasons. (These handy clichés are discussed more fully later.) Whenever a figure leaves the frame, hold the empty frame for a few seconds afterward to let the meaning sink in.

Slapstick is funnier when you delay the character's registration of the pratfall, and violent motions or explosions are more vivid when fragmented and shown repeating in quick cuts from different angles. Action sequences are by nature extremely difficult to improvise, however. To stay engaging, they must continuously ride the line between what is and isn't physically possible, and whether the conflict will turn one way or the other. This requires specific and precisely matched shots within a realistic-looking and perfectly internally consistent environment—which is not the kind of thing you can create on the fly. But if you're just trying to be funny or are OK with a videogame feel, then it doesn't matter.

Establishing Settings

Show a long-range establishing shot, like of a building or a forest, and everything that follows will be interpreted as taking place in that location, until the next establishing shot comes along. Sometimes it's nice to break up long scenes by re-establishing the setting at natural pauses. For example, if there's an extended interaction inside a car, break it up momentarily by cutting away to show the car going down the street.

"Parallel editing," one of the most basic cinematic devices, also keeps things interesting. This entails keeping two or more subplots running at the same time and switching between them at good suspense points. Each switch back and forth is flagged with a new establishing shot. On television series, these shots become familiar icons that need no more than a second or two to be read and understood: The office where they work, the apartment she lives in, the bar where they all hang out.

Stock Shots

Stock shots representing familiar concepts—printing presses and whirling headlines, the neon lights of the big city, spinning clocks and falling calendar pages, busy telephone operators, trains, airplanes, stampedes of buffalo, chain gangs—constitute an entire visual language of their own. These images may seem corny and clichéd in film, but their meanings are immediately clear and they don't require any sound, which makes them pure gold for VJs. They're also total retro-fun. No collection of clips should be without a nice assortment. Stills or short clips of famous city landmarks are also handy as backgrounds or establishing shots. Eiffel Tower? Bam—you're in Paris.

Basic Generative Grammar

With the rules above, it's possible to make a list of shots that you can mix together to generate a wide variety of situations. With characters and other foreground figures, they should be against a plain background in whatever color you're chroma-keying against (typically black, blue, green, or white).

Depending on your rig, some shots will need to be pre-prepared while others will be derivable (like, by applying an effect or flipping left-right). The results obviously won't look like custom animation. Instead, think *South Park* or Terry Gilliam's animations for Monty Python.

> Various characters—for each one:
> Front and side views, long and close-up
> Talking, each side
> Turning and looking, each way
> Variety of reactions
> Entering, leaving, and walking across frame from each side
> Engaging in characteristic activities
> Various interesting foreground props (for example, related to vices or
>   the supernatural) against plain background
> Fun variety of stock shots, establishing shots, and backgrounds

AUDIENCE AND IMPROVISATION ■ ■ ▨ ▨

As VJ emerges from its ancestral habitat of the dance club and steps into the open savannah of the performing arts, it enters a new period of exploration. No one can predict where it will go, but it may be possible to get some sense of which uncharted directions will prove most fruitful by examining other fields that VJ shares fundamental similarities with.

Technologies and specific content aside, what is the basic information dynamic of VJing? It's improvised and performed in front of a live and generally demonstrative audience, which makes it very different from movies or television. It has traditionally been in the background, ambient, but in new settings it is coming more to the fore. It can be abstract, representational, textual, symbolic, or any combination. All of these factors define how the form fits in with other media, and predict that in good hands, its cultural influence could be enormous.

Live audiences are important, whether they're watching something live or pre-recorded, because the dynamics within an audience enable people to measure and update their common values. Each individual audience member senses peripherally when others laugh, cry, fidget, or sit fight-or-flight on the edge of their seats, thereby obtaining a sample set of reactions for the society at large. Through these group "conversations," in response to the cultural offerings that probe them, the society collectively determines what is acceptable to laugh about, as opposed to crying; what characters are worthy of sympathy, rather than contempt; what is interesting, not irrelevant.

Many works steer the audience through a specific sequence of responses, and peoples' "thumbs up / thumbs down" assessments come down to whether or not the argument carried with them. For example, the movie *Blow* (2001), Johnny Depp portrays a drug kingpin as a sympathetic character, developing its defense case by explaining his life story. At one showing in San Francisco, a man stood up in the middle of this film, apparently furious at the overly-tolerant audience's sitting for such manipulative propaganda, yelled "This is fucked up!" and stormed out of the exit doors. This is the essence of "thumbs down."

The levels of audience feedback and involvement dictate different categories of entertainment, as described by the following HBS-style two-by-two graph. The two axes describe whether the audience has an effect on what's onstage or onscreen, and how actively they contribute to the overall environment. In one sense, these parameters run down and across from "cold" to "hot," not in McLuhan's sense (he described television as hot because it changed quickly), but in terms of how many ideas, reactions, and other bits of human communication are bouncing around. Approaches to content that suit each of these four categories are described below, and as with any such out-of-the-ass analyses, these characterizations are only valid to a point, if at all. There are plenty of successful exceptions.

		Audience Feedback	
		No	Yes
Audience Engagement Level	Passive / Reactive	Movies	Plays, VJ
	Active	TV / DVD (watched socially)	Vaudeville/Cabaret, Improv Comedy, Experimental Theater, VJ

Movie audiences are passive and have no effect on the entertainment being presented. Because of this, the successful movies must be perfectly honed, presenting their story or argument in a seamless and broadly understandable way, requiring no sensitivity or adjustments to specific audiences. This isn't a good medium for people to find their voice or work things out; they should know precisely what they want to convey and design the information as a complete package that's deliverable as a one-way informational payload. And thanks to their self-contained nature, movies are where the big bucks are. As products, they're duplicatable, distributable, and understandable anywhere, with no need for human involvement.

With plays, there is a feedback loop between performer and audience, with audience reactions such as laughter and applause affecting the action. But the audience is mostly passive, so they need to be felt and read, and the script is pre-determined, as with a movie. Because of the live audience, the evening-out gravity, the presence of discussion-encouraging intermissions, and lower budgets, plays are well-suited to ideas that are still too controversial or undigested to succeed on film. Theater audiences expect to be challenged and broadened as well as entertained, and the history of modern theater is largely the history of writers testing cultural boundaries. (Although many playwrights fool audiences into thinking they've been challenged simply by waving a few known culturally-divisive flags, permitting the audience to salute, and then congratulating them for being so sophisticated.)

A play's performers tune into each other and into the audience, and try to react effectively within the overall flow of the moment. This same approach works for VJ performances that are scripted in advance or that accompany music as background visuals. Tune into the vibe, and try to keep the crowd with you.

The "TV party" square in the above graph has its own dynamic. The audience is distanced from the content but engages actively with each other, commenting on what's onscreen, offering relevant gossip, etc. It's a form of conversation where the television provides a constant stream of possible new topics but is completely insensitive to what is being said, or laughed and jeered at. The remote control can affect what's being shown, for example, by shutting everything off, but it navigates unchanging, pre-recorded content nevertheless. With movies on DVD, the extra features work best when they support this social dynamic, acting as special, knowledgeable members of an audience conversation about the main title—in much the same way that search engines like Google can become members of a conversation.

The hottest environments of all are live performances in venues small enough that the audience can be actively engaged. Vaudeville, improvisational comedy, and some forms of experimental theater fit into this category. Given the infinite breadth and improvisational power of VJing, which lets performers show virtually anything they want and change it immediately, this also seems like the logical category for VJ performances, when they're center-stage in front of an attentive audience. If this analysis is correct, then what works with this category of setting and audience will also work with VJ.

Here, the venue is fairly intimate, and small enough for both performers and audience to hear each other's raised voices, which maximizes the bandwidth for feedback. Audiences are simultaneously impatient and forgiving. On one hand, the room has a sophisticated "everybody's a producer" sensibility. Acts are given the benefit of the doubt at first, but before long, they need to deliver. Audience members do more than just applaud and react involuntarily; they shout quick suggestions, make loud wisecracks, and even boo. If an act is bombing, it's pulled off the stage by a hook, someone in a gorilla suit, or another device, making way for the next one. The overall dynamic works like speed-dating, as applied to culture—it's a fast and efficient way to find the most promising prospects.

Meanwhile, the crowd is also very forgiving. No one expects perfection or polish. The audience understands that it's hit-and-miss, and they appreciate people's experimenting whether or not the results turn out to have much potential. Furthermore, entertainment often focuses more on the telling, the rendition, than on the content itself, which need not be new. Familiar shaggy-dog stories and striptease numbers serve as vehicles for the performer's own style. Pop standards like "Mack the Knife" inspire personal contributions to their established and proud performance histories.

VJs performing in these settings would do well trying out wild, gimmicky, high idea-density material that's geared toward short attention spans; things that tap into the news and current zeitgeist from a knowing, sophisticated point of view; and very personal, stylized renditions of familiar songs, stories, and other oft-contemplated cultural objects.

Many VJs have been discussing narrative in recent years with the one obvious question being how to do it. If the VJ is a solo storyteller, evidence points to the argument that they should decide on one story they want to tell and then stick to it without attempting to branch in different plot directions improvisationally. London's Light Surgeons have demonstrated a very successful way of incorporating a linear narrative; using a number of screens, they sample key scenes, retaining sound and dialog, from a single movie such as *The Fountainhead* (1949). They'll project these in plot order throughout the performance. The other visuals meanwhile key off of and comment on this primary text, taking its images of political idealism, skyscrapers, and destruction in new and interesting directions.

Branching narratives, in contrast, have been oversold in new media circles. Looking back thousands of years, Homer could have easily made *The Iliad* "fully interactive" by pausing to ask his audience questions like, "Okay now, does Hector kill Achilles or does Achilles kill Hector? How about a show of hands?" The epic tradition did not evolve in this way because people would rather listen to a good, time-tested tale than be bothered with such decisions. This point was ignored during the early and mid-1990s by the multimedia-CD mini-bubble, which pinned high hopes on branching stories, particularly for children, and devoted great attention to them because they were technically feasible. Hopefully, VJs will not make the same mistake.

The hives of audience feedback in the "hot" corner of the graph above are buzzing with ideas, so it's no surprise that historically, such settings bred many of the stock characters and situations that were later picked up by larger and more popular forms. Yiddish theater influenced early radio and television, for example. Weimar-era cabaret influenced theater and film, and the inspiration for numerous recent movies originated within the comedy-industrial complex based around Chicago's Second City and ImprovOlympics groups, which serve as farm teams for *Saturday Night Live*. The way *Saturday Night Live* is constructed makes it the closest thing television has to such memetic hotbeds, and the "Live" part is essential to the formula.

Improv comedy itself is a well-developed field with plenty of wisdom for VJ, including how to successfully improvise narratives. Most of these techniques are based on interactive role-playing, however, which won't be relevant to VJs until they start performing as teams within multi-player virtual worlds. Long-form improv techniques such as "The Harold," for example, harvest the players' group intelligence and unpredictability to concoct compelling on-the-fly narratives that would be impossible to map out in advance via a story tree. Prediction: VJ-improvised narratives will start getting interesting when VJs start performing together the way improv comedy troupes do.

Nevertheless, improv has other lessons for VJ that don't rely on interaction between characters. Here are some general recommendations, pulled and adapted for VJ from the Old and New Testaments of the field, Viola Spolin's *Improvisation for the Theater* and Charna Halpern, Del Close, and Kim "Howard" Johnson's *Truth In Comedy: The Manual for Improvisation*:

Merge with the crowd

Disconnect from the approval or disapproval of others. It's all good! Don't view the audience as judges or onlookers—instead, think of them as people you're sharing an experience with, enjoying it as it unfolds. Move from self-consciousness to group consciousness.

Recycle patterns

Create patterns and then revisit them later. Audiences love seeing things they recognize from earlier in the performance. Start, but don't finish patterns that you've established previously—leave the audience to complete them in their own minds. Look for clever ways to tie your patterns together at the end, like a visual pun that literally pieces everything together for the payoff.

The rule of threes

Nobody understands why, but third repetitions always work best for the punchline. You establish the pattern with one and two, and break it with three. Putting the payoff on four, however, would just be confusing. For instance, consider the following dialogue, spoken by nosy-neighbor housewives in a parody of an air-freshener commercial, from *Kentucky Fried Movie* (1977):

1. "Fish for dinner last night?"
2. "Harry still smoking those cheap cigars?"
3. "Jesus Christ! Did a cow shit in here?"

Identifying further examples is left as an exercise for the reader.

Play it straight

If you're going for humor, never acknowledge the ridiculousness of what you're doing. Make sure you always seem dead serious. Humor signifiers—clowns heads, rubber chickens, or whatever—should move reverently, like religious symbols, not bounce around to appear "wacky."

Don't fear silence

Silence (or blankness) creates tension and draws the audience in. This rule applies more strongly to actors onstage than to blank screens, but the point is that within reason, periods of inactivity are fine, even effective, for both.

DISCLAIMER AND ART RANT ■ ■ ■ ■

I INCLUDE THE FOLLOWING WORDS partially as a disclaimer, to cover my ass for the things I missed and got wrong in my attempt at the latest bringing-together of a broad field. But more importantly, I want to encourage questioning of all linear historical narratives. Language is a fantastically powerful compression scheme, but also lossy, and it's even more unreliable because everyone codes and decodes differently. Perhaps the most data of all is lost when language is used as a linear narrative, storytelling, to describe the sweeping generalizations that we call history.

When I read Carl Sagan's *The Dragons of Eden* as a teen, the part that changed my thinking the most and has stayed with me was his description of the origins of mammalian intelligence. While dinosaurs dominated the landscape, our ancestors were shrew-like creatures that survived underground. The dinosaurs could see and hear over distances, so they didn't need to create persistent models of reality. They simply recognized and reacted. But our shrewd ancestors had to build and navigate dark, underground tunnel networks and rely on internal, mental maps more than on sight or hearing. And our survival depended on everyone sharing the same map and agreeing on how to maintain and build out the tunnels.

With language and then writing, this innate drive to construct and agree on a shared model of reality blossomed, as evidenced by all the stories ever told and all the books ever written. When we turn this strategy toward empirical pursuits like scientific discovery or engineering (tunnel-building), it's enormously effective. The behavior of physical reality itself helps to keep people in agreement, except at the margins of understanding. But when it comes to historical or moral "reality," our species fights and dies over its conflicting descriptions. And when we try to describe culture, what we get as a result might just be an artifact of cultural politics and the shifting zeitgeist felt by the history-writing elite, rather than a more accurate description of the species' full creative output.

Hence, in a world full of billions of creative people, we develop and flock towards impossibly reductive characterizations such as, "after World War II, the center of the art world shifted from Paris to New York." And with this as background, socially ambitious artists get more support if they can convince the establishment that their work occupies a new and needed niche that connects back to the primary, shared narrative. In other words, they argue that the tunnel they're building is something that others will want to explore, because it links to everyone else's tunnels and goes in a promising new direction. They do this because no one wants to be lonely, and that's beautiful.

One result of this dynamic (if you grant the validity of the description-tunnel offered above) is that it overlooks the majority of artists, especially the ones who follow their own aesthetics out of love and personal vision, without scheming about how they might formulate their work to position it within the current cultural context. Put another way, it values cultural problem-solving and social skills above personal expression and aesthetics for their own sake. Now, let's think about this—which strategy will produce art that seems dated and indecipherable in the future (to non-art historians), and which will produce art that continues to connect?

If you want my advice, sell modern art short. Sooner or later, the bubble will burst. Take your investment out of the MoMA, out of the star system, out of all the indulgences, and put it into art created by your neighbors, friends, and family.

And so, I offer this formulation with the caveat that it's just one crackpot's point of view, based more on received ideas and hearsay than on personal experience, fact-checkable records, and empirically verifiable physical evidence. Please approach it with skepticism, and treat all other such histories and culture-crit posturings in the same way.

PREDICTIONS AND REFLECTIONS ■ ■ ■ ■

SPECULATIONS ABOUT VIDEO, VJ, AND THE FUTURE

The Clicker

An easy-to-understand user interface metaphor can push new technologies across the chasm from subculture to mainstream acceptance—witness the increased popularity of computers after the introduction of operating systems with the intuitive "desktop metaphor."

Currently, most VJ hardware and software uses a DJ metaphor: Two video-source screens (analogous to two turntables) appear on either side of a mixer. This is a versatile and time-tested arrangement, but it only makes immediate sense to people who are already familiar with DJing—a sizable population, but hardly a majority.

Some people DJ, but everybody watches TV. Therefore, a more universally-understandable metaphor for VJing might be channel-surfing. Everyone knows how to use their television's remote-control "clicker" to switch around improvisationally from a wide variety of video sources—a process which captures the essence of VJing. Perhaps the "clicker" metaphor can be extended, in either hardware or software, into a VJ tool that permits mixing and other video effects in addition to the simple selection of sources.

Such a device would also reinforce the way small groups sometimes use television socially, as a running source of discussion topics, rather than as an in-home theater for a passive and silent audience. (Search engines can sometimes also become "members of the discussion.") In such groups, people could pass the VJ clicker around and appreciate each others' video-surfing styles as personal creative expression, like karaoke, rather than fighting over the device out of the desire for control. Everybody should get their fair turn.

Puppetry: Growth Profession for the 21st Century

As we enter the post-rendering age of computer graphics, we're going to need all the puppeteers we can get—not to push sticks and pull strings, but to generate live spatial input for software. Real-time character generation, which got going with characters like Spike TV's Stripperella, is faster and cheaper than animation. The process only requires animators at first, to design the characters, to fashion the puppets by defining their appearance and the rules of their behavior. Once the puppets are built, a puppeteer, not an animator, wears the sensor glove, straps on the optical dots, or dons the Gypsy suit, and moves with grace and expressiveness, breathing life into the puppet.

Actually, the puppeteer's input device might even be a common joystick, rather than a glove or suit. One startup, Puppet3D, is developing software to control real-time character animation with off-the-shelf game components like joysticks and gamepads—inexpensive devices which many people already have considerable expertise with. This means that someday your child's video game prowess might actually have practical value.

Internet: Freedom of Speech :: Digital Projectors: Freedom of Assembly

Digital projectors are a powerful tool for democracy, when used in public places (for art or otherwise). What the internet has done for freedom of speech, projectors are starting to do for freedom of assembly—another First Amendment right.

The proud phrase "Freedom of Assembly" could do for some hip projector company what "Think Small" did for Volkswagen in the '60s. Imagine groovy summertime outdoor events, screening parties, neighborhood fundraisers, positive political activism—all grassroots, joyous human interaction. It's another view of the possibilities of digital projection that's recreational rather than productive (unlike office presentations), but more sociable and interactive than home theater.

Content-Secure Electronics

Traditional electronics design exposes all content ("invites piracy," some would say) by leaving analog, unencrypted signal accessible via external cables, and by allowing anyone to disassemble components easily with a screwdriver. Because of this, you can ultimately copy any content, no matter how it was protected during delivery, by tapping in to the wires that feed the speakers and the screen. As long as people have eyes and ears, this method will work.

Digital cable standards, however, can theoretically allow for encryption and decryption at each end, along with the addition of a traceable signature. A new standard that accomplishes this is certainly possible and would require no breakthrough beyond hashing out all the details. Combine such a cable standard with components (or, better, all-in-one systems) that are designed to discourage disassembly and physically destroy encryption circuitry when breached, and you lock out chances for piracy.

Under this hardware design philosophy, watt-hungry terminal components such as speakers and screens would each be powered separately, with their locally-decrypted signal boosted by single-channel amplifiers encased in the same inaccessible hard plastic as the decoder chips. Such all-digital, secure electronics would necessarily be disposable because they're designed to prevent any tinkering or repairs. Taking the idea further, they could also be designed to stop working entirely after an "expiration" date. Such electronics might well be housed in shapely cases that change seasonally, following fashion and design trends.

The home entertainment electronics industry could encourage adoption of such a design standard with a two-pronged campaign: legal lobbying aimed at criminalizing tinkering and home electronics repair (grandfathered against older equipment, if necessary), and a public-relations effort that paints analog-based equipment as old, boxy, and embarrassing, and the people who use and tinker with it as undesirable geeks.

VTTS: The Future of Lies

When everyone can easily manipulate video, what sources will we trust? Several universities and industrial research centers are developing video text-to-speech (VTTS) systems that literally put words into other people's mouths. The resulting video isn't perfectly realistic yet, but it gets better every year, and we can expect that before long, you'll be able to type in any words you want, and software will generate a believable image of any person—such as a politician—speaking those words with their characteristic inflection and expressions. In an article about VTTS systems from the *Boston Globe*, presidential politics expert Kathleen Hall Jamieson predicted: "We will probably have to revert to a method common in the Middle Ages, which is eyewitness testimony. And there is probably something healthy in that."

Iron VJ

It's a recipe for great television. The show starts with the contestants interviewed beforehand about how they feel and what their general strategies are. Then, just as *Iron Chef* unveils the feature ingredient before the cooking begins, *Iron VJ* unveils the Feature Story: "VJs, you will now create a performance based on 'Little Red Riding Hood.'" At the sound of the gong, they begin. You watch their performances, cutting back-and-forth between the visuals themselves and shots of the VJs twiddling knobs and sweating. Meanwhile, a panel of culture-critic types looks on and picks it all apart. At the end, the panel votes, and a winner is declared.

Flat Screen Décor

Increasing numbers of households have big flat-panel television screens mounted on walls. But what do they do with them when they're not watching? Companies such as ATMOS Pictures, producers of colorcalm, are founding a whole new industry dedicated to filling this decorative space with landscapes, abstract patterns, and other ambient visuals. It's a natural extension for publishers of VJ DVDs.

Meanwhile, for the same market, the MoMA will release a DVD of Andy Warhol's *Empire*. This eight-plus-hour experimental film consists of a motionless shot of the Empire State Building, originally shot in 16mm from the 44th floor of the Time-Life building back in 1964. It's a perfect way to add a quietly artsy touch to a living room, or even make it look like you have a window that faces midtown Manhattan in a time warp. Despite the film's epic length, *Empire* compresses easily onto a single DVD because it's black-and-white, it has no sound, and most significantly, it has no movement other than slow changes in lighting and the occasional bird flying. Finally, a way to put this notorious film to good use!

Live-Sports Aesthetic Ascendant

Forget the artist types—in fact, forget this whole book. The people who *really* understand live video are the ones who produce sports for television, juggling multiple cameras with instant replays, commentators, statistical graphs, animated "chalkboard" play diagrams, pre-game interview clips, and old archive footage. The people who sit at the helm and make the on-the-fly editing decisions for these broadcasts are absolutely brilliant in the way they make it all work as a smooth, logical, never-jarring package. They're probably also addicted to stress.

Look for other types of live events, such as political events, to start being produced with the same aesthetic—adding commentary and fact-check information in a text crawl underneath, and perhaps even showing instant replays. Live commentary on a presidential debate, for example, might come from Michael Moore, Jon Stewart, or Bill O'Reilly, depending on the network. Relevant images and facts, or wisecracks and visual puns, will be brought onscreen, not obscuring the speech, but adding a Greek chorus layer of mediation and interpretation. And as with some sporting events, "live" might mean on a slight delay, to allow more precious seconds for the writers to come up with good material.

Scriabin's *Prometheus* in Revival

Big-city symphony orchestras face aging audiences, and the demographic inevitability that society's next set of grownups will consist of rave kids and the MTV generation. With this in mind, they'll revive the visually-augmented concerts of yesteryear, luring younger audiences with spectacular visuals as well as great music. Equipped with such high-culture signposts as Alexander Scriabin and Leopold Stokowski, they will reassure themselves that they have not lost their way when accusations of pandering put them on the defensive. To get the ball rolling, they'll mount a historically-informed revival of Scriabin's *Prometheus* with original lighting.

Live Concerts: Last Bastion of Music Industry Profits

Wounded by unauthorized downloading, music companies are reducing wholesale CD prices and selling tracks for cheap through internet services. So, how will the industry continue supporting its legions of percentage-shaving schmooze-weasels? It's the concerts, stupid. The live concert experience can never by copied and distributed. You have to be there—and the only way to get there is to buy a ticket. The industry will begin treating recordings as advertisements for concerts, and the concerts will become even more spectacular, immersive group experiences that are nothing like what's available at home or anyplace else. The industry will de-emphasize distribution and focus on two things that computers can't do: manufacture celebrities, and provide the copy-proof experience of being in an audience.

Furthermore, for some live events, the performers won't even be physically present, which reduces costs considerably. Instead, bands will play at one high-profile venue, with their performance simulcast to other arenas across the country, projected large and supported by dazzling video effects and stage pyrotechnics. Naturally, the thousands of screaming fans, who are the main source of concert excitement anyway, will still be real. These lower-priced "Simulcast Tours" will begin with the bubblegum bands, and performers like Neil Young will probably never participate.

Abstract Sign Language Performance
Troi Lee's annual Deaf Rave in England proves that deaf and hearing people love to throw down together to a throbbing beat and wild visuals. But people who understand a sign language such as ASL or BSL can become among the most sophisticated practitioners and audiences for live video. By incorporating refer-ences to or suggestions of sign language into a performance, the VJ can add an entire level of meaning that's only understandable to the signers in the audi-ence. It's trivially possible to mix with clips of people signing, but in the future, motion-capture devices that read the entire arm, hand, and fingers will be more affordable, which will allow signing-literate VJs to generate video where signs are gracefully formed by animated characters, ribbons, abstract shapes or clouds, or anything else that the aesthetics demand.

My First Mixer
By many accounts, children immediately "get" VJ tools and want to play with them. Furthermore, the most common interface layout, two screens and controls on either side of a fader, is remarkably similar to gamepads that center a joy-stick in between clusters of buttons. Could this be mere coincidence—or is it incontrovertible proof of ancient astronauts? You decide. Anyway, some toy or game company should make a self-contained video mixer console for kids. They would make millions.

Trial by VJ
Live video can be very effective with a small, attentive audience. This was dis-cussed previously regarding entertainment, but juries are also good examples of such audiences. In making their arguments, trial attorneys are often allowed to present video evidence. And they must always tune into the moment, the set-ting, and the jury's reactions, and think on their feet. Sound familiar? Using VJ tools, an adept trial lawyer could razzle-dazzle a jury—lead them through an argument, weave together evidence, and tell a story with seamless, seeing-is-believing authority. Expect many of tomorrow's hotshot lawyers to possess mad VJ skills in addition to silver tongues, and perhaps law schools will offer courses in live video presentation for the courtroom.

QUOTES ■ ■ ■ ■

[T]he new clavessin... is susceptible to all manner of embellishments... For example, one can form the colors themselves with precious stones or counterfeits of the same color, the reds with garnets and rubies and carbuncles, the greens with emeralds, etc., and what brilliance and splendor a spectacle would possess where one could see appear from all parts and shine like stars, sometimes jacinths, and rubies, and sapphires—all of these accompanied with the light of torches in an apartment all hung with mirrors. It would be an infinitely brilliant spectacle as in immobile decoration... but what would it be like if movement and a regular, measured, harmonic, and quick movement animated all, giving it a sort of life? It would be a charm, a glory, a paradise!
> —Louis Bertrand Castel (1688–1757), inventor of the *clavessin oculaire*, quoted by
> Tom Douglas Jones, *The Art of Light & Color* (1972), p. 17

One could perform a play, in which entered human figures, angelic figures, animals, reptiles, etc., or, again, one could demonstrate all the sequence of the numbers of Euclid; one can give a play of flowers... so arranged that each touch of the hand would represent a flower-bed and the sequence a mobile diversity of flower-beds. All that one can paint one can put into a moving picture, and vice versa. I said that one could make as many color instruments as sound instruments, and one can make them according to a million tastes more different than ordinary music. Let all Paris have color clavessins up to 800,000!
> —Louis Bertrand Castel, ibid., p. 18

The reader... may gain some faint anticipation of the Colour-art of the future, if he will try to recall... the exquisite tints painted upon the dark curtain of the night at a display of fireworks. I select fireworks as an illustration in preference to the most gorgeous sunset, because I am not speaking of Nature but of Art... and I select pyrotechny instead of painting of any kind, because in it we get the important emotional property of velocity, necessarily absent from fixed colouring.... But the Colour-art must first be constituted, its symbols and phraseology discovered, its instruments invented, and its composers born.
> —Rev. H.R. Haweis, "Music and Morals" (1875), quoted by Adrian Bernard Klein,
> *Coloured Light: An Art Medium* (1937), p. 5

In writing these pages, I have felt myself to be addressing two classes of readers, namely, those who know something of the art of Mobile Color, its past history, its hopes and its aims; and others who have never even heard of the subject... [F]rom the latter, I would ask for as open-minded a consideration of the subject as they can give me.
> —Alexander Wallace Rimington, *Colour-Music* (1912), p. v

To sit at this instrument and improvise for half an hour whilst watching the ever-varying combinations of colour on the screen produced by the playing is not only an unspeakable delight, but of real health-giving effect on the sense of color.
> —Alexander Wallace Rimington, ibid., p. xiii

[I]t would almost seem as though an advancing material civilization were inimical to colour... [A]mongst large sections of the population in many nations it is no exaggeration to say that any real feeling for color has died out.
—Alexander Wallace Rimington, ibid., p. 9

In music we are perfectly satisfied with compositions which do not express definite ideas, and in colour there seems to be no reason why this should not also be so if our colour sense is sufficiently developed. If stringed instruments had never been invented, could it have been for a moment supposed that a whole audience would sit spell-bound under the sounds produced by drawing a horse-hair bow over a tightened gus-string without definite words or ideas attached to such sounds? It is simply the insufficient training of the colour sense in many people that makes them demand form in addition to colour.
—Alexander Wallace Rimington, ibid., p. 72

[T]he great majority of the lower middle and working classes are not only absolutely inartistic in their tastes, but, as far as colour is concerned, incapable of appreciating good colour to an extent which it is difficult for some of us who have always lived in the art world to realize.
—Alexander Wallace Rimington, ibid., p. 74

The craftsmen of China and Japan are still able to design in colour... If it be argued that the colour sense in Eastern nations has from very early times been stronger and better than in Western ones, surely the reply is that we should profit by their example.
—Alexander Wallace Rimington, ibid., p. 76

As music the composition is on a level with some of the most modern developments in cacophony and impotent invention. Only the barest outline of thematic material is to be discerned, and that of a quality that bears little relation to what has hitherto been understood as musical.... So far as the lights were concerned it could not be discovered how they added to or intensified the meaning of the 'music.' They were continually shifting and melting, but without visible relation to the sounds... The composer's clue was not entrusted to the lights, and to the first bewildered beneficiaries of the new art, it seemed still to be a sealed book.
—*New York Times*, 21 March 1915, review of the Carnegie Hall debut of Scriabin's *Prometheus*, reprinted in Klein

The manipulation of light is now in the hands of the illuminating engineers and its exploitation (in other than necessary ways) in the hands of the advertisers... Some results of their collaboration are seen in the sky signs of upper Broadway, in New York, and of the lake front, in Chicago. A carnival of contending vulgarities, showing no artistry other than the most puerile, these displays nevertheless yield an effect of amazing beauty. This is on account of an occult property inherent in the nature of light—*it cannot be vulgarized*. If the manipulation of light were delivered into the hands of the artist, and dedicated to noble ends, it is impossible to overestimate the augmentation of beauty that would ensue.
—Claude Bragdon, *Architecture and Democracy* (1918), archived online by Project Gutenberg

Let us therefore attempt to classify the colors of the spectrum according to this theory [based on principles of dramatic expression by François Delsarte], and discover if we can how nearly such a classification is conformable to reason and experience... The red end of the spectrum, being lowest in vibratory rate, would correspond to the physical nature, proverbially more sluggish than the emotional and mental. The phrase "like a red rag to a bull," suggests a relation between the color red and the animal consciousness established by observation. The "low-brow" is the dear lover of the red necktie; the "high-brow" is he who sees violet shadows on the snow. We "see red" when we are dominated by ignoble passion. Though the

color green is associated with the idea of jealousy, it is associated also with the idea of sympathy, and jealousy in the last analysis is the fear of the loss of sympathy; it belongs, at all events to the mediant, or emotional group of colors; while blue and violet are proverbially intellectual and spiritual colors, and their place in the spectrum therefore conforms to the demands of our theoretical division. Here, then, is something reasonably certain, certainly reasonable, and may serve as an hypothesis to be confirmed or confuted by subsequent research. Coming now finally to the consideration of the musical parallel, let us divide a color scale of twelve steps or semi-tones into three groups; each group, graphically portrayed, subtending one-third of the arc of a circle. The first or red group will be related to the physical nature, and will consist of purple-red, red, red-orange, and orange. The second, or green group will be related to the emotional nature, and will consist of yellow, yellow-green, green, and green-blue. The third, or blue group will be related to the intellectual and spiritual nature, and will consist of blue, blue-violet, violet and purple. The merging of purple into purple-red will then correspond to the meeting place of the highest with the lowest, "spirit" and "matter." We conceive of this meeting-place symbolically as the "heart"—the vital centre. Now "sanguine" is the appropriate name associated with the color of the blood—a color between purple and purple-red. It is logical, therefore, to regard this point in our color-scale as its tonic—"middle C"—though each color, just as in music each note, is itself the tonic of a scale of its own.
  —Claude Bragdon, ibid.

After my years of study and training with Leschetzky, I came back to America fully equipped for, and keenly anticipating, concert work. For months I went from one manager to another, hoping to find an opportunity for the public expression of my musical art. But everywhere the doors seemed closed to me. There were more than enough pianists on the market, they told me rather brutally—talent, even genius, was no longer the basis of success for a pianist, unless there was something sensational and startling about the personality of the performer herself.
  I went home and thought the matter over. Should I take on freakish personal attributes in order to draw to myself the attention of the managers and the public? No, I decided, I could never do that. The idea came to me that I must find something new—even something startling—not for myself, but for my art. Then came the flash—sunlight makes the world sing; why shouldn't light help the song sing? The vision, which resulted in the invention of the color organ, came for an instant, and since then sixteen years have been devoted to the realization of that momentary flash. For sixteen years I have devoted my time and energies not only to the esthetic side of this new art, but to its mechanical side, which meant learning about electricity, physics, engineering, in addition to everything under the sun about colors. I have drawn the plans and practically built every part of the color instrument myself.
  —Mary Hallock-Greenewalt, quoted by Rose Rosner in "New 'Color Organ' to Interpret Music," *New York Times*, 12 November 1922

I truly believe that the loveliest fine art of all will be this sixth to come into existence. With what strength it will speak, compared to the powers held among the others, no one can foretell.
  —Mary Hallock-Greenewalt, ibid.

[W]hat pleasure we got from the afternoon, apart from the passing interest of its novelty, consisted in the seizure of certain moments when the forms fell into beautiful pattern or suggested known objects. One wanted at these moments to cry 'Halt!' to the machine and examine the pattern at greater length... it is in the movement (or rhythm) that the new idea fails, for the patterns did not continue to be beautiful all the time. And even if they did we do not think that it would constitute a new art... So one sees in the 'Clavilux' no real creation of a new art, but a machine capable of producing occasional pleasure... and fraught with infinite possibilities of boredom.
  —*The Times*, 18 May 1925, review of Clavilux performance by Thomas Wilfred at Queen's Hall, London

The apparatus is admittedly not perfect, as yet the colours are still a little crude and speed is restricted, but the 'compositions' already have a haunting beauty that is almost disquieting in its novelty. One seems to look as in a dream on some unearthly aquarium where strange creatures float and writhe, and where a vegetation of supernatural loveliness grows visibly before the spectator... If the 'Clavilux' develops as one sees it will, the totally deaf will henceforth have some conception of what music is like.
 —*Manchester Guardian*, 18 May 1925, review of same performance by Wilfred

At times the whole relation of performer to audience becomes a game to see which will submit to the other. After all, the passivity of the audience in its attitude toward the speaker is only relative and never absolute.
 —Kimball Young. "The Psychology of the Audience." Chapter 22 in *Social Psychology: An Analysis of Social Behavior*. New York: Alfred A. Knopf (1930): 537-5, paraphrasing R. H. Barnard, *A Study of the Control of Hostile Audiences in the Anti-Slavery Speeches of Wendell Phillips*, M.A. thesis 1929, University of Wisconsin. Published on the Mead Project website, Brock University

Most actors say that they can "feel" the responses of the audience. They "sense" whether the play is "going over" or not. The problem of the mechanism of this effect needs much careful investigation, but observation seems to indicate that the actors are influenced by the subliminal stimuli of slight noises of the audience. Certainly they are affected by the laughter or tears of the audience. It is common knowledge among actors that the first laugh by the audience is important for the success of the first act, if not indeed for the success of the whole comedy. Clever humor, witticisms, and foolish gestures set off the audience. They are devices to release the inhibitions of the audience. They produce a receptive mood. If the play drags, the audience settles back, to assume critical attitudes, or to become passive or indifferent. Actors say that they can "feel" this change in the responses of the audience.
 —Kimball Young, ibid.

This age insistently demands from the artist satisfaction of its craving for nerve stimulation. The feeble efforts of the experimentalist will not have the remotest chance of attracting attention. So for colour-music to be both popular and a commercial success it must start from the very beginning with an overwhelming display of light and colour. And to achieve this will require the expenditure of a lot of money.
 —Adrian Bernard Klein, *Coloured Light: An Art Medium* (1937), p. via.

Coloured light... is the most powerful element by means of which the advertising expert succeeds... The fertility of invention in this field has been remarkable. Some of the great coloured electric "signs" of the American cities, and to a lesser degree those of Europe, are quite beautiful. The future lighting artist can find here much that is instructive. Many "signs" present colour sequences which, though simple, are worth study.
 —Adrian Bernard Klein, ibid., p. vi*b*

The modern artist withdraws himself from the world of common concepts and ordinary feelings... As he becomes more and more intellectual his field of influence narrows. His public may therefore consist finally only of the one or two eager minds who have made a special study of his particular idiom. Indeed, the artist in this is not dissimilar from the great mathematician, who may perhaps count on the fingers of one hand the number of his contemporaries who are competent to comprehend his discoveries... This state of affairs has not always existed. It is obvious that the common people could make something out of the Sistine Chapel.
 —Adrian Bernard Klein, ibid., p. xi

Young men are always ready to push the advance yet a little forward from the position gained by unselfish pioneers. They are, as ever, heedless of their debt to predecessors. They are always the "inventors" of colour-music. Who cares in our exclusively commercial civilization who originated an idea, or whether it was stolen, or whether it was the outcome of artistic conviction? Nobody cares about any of these questions. We care only if there is money to be made. Then, and then only, we can get something done.
  —Adrian Bernard Klein, ibid., p. xvii

Painting is no longer a vital art.... A framed picture hanging on a wall is a preposterous anachronism, and sooner or later this will be generally recognized.... Painting is either a speedy route to réclame and wealth, a cloak for indolence, or the refuge of those incapable of adaptation to the conditions of the industrial epoch.... Inversely as painting has declined music has grown. *Music is pre-eminently the important art of the age.*
  —Adrian Bernard Klein, ibid., p. 31

It seems hardly necessary to observe that in order to gain the maximum effect upon the observer, anything in the nature of a frame, or screen, or limited illuminated area, must be rejected as inadequate... Obviously a small screen placed in the middle of an orchestra will tend to arouse hilarity rather than awe.
  —Adrian Bernard Klein, ibid., p. 146

There are those who insist that music owes its expressive power to the fact that we ordinarily express our emotions and thoughts by the faculty of speech, and that as we are unable to radiate light in the way that we can, so to speak, radiate sound, light can never have the significance that sound has for us. But does not this view ascribe too much importance to the power of music to awaken emotions by means of sounds which are associated with those which the human being utters to express intense emotions? ... [I]t is a hopeless task to attempt to differentiate between the characteristics of one Bach fugue and another in terms of shrieks of despair, moans of the anguished, chuckles of the amused, snorts of the angered, hurrahs of the enthused!
  —Adrian Bernard Klein, ibid., p. 222

If there were only a hundred people in the world who could derive genuine pleasure from colour-music it would be worth while composing for them. Artists... are notoriously bigoted, and only in the rarest instances are they equipped... to form a just estimate of the significance of an aesthetic experiment perhaps a century in advance of the receptive powers of their own time.
  —Adrian Bernard Klein, ibid.

Mr. Wilfred has completed some new compositions, several of which are among the finest things he has yet done in the field of, so to speak, "silent music." This is pioneering work of the utmost significance.
  —"Art Notes," *New York Times*, 10 November 1940

Whether or not Bach or Beethoven needs the explanatory assistance of even so great an artist as Mr. Disney is unimportant. Nor is it important that epic music has been visually interpreted. It is the fusion that is important, the fusion of music, drama and graphic art that Wagner strove to attain. *Fantasia* is the first work that clearly indicates the possibilities. And it is for this reason that Mr. Disney has made history.
  —"Mr. Disney and *Fantasia*" (editorial), *New York Times*, 15 November 1940

The experimentation of electronic media mix techniques that have introduced the discotheque and "total theater" are a result of the attempts of artists, poets, engineers, photographers, filmmakers, etc. to produce the psychedelic state without LSD. However, it is significant and perhaps more important that they reflect a recognition of McLuhanistic mysticism which charges us to get involved in it all.
    —George X. Charisma, "Zoom Senses," *Context* vol.1 no.1 (Sept. 1966).

Stewart Brand, a local photographer whose "America Needs Indians - Sensorium 9" kicked off The Trips Festival, anxiously asked, "Why don't we have a photograph of the whole earth." On August 25, he was answered by Lunar Orbiter.
    McLuhan says the planet has become the content of a new space and in the next few decades "we will caress and shape and pattern every facet, every contour of the planet as if it were a work of art." And he adds, "I think the computer is admirably suited to the artistic programming of such an environment."
    —George X. Charisma, ibid.

Having been to the Fillmore & the Avalon, among other such resorts, and having heard endless gassed chatter about Acid Tests, Trips Festivals et psychedelic cetera, we have decided quote fuck it close quote that we are going to prove that the rock dance can & ought to be a genuine Art Form.
    The trouble with the events mentioned above is everything. First, the lights tend to be projected against either a screen or the band, giving the customer much the same sense of participation he gets from a technicolor movie. This is clearly bullshit. You're not supposed to see the light show; it's supposed to happen to you.
    Second, all the light shows are pretty much alike. Our vaunted light artists are playing the same piddling liquid light & lantern slide games we were playing with Mr. Sulks & John Brent on the Lower East Side in 1957. The only progress made in ten count 'em ten years is that now some of the lantern slides are just a bit erotic. Yet more bullshit.
    Third, light show colors are pallid, pastel, puny & unimpressive, instead of brilliant & compelling. And for this millions benighted teenies pay their daddies' hard earned bread. One more heap of bullshit....
    In other words... all rock dances & similar shivarees have been produced by people who (a) have never read Marshall McLuhan, (b) don't know anything worth mentioning, & (c) are unaware of their all-embracing ignorance....
    We feel that a rock dance should change your life, & we intend to see that it does.
    To this end we are embarked upon an evolutionary process. We have, so far, three dances planned: Bedrock One, Bedrock Two and Bedrock Three. (We are nothing if not orderly.) The first will be better than sex, the second will be better than the first, and we expect to have to flee the city after the third.
    We have a dedicated crew of environmental artists... We'll be able to tune the audience like a guitar. In fact, we intend to play the audience like a guitar. An electric guitar. Hard.
    —Chester Anderson, "Bedrock One" handbill, Feb 1967 (from San Francisco Public Library
    Hippies Collection, Box 1, Folder 6—*Ephemera / Street Raps: A Com/Co Annotated Anthology*

Dynamic, ever-changing color is more than beautiful and stirring. It can be psychological dynamite. It reacts not only on the conscious mind of the beholder, but on deep unconscious levels as well...
    To the creative person, who is likely to be in better communication with his own unconscious, the impact of moving color poses little threat. He can "have" this art-form comfortably. To more rigid, non-creative people, particularly those who are imitative and exploitive "second handers," the syndrome is quite different... The greatest single threat to [his] ego image is the power of womanhood... On some obscure unconscious symbolic

level, dynamic moving color represents this very power, and is the softness and beauty and accdeptance that the imitative-exploitive character regards as a hunger, defect, or threat... which must be destroyed...

—Dr. Henry Hill, "Color Game Traps," from *Color Games: Light Show Manual*, 3rd edition, by Robert. C. Beck (1966)

There are two major roles in which the spoiler masquerades. We call them (1) the "PROMOTER" and (2) the "ICDIB", a name derived from the phrase "I Can Do It Better."...

The "PROMOTER" is a person who has been exposed to color and instantly "intends" to use color in some commercial venture immediately... His behavior is amazingly predictable, but nonetheless dangerous... THERE IS SOME SUBLIMINAL FACTOR IN DYNAMIC, MOVING COLOR THAT BRINGS OUT DESTRUCTIVENESS IN THE NON-CREATIVE PERSON WHO ATTEMPTS TO EXPLOIT IT COMMERCIALLY.

His tactics run as follows: (1) He opens by making great promises and building you up (2) he steals a great deal of your time and systematically picks your brain and ideas, (3) he begins to subtly find fault with your devices and with the whole idea of color, (4) when confronted directly on the issue of finances, he stalls at first and later diverts the real issues by endlessly quibbling over pennies when at first he had been talking about dollars, (5) he progressively finds more and more fault with you (this is a process whereby you have become the victim of his own projections and basic insecurities) and finally, (6) he aborts the game by completely negating and abandoning the dynamic use of color, or by hiring someone other than yourself to install the color in a greatly reduced, devitalized, emasculated and insipid application which must always be a washout.

No matter how promising and businesslike your initial meetings with the "color promoter" may be, in time contact becomes a frantic, ridiculous farce where you are progressively victimized.... There are ways of handling this, and one is that you should ask for a substantial advance payment of "front" money at the very first interview... Otherwise he will ALWAYS change his mind again and again. Losing your temper does no good, you are dealing with a sick person, not a normal businessman.

—Dr. Henry Hill, ibid.

The "I can do it better" person is... a destructive and diversionary force who will thwart your efforts if you let him.

The typical ICDIB is a person with some degree of knowhow and skill, usually in the fields of electronics, optics, photography, or color... He undoubtedly entertains the notion that someday he will himself build a colored light device better than anyone else's...

In spite of his technical knowledge... the ICDIB is, and always will be essentially a non-creative person, or a "second-hander," and can never really get around to constructing any such device in actuality because somewhere inside himself is that doubt that it just may reveal to the world his mediocrity... So his behavior is oriented toward discrediting or disrupting the existing creative efforts of others who while less technically able than he, are nonetheless considerably more creative and in motion....

He delights in pointing out to you that "you are doing it the hard way." He delights in technical name-dropping, and referring to technology and hardware that will invalidate you, like, "why are you using that antique, obsolete thingamabob when any fool knows that a whoosisified whatchamaroodle would work MANY TIMES better..." There is a sure-fire way to handle the superior and ridiculing ICDIB. Take him back DOWN the abtraction ladder. Inform him politely, firmly, and unequivocally that you prefer building your own instruments in your own way and you would be delighted if he would go ahead and build his own in his own way.... He won't.

—Dr. Henry Hill, ibid.

[D]on't get caught up in your fantasies about building better and more complex effects. This leads to a state of non-productive inactivity. The only color devices that fly are the ones that get built.

Another internal trap is turning yourself into a color prima donna. We've know a few mystical types who have fallen into the bag of deluding themselves that they have some-how been chosen by the Powers that Be to bring the message of Color to suffering humanity. This New Age Miracle should be disseminated in the Temples, and You are the Messenger. The end state of this bag is a paranoia where the player fearfully hides the color devices in the hall closet apprehensive that someone else might come and discover the principle and steal the idea.

"Color Heads" have been observed to fall into the internal trap of excessive jealousy which grows out of comparing their color devices with the work of others. And the end result is the tight bind of paranoia rather than the desired expanded awareness.
—Dr. Henry Hill, ibid.

[A]ll the effort that has gone into the development of the colorscopes is a part of the crea-ture's search for the Creator. It is not all of that search any more than the stained glass win-dows are all of the cathedrals. Just part of it.
—Robert Moore Williams, "This Shout of Wonder," from *Color Games: Light Show Manual*, ibid.

Probably the most up-to-date technique involves the setting up of a closed circuit television system, preferably with a TV projector. The camera, with zoom and close-up lenses is led by a follow-spot which illuminates the dancers, who see huge images of themselves projected on the screen. This is about as expensive as anything could get and is only possible at a university or other facility which owns such equipment.
—Herbert H. Wise, *Professional Rock and Roll*, p. 60. New York: Amsco Music
Publishing Company (1967).

The wet show has been most fully exploited in the West Coast rock ballrooms... To keep a show of this kind interesting all night takes genius.
—Herbert H. Wise, ibid.

Blowing fuses during a performance doesn't make it at all.
—Herbert H. Wise, ibid.

[Louis Bertrand] Castel wrote of spectacular color effects that today have been unknowingly attempted in the modern discotheques. It is doubtful, of course, that he actually achieve what he described, but his imagination well echoes the visions of persons under the influ-ence of hallucinogenic drugs.
—Tom Douglas Jones, p. 16

[D]uring the nineteen sixties... the sophisticated nightclub, patronized by well-dressed adults, gave way to the discotheque, the electric circus, frequented by youngsters in dungarees and with bare feet. Rock and roll music, amplified to a cacophonous din, demanded all that the senses could bear—which meant vivid color, flashing light, dizzying motion, stroboscopic vibration.
—Tom Douglas Jones, p. 28

We are trapped by the constant hope that the next video will finally satisfy and, lured by the seductive promise of immediate plenitude, we keep endlessly consuming the short texts.
—E. Ann Kaplan, *Rocking Around the Clock: Music Television, Postmodernism,
and Consumer Culture*, p. 4. New York: Methuen (1987).

MTV appears symptomatic of Reagan's America in its unquestioning materialism.
—E. Ann Kaplan, ibid., p. 30.

The story of film begins around a fire, in darkness. Gathered around this fire are primates of a certain species, our ancestors, an animal distinguished by a peculiar ability to recognize patterns. There is movement in the fire: embers glow and crawl on charcoal. Fire looks like nothing else. It generates light in darkness. It moves. It is alive [....] They see the faces of wolves and of their own dead in the flames. [....] They crouch, watching the fire, watching its constant, unpredictable movements, and someone is telling a story. In the watching of the fire and the telling of the tale lie the beginning of what we still call film.
—William Gibson, from a talk given at the Directors Guild of America's Digital Day,
17 May 2003 (posted to Gibson's blog 21 May 2003)

Any linear narrative film...can serve as the armature for what we would think of as a virtual reality, but which Johnny X, eight-year-old end-point consumer, up the line, thinks of as how he looks at stuff. [....] Somewhere in the countless preferences in Johnny's system there's one that puts high-rez, highly expressive dog-heads on all of the characters. He doesn't know that this setting is based on a once-popular Edwardian folk-motif of poker-playing dogs, but that's okay; he's not a history professor, and if he needed to know, the system would tell him....

But later in the afternoon he's run across something called *The Hours*, and he's not much into it at all, but then he wonders how these women would look if he put the dog-heads on them. And actually it's pretty good, then, with the dog-heads on [...] And what has happened, here, in this scenario, is that our ancient project, that began back at the fire, has come full circle. The patterns in the heads of the ancestors have come out, over many millennia, and have come to inhabit, atemporally, this nameless, single, non-physical meta-artifact we've been constructing. So that they form an extension of Johnny's being, and he accesses them as such, and takes them utterly for granted, and treats them with no more respect than he would the products of his own idle surmise....

I can only trust that Johnny's entertainment system, and the culture that informs it, will be founded on solid curatorial principles. That there will be an ongoing archaeology of media-product in place to insure that someone or something is always there to categorically state, and if necessary to prove, that *The Maltese Falcon* was shot in black and white and originally starred Humphrey Bogart.
—William Gibson, ibid.

Movies may never be downloaded as often as music, because the two are consumed so differently. In general, movies aren't replayed again and again. We don't rearrange the scenes or build playlists of our favorite car chases.
—"MEMO: To: The next head of the Motion Picture Association of America" (editorial),
Wired magazine, Jan. 2004. New York: The Condé Nast Publications, Inc.

The similarities between Color Field painting and contemporaneous experiments with color projection are striking. It is interesting to learn, in Kerry Brougher's essay for [Los Angeles MOCA and Hirshhorn Museum exhibition] *Visual Music* (p. 166), that Sam Francis helped Single Wing Turquoise Bird provide light shows for Grateful Dead concerts. But I doubt that [influential mid-century art critic Clement] Greenberg was in attendance.
—Harry Cooper, "An Eye for an Ear: Art & Music in the Twentieth Century," *Artforum*,
Summer 2005 (vol. 43 No. 10). New York: Artforum International Magazine.

RECIPES ■ ■ ■ ■

VJ Aix's Reverse Feedback Flow

This effect generates a visual flow with trails and works particularly well with source video of small light objects against a dark background, like a zooming star field. It was first performed by VJ Aix in 2001.

You need:

1 Videonics MX-PROdv, or other video mixer with more than one output jack
2 Video source (DVD player, camcorder, etc.)
3 RCA or S-Video cables

Instructions:

1. Connect video source to mixer's Channel 1 input jack. Verify that visuals are playing through to the mixer output.
2. With a cable, connect the mixer's Master output jack to the Channel 2 input jack. The video input on channels 1 and 2 should now look identical.
3. Flip Channel 2 picture either horizonally or vertically.
4. Activate the luma or chroma key function.
5. Set the T-bar to fade, and move it to halfway between channels 1 and 2.
6. The reverse feedback flow effect should now be visible. Adjust T-bar to taste.

Complex's Trick BSoD

Your performance interrupts suddenly with what appears to be a system error screen, Windows' notorious Blue Screen of Death (BSoD). The audience thinks your computer has crashed. But then the BSoD takes on a life of its own, morphing through effects and mixing with other clips, proving that you have had complete control all along. This piece was first performed at a +8 Records Tour at Mono in Dublin, Ireland, with Ritchie Hawtin.
You need:

1 Short (3-4 sec) clip facsimile of the BSoD. You can create your own, or download Complex's original After Effects file at *http://www.complexvisuals.com/bsod*.

MacOS users may substitute "Bomb" or "Unhappy Mac" screens.
2 Motion Dive, or other VJ software

Instructions:

1. During performance, suddenly cut to BSoD clip. Show uninterrupted for a couple of seconds.
2. Apply slight effect or slowly fade in another clip, then back off momentarily, or continue increasing intensity of manipulation.
2 (alternate version). Immediately cut away from BSoD and continue performance, just as before. Watch as puzzled audience members ask each other, "Wait—did you see that?"

Hand Shadows with Video

At first, this low-tech / high-tech dissonance is good for a laugh. For a greater challenge, take the combination more seriously by developing it, matching duck shadows to swirling lake backgrounds, etc.

You need:

1 Video projector, positioned so you can easily reach into beam
2 Hand shadow knowledge (available from Bursill, Henry: *Hand Shadows*. London: Griffith & Farran (1859). Reprinted by Dover and available online at The Gutenberg Project, *http://www.gutenberg.net*)
3 Hands and (optional) utensils, implements that can be cast into recognizable shadows

Instructions:

1. Project visuals that establish modern, comfortable VJ mood.
2. Interrupt beam with hand shadows. "Duck," "Doggie," and "Grandpa" are popular favorites.
3. Let hilarity ensue.

Pall Thayer's PD Live Text Scroll

This recipe adds your own news network-style text crawl to the bottom of any video input, live. You type in lines of text, and they scroll along the bottom— a powerful way to add commentary to events as they happen. It runs on Linux machines using PureData, a free, open-source programming environment, and a couple of Perl scripts. With some adjustments, this recipe should also work on Mac OSX.

You need:

1 Linux machine running PureData, with libraries pdp, pidip, and zexy. These are available online at the Planet CCRMA archive, at *http://ccrma.stanford.edu*
2 The three scripts readchk.pl, txtinsrt.pl, and txtrll.pd, written by Pall Thayer are available as ready-to-use files at *www.thevjbook.com* website, linked to *http://www.feralhouse.com*
3 Video source input to PureData

Instructions:

1. Within a shell window, create a project directory containing the files readchk.pl, txtinsrt.pl, and txtrll.pd.
2. Create a blank file lines.txt with full read-write access (chmod 777 lines.txt, from the prompt). This file is where the lines you type in will be stored and read from.
3. Open two more terminal windows / shell windows in your directory. Run readchk in one, then run txtinsrt in the other.
4. From your original window, launch PureData with the command "pd," loading the libraries pdp, pidip, and zexy. You can include the library paths in the command line itself ("pd–lib ‹location of pdp›–lib ‹location of pidip›–lib ‹location of zexy›" or else just list them line by line ("-lib ‹location›") in your .pdrc file.
5. From the PureData window, run txtrll.
6. Enter lines of text into the console window within PD, and watch them scroll underneath the video, in the pdp window. Text entered faster than it can scroll is temporarily buffered, and displays after it waits its turn in line.

Code can be found online at www.feralhouse.com and thevjbook.com.

RESURCES ■ ■ ■ ■

VJ

VJ Central—*http://www.vjcentral.com*
VJ tutorials, news, reviews, forums, and chat.

Audiovisualizers—*http://www.audiovisualizers.com*
Reviews, forums, software listings, and the VJ Loop Server, a shared pool of video clips.

Eye candy—*http://groups.yahoo.com/group/eyecandy*
General forum for VJs on Yahoo! Groups.

VJs.net—*http://www.vjs.net*
VJ news and resources, sponsored by a UK government grant.

Electronica-Optica—*http://www.eoptica.com*
VJ information and products.

VJTV—*http://www.vjtv.net*
VJ interviews and visuals archives (affiliated with Electronica-Optica)

oxff List—*http://music.columbia.edu/mailman/listinfo/0xff*
Advanced-user email discussion list dedicated to real-time video.

LOCAL VJ GATHERINGS AND RESOURCES

Eyewash—*http://www.forwardmotiontheater.org/Events*
Weekly (approx.) show-and-tell for NYC area VJs, at Remote Lounge, hosted by Forward Motion Theater.

LAVA (Los Angeles Video Artists)—*http://www.la-va.org*
L.A. area VJ online community, news, clips, and events.

Synapse—*http://www.terpsichoregroup.org/events.html*
Bi-weekly (approx.) multimedia show in Los Angeles, at Monroe's Bar, hosted by
The Terpsichore Group.

Video Salon—*http://www.dimension7.com/videosalon.html*
Monthly (approx.) show-and-tell for San Francisco-area VJs, hosted by Dimension7.

VJ FESTIVALS

AVIT—*http://www.avit.info*
Annual international VJ conference.

ContactEurope—*http://www.contacteurope.org*
Annual VJ festival held in various locations in Europe.

Cimatics—*http://cimatics.com*
Annual VJ festival in Brussels.

Machinista—*http://www.machinista.org.uk*
Annual new media festival held in various locations in the UK.

PixelACHE—*http://www.pixelache.com*
Annual festival for VJing and other new media.

General media-arts conferences that include VJing:
Netmage, Italy—*http://www.netmage.it*
Transmediale, Germany—http://www.transmediale.de

VISUALS DVDS AND DVD "LABELS"

Lightrhythm Visuals—*http://www.lightrhythm.com*
Explicitly VJ-oriented DVD label.

Microcinema / Blackchair—*http://www.microcinema.com*
Massive selection of independent visuals and other DVDs.

Lowave—*http://www.lowave.com*
European film and video art.

YouWorkForThem—*http://www.youworkforthem.com*
DVDs, etc. for professional artists and designers

Reline—*http://www.reline.net*
Multi-artist video DVD

CONTENT

Common Content—*http://commoncontent.org*
"An open catalog of Creative Commons licensed content."

Prelinger Archives—at the Internet Archive, *http://www.archive.org*
Massive collection of ephemeral films, all downloadable in various formats and in public domain.

Something Weird Video—*http://www.somethingweird.com*
"Lost" films on VHS and DVD, including Special Edition digitally-remastered DVDs.

Super Happy Fun—*http://www.superhappyfun.com*
Foreign and obscure films on VHS and DVD.

Big Reel Magazine—available through *http://www.collect.com*
Monthly for film reels and other Hollywood collectables.

GENERAL VIDEO

Projector Central—*http://www.projectorcentral.com*
Reviews, news, and discussion of digital projectors.

AVS Forum—*http://www.avsforum.com*
Video Help—*http://www.videohelp.com*
Two favorites among the many video and home theater websites that feature how-to articles, forums, and reviews.

Machinima.com—*http://www.machinima.com*
Main info site for machinima, using game software and utilities to make animated movies.

Doom9—*http://www.doom9.net*
To preserve plausible deniability, this site calls itself "the definitive DVD backup resource."

OPTICAL

Rainbow Prism Atomic Lightshow—*http://www.lightshow.cc*
Sources and resources for DIY psychedelic light shows.

Beck, Robert C. (Bob): *Color Games: Light Show Manual*, 3rd Ed. Los Angeles: Pericles Press, 1966. A copy of this excellent self-published book is at the San Francisco Public Library.

International Laser Display Association—*http://www.ilda.wa.org*
Laser industry links and resources.

LEGAL

Creative Commons—*http://creativecommons.org*
Create your own legally-binding contract according to how you want your work to be used and credited.

Electronic Frontier Foundation—*http://www.eff.org*
"Defending Freedom in the Digital World."

HISTORY

Betancourt, Michael: *Visual Music Instrument Patents (volume 1)*. San Bernardino, California: Borgo Press, 2004.

Rimington, Alexander Wallace: *Color-Music: The Art of Mobile Color*, Elibron Classics Replica Edition. Chestnut Hill, MA: Adamant Media Corporation, 2004. Originally published in 1912 by Hutchinson & Co., London.

Klein, Adrian Bernard (Adrian Cornwell-Clyne), *Coloured Light: An Art Medium*. London: Technical Press, 1937. A copy of this is at University of California, Santa Barbara, available via interlibrary loan.

Jones, Tom Douglas: *The Art of Light & Color*. New York: Van Nostrand Reinhold Company, 1972.

pOoTer's pSycheDelic shack—*http://www.pooterland.com*
History and archives of psychedelic-era light shows.

RhythmicLight—*http://www.rhythmiclight.com*
History, archives, and bibliography of classical light performance.

ARTICLES

Scotese, Amanda: "Visual Riot: Live Projected Art in Clubland," *San Francisco Bay Guardian*, 18 June 2003.

Romero, Dennis: "Mixing Up a Visual Storm," *Los Angeles Times*, 16 Feb 2003.

Tomas, Juan-Carlo: "Mix Masters," *Sydney Morning Herald*, 22 Nov 2002.

Glaser, Mark: "Making Images Dance to a Rock Beat," *New York Times*, 19 Sep 2002.

INDEX ■ ■ ■ ■

221

About the VJ DVD

Produced by Melissa Ulto (VJ Miixxy)

This is a dual-use DVD/DVD-ROM. The DVD presentation and DVD-ROM sections are explained below. This DVD will play in most commercial DVD players; however, there may be an issue with computer DVD players. The DVD-ROM will most likely load instead on most computers, with clear access to the software and samples directories. If you wish to play the DVD presentation on your computer, mount the VIDEO_TS folder in your DVD player application.

If you are reading this, the disc is probably in a DVD player, and from here, you can simply play the clips from the main menu and watch them in couch-potato mode.

Please note: The VJ clips presented on this DVD are for viewing only. All text, photographs, audio, video, and graphic contents of this DVD are copyright (c) 2005 Feral House or their respective copyright holder (see Artist List above). All rights reserved. No other party may modify, copy, distribute, transmit, broadcast, display, reproduce, publish, license, create derivative works from, transfer, or sell materials or information that is subject to such copyright, directly or indirectly, in any medium, without advance express written permission.

DVD-ROM FILES: Also included is a selection of VJ software for both Mac and PC users—Vidvox's Grid and VDMX, Soyuz, and Isadora. Additionally, VJ Miixxy and VJ MonkeyDaddy (http://www.motiongraf.com) have included clips from their own libraries, as samples for the budding VJ to practice with. The software and samples can be found in the following directories:

ADDITIONAL MUSIC:

VJ SAMPLES: To mix with these clips, you need to install the sample VJ software and copy the clips over to your computer's hard drive.

SOFTWARE-MAC:

To install the software, put the DVD into a Mac OS or Windows-compatible computer, navigate to the Software-PC or Software-MAC folder, and then choose the software subfolder, as appropriate. Inside the subfolders, you'll find installer files for a variety of VJ applications. Launch the ones you want to try, and follow their installation procedures.

SOFTWARE-PC:

You can copy VJ clips from the top-level folder VJ Samples directory, or load each VJ subfolder separately.

VJ SAMPLES:

Enjoy!
Paul Spinrad & Melissa Ulto, August 27, 2005

1. **BEN NEILL:** http://www.benneill.com

2. **BENTON-C BAINBRIDGE:** http://www.benton-c.com/

3. **BILL COTTMAN:** http://www.salon1016.org/

4. **CHRIS JORDAN—SEEJ:** http://www.seej.net/

5. **EYEWASH (HOLLY DAGGERS & ERIC DUNLAP):** http://www.forwardmotiontheater.org

6. **GEORGE STADNIK:** http://www.photonlightguitars.com/

7. **GILES HENDRIX:** http://www.gesture.org/ **HENRY WARWICK**: http://www.kether.com/

8. **LASERIUM (IVAN DRYER):** http://www.laserium.com/

9. **JOEY CAVELLA:** http://joeycavella.com/

10. **JOSH GOLDBERG:** http://goldbergs.com/

11. **LIVID (JAY SMITH):** http://lividinstruments.com/

12. **MARC CONIGLIO:** http://www.troikaranch.org/

13. **MELISSA ULTO—VJ MIIXXY:** http://www.miixxy.com   http://www.multo.com

14. **MISSY GALORE:** http://feedbuckgalore.com/

15. **NORMAN PERRYMAN:** http://www.normanperryman.com/

16. **OPTICAL DELUSION:** http://opticaldelusion.com/

17. **PETER METTLER:** http://www.gambling-gods-and-lsd.ch/

18. **SCOTT ARFORD:** http://www.7hz.org/s_arford/s_arford.main.html

19. **STEFAN G:** http://www.vjcentral.com/members/view/id/3735

20. **SUEZ HOLLAND:** http://homepage.mac.com/zuendo/iMovieTheater9.html

21. **VIDEO OUT (FILM BY 13BIT PRODUCTIONS):** http://www.13bit.com/videoout.html

22. **OLI SORRENTINO—VJ ANYONE:** http://www.anyone.org.uk/

23. **DORON ALTARATZ—VJ SPUTNIK:** http://vjsputnik.com/

1. **CATHERINE WENTWORTH—DJ CAT:** http://www.djcatnyc.com

2. **MIGDOEL—SOULisETERNAL:** http://artists.iuma.com/IUMA/Bands/SOULisETERNAL/

(Migdoel AKA SOULisETERNAL appears courtesy of Robust Records.)

ISADORA: www.troikatronix.com/isadora.html

LIVID UNION DEMO: www.lividinstruments.com/software_union.php

SOYUZ: www.vjsputnik.com/simple/soyuz.html

VIDVOX: www.vidvox.net

GRID: www.vidvox.net/grid2.php

VDMX: www.vidvox.net/products/vdmx

ISADORA: www.troikatronix.com/isadora.html

VIDVOX: www.vidvox.net

GRID: www.vidvox.net/grid2.php

VDMX: www.vidvox.net/products/vdmx

VJ MIIXXY SAMPLES

VJ MONKEYDADDY SAMPLES

ALSO FROM FERAL HOUSE

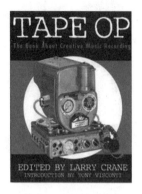

TAPE OP
The Book About Creative Music Recording
Edited by Larry Crane, Introduction by Tony Visconti
Forget the glossy trade mags, only *TAPE OP* opens the door to the minds and techniques of the most innovative recording engineers, producers and artists around. Creativity, ingenuity and using whatever facilities are available are the keys, from amazing albums recorded on 4-track cassette by the likes of Pavement, Quasi, Man or Astroman?, to full studio productions with Steve Albini [Shellac, Nirvana], Don Zientara [Fugazi, Minor Threat], Steve Fisk [Unwound], and Don Dixon [early REM]. Inside there's a wealth of practical information for the home-recordist, musician, record producer or the curious on how to get the most out of any recording scenario.
8 x 11 • 222 pages • $19.95 • ISBN 0-922915-60-1

SUICIDEGIRLS
Edited by Missy Suicide
The book is here! 160 pages of full-color photos of pre-eminent SuicideGirls in a finely-printed, strikingly designed hardcover. The book contains Missy Suicide's great pin-up photography as well as SuicideGirls' self-portraits with major diary excerpts. SuicideGirls.com started it all, a place where punk/emo/goth girls can be themselves and where their creativity and uniqueness define their beauty. SuicideGirls is a fast-growing new alternative community that appeals equally to women and men.

11 x 8 • 160 pages • color photos throughout • $22.95 • ISBN: 1-932595-03-1

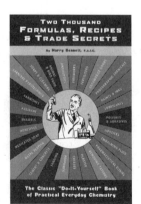

TWO THOUSAND FORMULAS, RECIPES AND TRADE SECRETS
The Classic "Do-It-Yourself" Book of Practical Everyday Chemistry
By Harry Bennett
During the Great Depression, books of pharmaceutical and chemical formulas were reformatted for layman readers, promising that they could "save hundreds of dollars by making things for yourself and your friends," and seen in most homes next to yearly almanacs and Webster's Dictionaries. The most practical and scientifically correct formula book, edited by the chemist Harry Bennett, is now available again from Feral House.
   "*Two Thousand Formulas* has a geeky charm."—*Village Voice*

5 1/2 x 8 • 336 pages • $14.95 • ISBN: 0-922915-95-4

TO ORDER FROM FERAL HOUSE:
Individuals: Send check or money order to Feral House, P.O. Box 39910, Los Angeles CA 90039, USA. For credit card orders: call (800) 967-7885 or fax your info to (323) 666-3330. CA residents please add 8.25% sales tax. U.S. shipping: add $4.50 for first item, $2 each additional item. Shipping to Canada and Mexico: add $9 for first item, $6 each additional item. Other countries: add $11 for first item, $9 each additional item. Non-U.S. originated orders must include international money order or check for U.S. funds drawn on a U.S. bank. We are sorry, but we cannot process non-U.S. credit cards.

www.feralhouse.com